Rescued
Obscu

... the continuing story of the ...
Hereford & Gloucester Canal

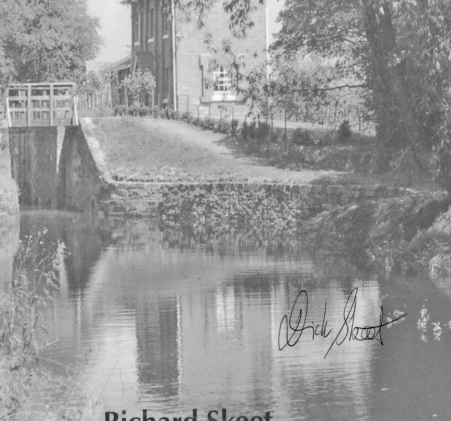

Richard Skeet

Rescued from Obscurity

... the continuing story of the ...

Hereford & Gloucester Canal

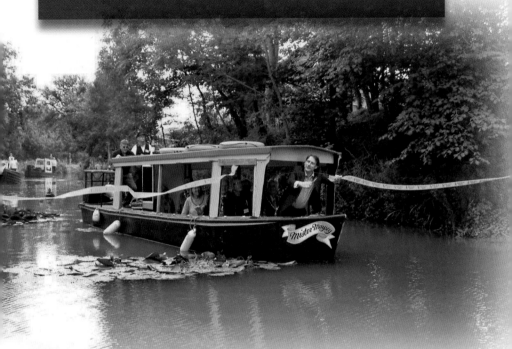

"Throughout the length and breadth of England, no major navigation is so lost in obscurity as the Hereford and Gloucester Canal"

David Bick, in his introduction to "The Hereford and Gloucester Canal" written in 1979. By kind permission of the Oakwood Press

HEREFORDSHIRE & GLOUCESTERSHIRE CANAL TRUST

Working *together* in the present to revive the past and secure a better future.©

Rebuilding 34 miles of canal between Gloucester and Hereford

Charity No. 1010721

4

First published in Great Britain in 2014 by
The Herefordshire and Gloucestershire Canal Trust

British Library Cataloguing Data

A catalogue record for this book is available from the
British Library

ISBN 978-0-9929441-0-0

Designed by Maggie Jones

Printed by Print Plus, 126, Widemarsh Street,
Hereford, HR4 9HN

Cover photo:
Oxenhall Lock and Cottage *(Dick Skeet)*

Title page photo:
James Pullen of Gloucester Quays cuts the Vineyard Hill ribbon *(Cliff Penny)*

Contents

	Acknowledgements	6
	Foreword	8
CHAPTER	Introduction	9
1	Canal Mania	12
2	Early Schemes	18
3	Gloucester to Ledbury	28
4	Ledbury to Hereford	46
5	An Exceptional Man	56
6	Uncertain Times	64
7	Dark Ages	87
8	A New Beginning	106
9	The Herefordshire and Gloucestershire Canal Trust	114
10	Restoration in Herefordshire	123
11	Restoration in Gloucestershire	137
12	The Wharf House	159
13	Llanthony Lock	165
14	The Canal Trust's fleet	170
15	Other Reminders	176
16	The Road Ahead	185
	Appendix	193
	Index	196

Acknowledgements

I find it difficult to imagine how this book could have been written without the help and support from members of the Hereford and Gloucester Canal Trust and others who have supplied me with advice, information, photographs, source material and practical help.

I am particularly grateful to Glen Atkinson, Ted Beagles , David Blagrove, Roger Byard, John Chappell, Peter Cross-Rudkin, Graham Every, Martin Danks, Colin Dymott, Brian Fox, Will Frecknall, Chris High, Pamela Hurle, Nigel Jefferies, Caroline Jones, Maggie Jones, Michael Handford, Paul Henshaw, Chris Johnson, Wilf Jones, Alan McBride, Peter Moore, Janet Moult, Cliff Penny, David Penny, Dr. Sylvia Pinches, Mike Potts, Robin Stiles, Martyn Tilford, Mike Turpin and Andrew Wynne who between them supplied most of the photographs, archive material and advice. Sadly, constraints of space meant that I was not able to use everything I was given that I would have wished to.

I am grateful to other individuals who provided photographs and these are credited in the text. In some cases the owner of the photograph may not have been the original photographer. Great care has been taken to ensure that illustrations have been accurately credited but that has not always been achievable and, particularly in the case of older photographs, it is possible that mistakes have been made. The author apologises for this and welcomes any corrections which are necessary.

Particular thanks are due to Lyn Ballard for kindly allowing me to quote heavily from Stephen Ballard's diaries and to reproduce his portrait. I am grateful also to Dr. Mark Baldwin for permission to quote from Charles Hadfield's letter to David Bick and to James Hervey-Bathurst for providing the Foreword.

Richard Cornwell, Fiona Macklin (Malvern Hills Conservators) Lauren Price (Hereford Library), John Hammond and Dr. David Skeet all provided valuable practical help.

Photographs of the Canal Company's Minute Books taken by the author are reproduced by permission of the Canal and River Trust and the National Archives, Kew.

Every effort has been made to ensure that no copyright or personal material has been used without permission. Again, should any mistakes have been made, the author apologises and welcomes any necessary corrections.

I am grateful to the following for their permission to use published or archived material:

British Newspaper Archive
Canal Boat
Herefordshire Community Foundation
Hereford Journal
Hereford Library
Hereford Archive Service
Hereford Times
John Goodwin FRICS
Ledbury Civic Society
Ledbury Reporter
Logaston Press
Malvern Hills Conservators
Oakwood Press
Portico Library and Gallery, Manchester
Ross Gazette
The Canal and River Trust
The National Archives
The Society of Authors
Waterways World
Worcester News

Almost the last word of thanks must go to Maggie Jones who gave a great many hours of her professional skills, converting my poor attempts at laying out a book into something far more attractive and easier to read.

Finally though, I must thank Pat, my wife, who has given me constant support, and excused me many of the household chores. She has put up with long hours of my being shut up in my study in a state of "Do not disturb", untangled my more convoluted prose and above all, kept me sane. Almost.

Dick Skeet May2014

Foreword

I am delighted that Dick Skeet has revised and updated David Bick's *"The Hereford & Gloucester Canal"* which I enjoyed reading when it first came out. He has done a very good job.

As a boy, I had explored the tunnels at Oxenhall and Ashperton and also travelled to Gloucester and back on the branch line, but without appreciating its intimate connection with the canal, and so the original book provided a great source of interesting local information on those important transport links. My family's links to the canal are obvious, not only through my mother's ancestor, Earl Somers, but also because all the external building stone for Eastnor Castle was transported from the quarries in the Forest of Dean by canal to Ledbury so, without the canal, I am sure construction of the house would have been much slower and more expensive. I am very much aware of the importance of the canal in our own family history.

This publication comes at a time when the restoration of the canal is well under way in various sectors through the hard-working volunteers in the Herefordshire & Gloucestershire Canal Trust; it is well timed and will lend weight to the efforts to finish the project, which will be a very valuable asset for local tourism and for wildlife. I hope it will also encourage wider support for the project from members of the public and grant-giving bodies.

I look forward to a delivery of new Forest of Dean sandstone by canal in due course, made possible partly as a result of this excellent revised history.

James Hervey-Bathurst CBE DL
Eastnor Castle, Ledbury
Vice President
Herefordshire & Gloucestershire Canal Trust

Introduction

When I foolishly agreed to update the late David Bick's book, "The Hereford and Gloucester Canal" which was first published in 1979 and ran to a third edition in 2003, I envisioned a slimmer, less academic volume with a smaller amount about the past and more about the present and the future.

I intended to tell the story of the canal, as far as possible, in the words of the people of the time using newspaper cuttings, letters, Parliamentary Proceedings, Company Minutes, Stephen Ballard's dairies and the like. The elegant language of Georgian and Victorian England, if now often sounding somewhat pompous and stuffy, sometimes makes us smile - but we are the better for that.

Whether or not this was a bad mistake I leave my readers to decide, but the result was a huge amount of material to be sifted and organised. Then the emails and phone calls from members of the Trust began to arrive providing me with even more bits and pieces, so fascinating, to me at least, that there was none I wanted to exclude. My hopes of brevity soon disappeared as rapidly as water is wasted from a leaky lock.

I also wanted to speak to an audience wider than industrial archaeologists and to include the sort of people we bump into at the Canal Trust's events, both local and far from the two counties – the sort of people who tell me that they have lived all their lives in Hereford but were only vaguely aware that there was once a canal in the heart of the city.

I thought it was important not to attempt to write the Fourth Edition of David Bick's book, but to try to bring something new to the story. Probably more than anything else, David's deep knowledge of the canal's history and his determination that the memory of it should not disappear altogether, was the single most important factor in the establishment of the Hereford and Gloucester Canal Society in 1983. It is somewhat ironic that the man who 'started it all' never really believed that full restoration of the

canal was a possibility. In his later years he must have felt rather like Dr. Frankenstein whose creation got so badly out of control. In this important respect David and I part company, for I believe that, if we want it enough, one day there will be boats arriving in Hereford having travelled all the way by canal from Gloucester and far beyond.

While the correct title of the canal was the "Herefordshire and Gloucestershire Canal Navigation", I have followed the convention of most authors and adopted the shorter title of "Hereford and Gloucester Canal". I think the minutes clerk recording the proceedings of the Company Committee and General Assembly would have envied me.

Since the names of some of the locks on the canal do not appear on early maps I have used the lock names as they appear in the Minute Books. Most of these will be familiar, but "Thingwell" Lock which appears in Bick's book and almost everything else since, I believe to be a corruption of "Thinghill". The Minute Books mention "Kymin" Lock which is a far more logical name.

More mysteriously we read that Humpidge's Lock and Morgan's Lock were in need of new gates in 1831, oak timber for new gates at Bullock's Lock, Newent had been purchased in 1867 and, strangest of all, that in 1840 "the Lock gates are being put in to the Skewbridge Lock." Whether these were alternative names for locks or whether they were the names of stop locks with a single pair of gates to prevent loss of water has still to be discovered.

When I had the privilege of being Chairman of the Canal Trust I once included a story in my column in the Trust's quarterly magazine, The Wharfinger, relating a tale about Sir Christopher Wren who liked to make incognito visits to the building site that was to become St. Paul's.

It is said that on one occasion he spoke to a man who was working with a yardstick on a piece of bare earth and asked him what he was doing. "I am a surveyor" the man replied "and I am marking out the course of a great wall". The next man Wren spoke to was chiselling away at a vast piece of stone and Wren asked him the same question. "I'm a Master Mason" he replied, "and I'm shaping the keystone for that soaring arch over yonder. Next Wren spoke to a carpenter who proudly informed him he was preparing one of the great beams which would support the roof of the nave. Nearby was an elderly woman, bent double over her birch-twig broom sweeping up the shavings the carpenter was making. "And what are you doing, my good woman?" Wren asked. She straightened her back

as much as she could and looked him straight in the eye. "Why Sir, I am helping Mr. Wren to build his cathedral."

This book is dedicated to all those incredibly devoted and skilled people who have done (and are doing) so much to make the dream of a canal once again connecting these two ancient cities become a possibility. This may be in the seat of an excavator or a dumper truck, in mud or undergrowth with a spade or slashing hook, surveying, planning and designing projects, at home drowning under the mass of paperwork required to manage the Trust's activities, assets and finances and to secure grant aid, in a committee room late into the night, negotiating with developers, landowners, local authorities and other agencies, representing the Trust at hearings and inquiries, liaising with the media, writing, designing and producing the Trust's own magazine and promotional material, in a hot kitchen making chocolate cakes or leek and potato soup, or on a cold, wet display stand promoting the work of the Trust and selling cuddly toys, draw tickets or even copies of this book to reluctant members of the public.

And, of course, to those who clear up the mess others have made.

Richard Skeet

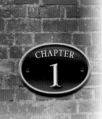

Canal Mania

The Hereford and Gloucester Canal was conceived at the height of the Canal Mania, a phenomenon which swept through Britain during the last decade or so of the 18th century. Its seeds were sown in the 1760s following the Duke of Bridgewater's construction of a canal to link his mines at Worsley with the growing cities of Manchester and Salford four or five miles away.

The Duke's canal, opened in 1761, was not the first in Britain, nor even in Lancashire, as the Sankey Canal had opened four years before, connecting St. Helens to the River Mersey. This had been planned partly as a river navigation along the line of the Sankey Brook but was actually built as an entirely new artificial cut. The Fossdyke in Lincolnshire was much older, parts of it dating back to Roman times, but it was the Duke's Canal which caught the imagination of the entrepreneurs of 18th century Britain.

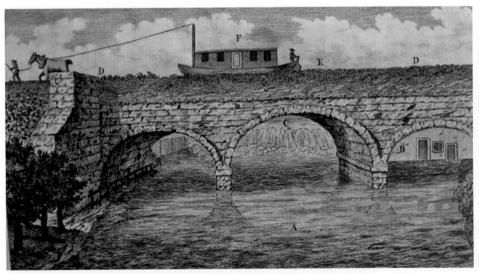

Figure 1: The Barton Aqueduct over the River Irwell on the Bridgewater Canal, from a drawing by Arthur Young, about 1769. *(Portico Library, Manchester)*

From his single line branches and extensions soon developed. Their construction was funded by the Duke himself, though to do so he had to mortgage his country estates and London home, and borrow from relatives and from some Manchester factory owners who had the foresight

to recognise the potential of a better system of transport for their goods. The cost was upwards of £220,000 but almost as soon as the canal was in operation the annual income was well over half that sum. Much of the credit in the early years of planning must go to the Duke's agent John Gilbert and to James Brindley, his engineer from 1759.

Journals of the House of Commons Volume 94

Priestley, Joseph: Historical Account of the Navigable Rivers, Canals and Railways of Great Britain, 1832 p. 92

Development was slow at first, but within ten years canals were beginning to criss-cross England as the Industrial Revolution swept through the country. Share prices rose astronomically and great fortunes were made. By 1772 the Staffordshire and Worcestershire Canal connected the Birmingham Canal to the new inland port of Stourport on the River Severn and to the Trent and Mersey Canal which linked to the Bridgewater Canal. Five years later the Trent and Mersey linked Manchester to the East Coast ports of Goole and Hull by its connection with the River Trent. By 1790 the Thames and London were connected to the north and the midlands by the Coventry and Oxford canals. Although Brindley designed these canals, he did not survive to see all of them completed. His son-in-law and assistant Hugh Henshull, who will feature in a later part of our story, was responsible for completing most of Brindley's unfinished projects.

Famously, the Duke declared that "A navigation should have coals at the heel of it" and over half of the canals built over the next 40 years were built to serve collieries. In the last decade of the 18th Century scores of enabling acts were passed. In 1793 alone the construction of 20 new canals was authorised by Parliament.

There were, of course, river navigations long before the Duke's Canal. From about the thirteenth century attempts were made to improve the natural rivers by dredging, weed cutting and bank protection. When major improvements were planned an Act of Parliament was required, the first of these being for maintenance of the River Lee from Hertford to the Thames.

Gloucester had relied on the River Severn since earliest times, the first Severn Trows being built in the 15th Century. Hereford was served by the Wye which was clearly much more navigable in the past than it is now. Today's visitors to the Wye in Hereford will have little idea of the waterside activity which would have been taking place 200 and more years ago, despite the undoubted challenges the Wye presented to the boatmen of the 18th Century. A spell of dry weather in Summer often stopped traffic altogether as water levels fell and during the winter months flooding made the river extremely dangerous, if navigable at all.

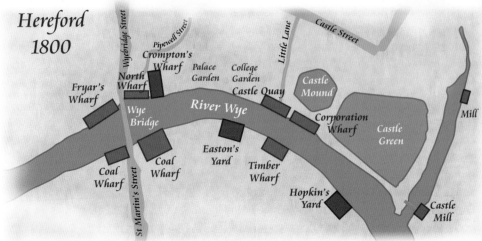

Figure 2: Principal wharves and boatyards on the Wye in Hereford about 1800. *(From Hurley 2013)*

Hurley, Heather: Herefordshire's River Trade, Logaston Press, 2013

Heather Hurley's encyclopaedic description of trade on the Wye and Lugg reveals much of the importance of the river before the canal and railway age. There were wharves on the whole of the river from Chepstow to Glasbury, though little traffic was possible for much of the year on the uppermost reaches. In Hereford, on both sides of the river there were wharves handling a wide diversity of cargoes including coal, iron, timber, bark, building materials, agricultural goods and, of course, cider. There were several boatyards in which craft of varying types were built including many 'standard' Wye barges 50 feet long with a beam of 11 feet. The weight of cargo carried would have varied according to the depth of water available, but in good conditions they might carry as much as 40 tons.

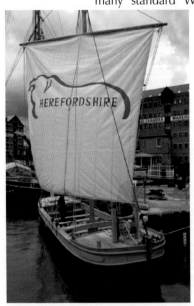

These barges would generally be bow-hauled by teams of men or horses, an often difficult and sometimes dangerous task.

Wye trows were generally larger, up to 70 feet long with an 11 feet beam. A square sail provided assistance where possible.

No original Wye trow has survived but a replica was built for the Royal Jubilee in 2012 and was rowed in the Jubilee Pageant by members of the Hereford Rowing Club.

Figure 3: The Hereford Bull, a replica Wye Trow built to celebrate the Queen's Diamond Jubilee in 2012. *(Bob Tabor Herefordshire Community Foundation)*

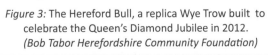

Even steam-powered vessels weighing as much as 140 tons were built in Hereford, though these could not have worked on the Upper Wye. Over the years attempts had been made to improve things by the building of weirs. Navigation through the weirs was achieved by flash locks which were basically removable sections of the weir. Travelling downstream, boats would be flushed through with a total disregard of the boatmen's safety. Travelling upstream, the boat would have to be laboriously bow-hauled through at precisely the right moment while there was sufficient water to keep the boat afloat but with a low enough flow the make the task possible at all.

Constant disputes with mill owners made improvements hard to achieve. Under an Act of 1695 all but one of the flash locks on the Wye were ordered to be removed, the exception being that at New Weir, Symonds Yat. Despite several schemes proposing pound locks (the sort we use today) on the Wye, none were ever built, though some were constructed on its tributary, the Lugg, the scant remains of which are still visible today. The lock at Mordiford is a Grade II listed structure, but has sadly deteriorated over the last 20 years such that nothing visible apparently now remains, while at Tidnor, the next lock upstream, one complete lock wall (unlisted!) can be seen from the river. Traces of

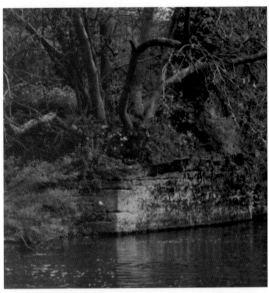

Figure 4: Remains of Mordiford Lock on the River Lugg in 1993. *(Will Frecknall)*

the lock at Hampton Court can also be found. Considerable efforts were made to improve the Lugg in the early years of the 18th century including the raising of several bridge arches to allow the passage of larger boats. Evidence of these improvements is clearly visible today.

From Hereford to Gloucester by river involved a difficult and dangerous journey of 115 miles. The alternative was the coach road and it would be surprising indeed if the road between these two cities was any better than most others in the country, rough and uneven, dusty in the summer and a quagmire in winter. On the better roads a horse-drawn cart might move two tons; on the much more common poor roads a pack horse could only manage 2½cwt.

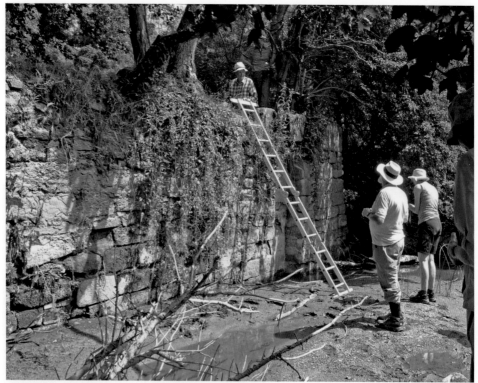

Figure 5: Tidnor Lock on the River Lugg, the only substantial remains of a lock on the navigation visible today. *(Author)*

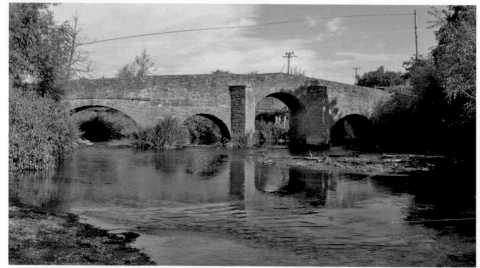

Figure 6: River Lugg: Marden Bridge showing the arch raised in the early 18th century. *(Paul Young)*

With news of the profits from Brindley's canals and the words of The Duke of Bridgewater ringing in their ears, it is hardly surprising that the entrepreneurs of the cities of Gloucester and Hereford cast their eyes on the collieries around Newent and scented that here was a fortune waiting to be made.

Newent lies on the northern limit of the Forest of Dean coalfield and there had been long established mines at Kilcot and Boulsdon, but neither were producing enough coal to justify the building of a canal. Brian Smith estimates that only about 66 tons of coals were being produced from these mines annually. A more successful mine was to be found at Mamble, just over the Herefordshire border into Worcestershire near Cleobury Mortimer. The coal was of indifferent quality though considerable quantities were there to be mined if transport away could be managed. This was an age of great optimism and even if little coal was being produced at present, what was there to stop a great expansion of the mines in the future?

It was in this ferment of canal enthusiasm, often badly misplaced, that the Herefordshire and Gloucestershire Canal was conceived.

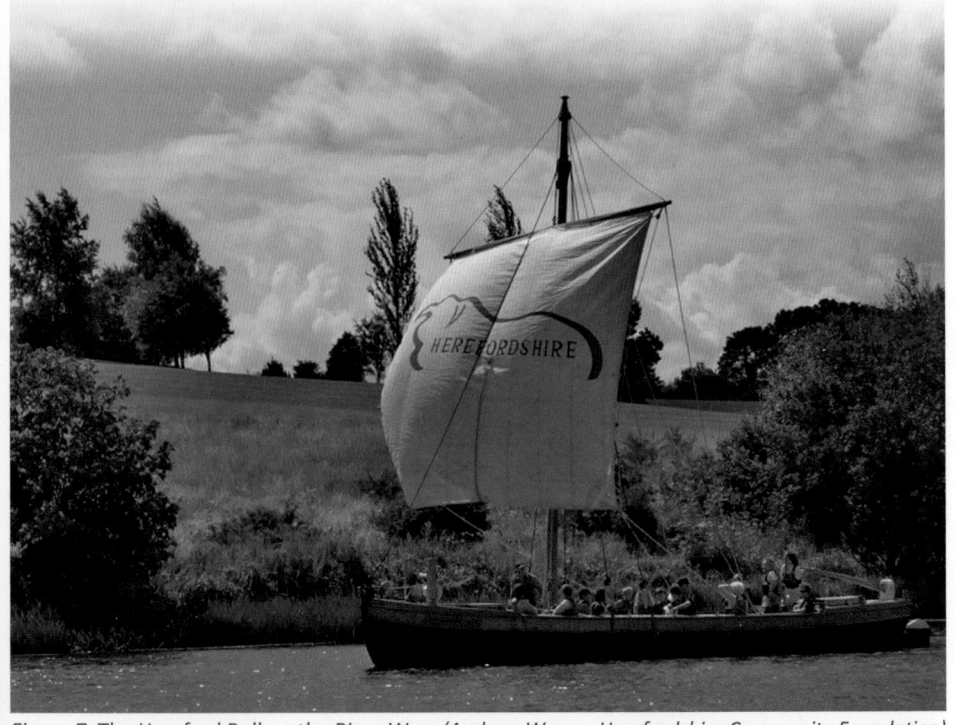

Figure 7: The Hereford Bull on the River Wye. *(Andrew Wyne – Herefordshire Community Foundation)*

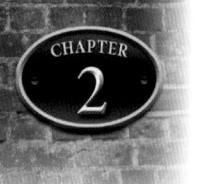

Early Schemes

Given that Herefordshire today has less water navigable by anything larger than a canoe than any other county in the Midlands, it is surprising to discover that Herefordshire was particularly afflicted by the Canal Mania. In the 1770s all manner of schemes were being dreamed of. Perhaps because the Wye was carrying a considerable amount of goods from Hereford to the south, most of the canal schemes focussed on the north and east of the county with the aim of linking with the Midlands. Figure 8 shows the possible canals considered by the eminent engineer and surveyor Robert Whitworth in his report of 1777.

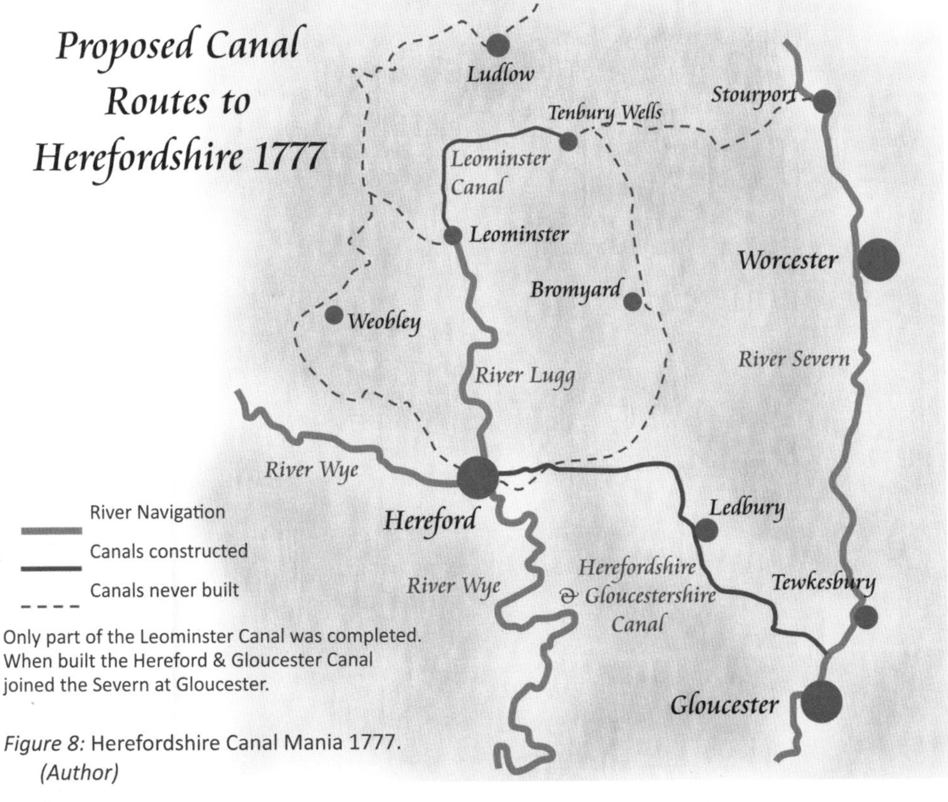

Proposed Canal Routes to Herefordshire 1777

Ludlow
Tenbury Wells
Stourport
Leominster Canal
Leominster
Worcester
Bromyard
Weobley
River Lugg
River Severn
River Wye
Hereford
Ledbury
River Wye
Herefordshire & Gloucestershire Canal
Tewkesbury
Gloucester

River Navigation
Canals constructed
Canals never built

Only part of the Leominster Canal was completed. When built the Hereford & Gloucester Canal joined the Severn at Gloucester.

Figure 8: Herefordshire Canal Mania 1777. *(Author)*

The front runner in Herefordshire in these early days was a proposed line from Leominster to Stourport which would serve the collieries at Mamble

and reach Hereford by way of the River Lugg Navigation. Whitworth recognised that, although much of the line could quite easily be built, the descent into the Severn Valley to Stourport would be "not so easy". Other ideas considered were using the Frome valley to Tenbury via Bromyard and even one from Bridgnorth to Ludlow, Leintwardine and the Yazor Valley to Hereford. One other option was a link to the Severn just below Tewkesbury via Ledbury.

The Leominster Canal eventually received its enabling Act in May 1791 and by 1796 coal was being carried from the mines at Mamble to Leominster. In the planning stages this must have looked an attractive opportunity for those considering a line to Hereford as the River Lugg provided an easy connection, but it must already have been clear that the expense of extending to Stourport was likely to be prohibitive.

The Leominster Canal, though operational for 60 years, never reached either Stourport or Kington as was later proposed and remained an isolated waterway. Wisely then, Whitworth's idea for a canal from Hereford via Ledbury to the Severn was resurrected in a proposal by the surveyor Richard Hall.

On Thursday, March 18th 1790 a meeting was held at which it was agreed to set up a company to build a canal between Hereford and the Severn. A "Committee of the Proprietors of the Herefordshire and Gloucestershire Canal Navigation" was formed. Shares in the Company would cost £100 and Josiah Clowes was appointed Engineer. Clowes was a wise choice. He had worked on the Chester Canal and the Stroudwater Navigation. More recently he had worked as Robert Whitworth's assistant on the Thames and Severn Canal and was largely responsible for the construction of the Sapperton Tunnel, 3817 yards long. Whitworth was also asked to "complete his survey".

Clowes obviously came under pressure from the canal promoters to revise Whitworth's route to take it closer to Newent and the mines at Kilcot and Boulsdon. In a letter to the promoters, no doubt recalling the engineering difficulties experienced in the building of Sapperton Tunnel, he advised as follows:

> 66 Upon a careful examination of the country from Ledbury to Newent, I find it so much intersected with hills, that it is impracticable to carry the main line by way of Newent. But a lateral branch to Newent may be made as laid down in the plan by Mr. Hall, which in my opinion will answer every requisite purpose. 99
>
> *Clowes, Josiah: Letter to the Promoters, April 27th 1790*

Clowes did, however, change Richard Hall's route beyond Ledbury, to use the Leadon Valley, joining the Severn in Gloucester rather than five miles upstream at Wainlodes.

The planned route included two tunnels, one in Hereford of 440 yards and a much longer one near Ashperton of 1,320 yards. Aqueducts were required to carry the canal over the rivers Lugg and Frome. The line involved over 20 locks in its 35½ mile course. It was designed to be slightly larger than Brindley's seven foot gauge narrow canals, to accommodate vessels 70' long and 8' beam.

In promoting the canal much was made of the Newent coalfields, Clowes estimating that some 20,000 tons of coal would be carried along the canal annually. As part of the promotion a series of exquisite fans made of paper and ivory was made for "the ladies of the shareholders" showing the line of the canal. One survives in the Hereford Museum and is shown in Figure 9.

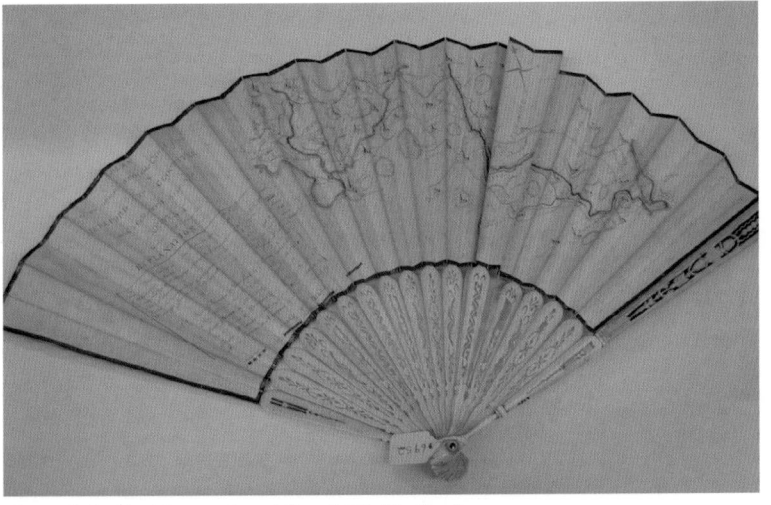

Figure 9: Ladies' Promotional Fan 1791. *(Author)*

A detail of the map is shown in Figure 10. The section from Ledbury to the Severn can be seen clearly, as can the branch to Newent. There is nothing new in sales. "Buy shares in our canal and get a free ladies' fan!"

On March 2nd 1791 a Bill for "Making and Maintaining a Navigable Canal from the City of Hereford to the City of Gloucester, with a Collateral Cut from the same to the Town of Newent in the County of Gloucester" was laid before Parliament, though not everyone was impressed. Protests drawing attention to a dubious business case, inadequate funding and vandalism of

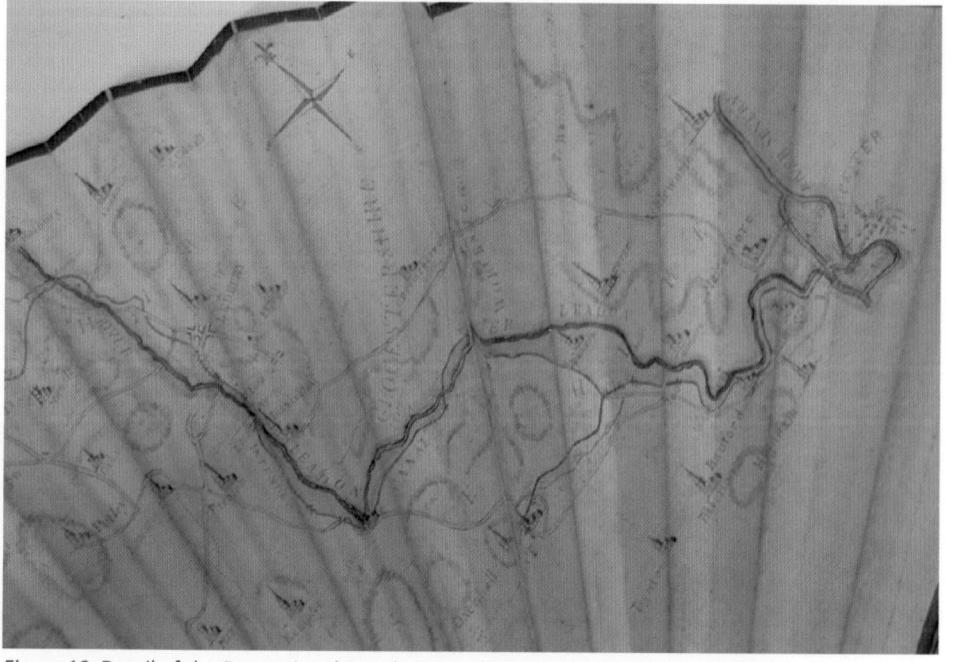

Figure 10: Detail of the Promotional Fan showing Clowes' proposed route of 1791. *(Author)*

the countryside, remarkably reminiscent of the present counter-arguments to High Speed 2, were expressed in petitions considered by the House of Commons where "several Gentlemen, Freeholders, Farmers, and others, Proprietors and Occupiers of Land on or near the line of an intended Navigable Canal" pleaded:

> ❝ That the Scheme of the said intended Canal is merely speculative, and by no Means ascertained so as to justify the Undertaking, and that the Land in general, through which the said Canal is intended to pass, is very rich Meadow and Pasture Ground, great Part thereof fertilized by the adjacent Streams of Water, which will be either destroyed or rendered useless by the said Canal; and that the Land and Property of several of the Petitioners, from the peculiar Situation thereof, will be more injured and affected by the said Canal than any other Individual having Land on or near the said Line, and all the lands on or near the Line will be considerably lessened in Value, and rendered extremely incommodious in the Cultivation thereof; and that the Line of the said Canal is nearly Central to (and at only a short distance from) the Navigable Rivers Severn and Wye which, it is presumed, are amply sufficient and convenient for the Uses and Purposes of the surrounding Country. ❞
>
> *Journals of the House of Commons Volume 46 p. 254-5, 261*

From Ledbury "Several Gentlemen, Tradesmen, and others", with clear evidence of collusion, had even more to say :

> 66 That the Scheme of the said intended Canal is entirely speculative, and by no Means ascertained, so as to justify the Undertaking, and it is very uncertain whether any Colliery can be established at or near Newent, and, if the same should take Effect, the Coals produced therefrom are of such an inferior and bad Quality, it is presumed they would be unfit for general Use; and that the Turnpike Tolls of Ledbury aforesaid will be materially lessened, whereby the Securities thereon, amounting at present to £5,000 and upwards, will be greatly injured ; that the Markets and Trade of Ledbury will be wholly lost, and many of the Inhabitants thereof ruined, and the Property of many Land Proprietors and Landholders, on the Line of the intended Canal, will lie greatly injured, particularly so as such Line runs through a very rich Tract of Land, the greater Part whereof is Meadow and Pasture Ground fertilized by the adjacent Streams of Water, which will either be destroyed or rendered useless by the said Canal ; and that the Estimate for making the said Canal is by no Means adequate to the Execution of the Scheme, and the present Subscriptions bear but a small Proportion to such Estimate, and that the Projectors of the intended Canal themselves aver the Scheme cannot be carried into Execution for less than £100,000, although the present Estimate is no more than £74,581.18s 4d.; and that the Line of the said Canal is nearly Central to (and at only a short Distance from) the Navigable Rivers Severn and Wye, which are, it is presumed, amply sufficient and convenient for all the Uses and Purposes of the Inhabitants of the surrounding Country; 99
>
> *Ibid.*

The gentlemen of Hereford, expressed similar views:

> 66 … the River Wye flowing through the Centre, and from the one Extremity to the other, of the County of Hereford, will always afford a more speedy, safe, and cheap, Conveyance than the proposed Canal, for the various Articles of Cyder, Corn, Timber, Bark, Wool, and Hops, which Articles exclusively comprehend the Whole of the Export Trade of the City and County of Hereford, and are always ready for the Market in those Seasons of the Year, when the Navigation of the Wye is scarcely ever known to have failed; and that the Petitioners apprehend, in case a Colliery should be established at Newent, the Coals to be produced there are of a Quality so very indifferent and bad, as to be unfit for general Use, and that they cannot be rendered to

> the Inhabitants of the City and Neighbourhood of Hereford, cheaper than those of the Forest of Dean Coals of an unexceptionable Quality, which always have, and now do, abundantly supply the Inhabitants of the City and Neighbourhood of Hereford by the Barges and other Craft navigating the River Wye; and that the Navigation afforded by the River Wye is more than adequate to all the Purposes which the Trade and Business of the City and Neighbourhood of Hereford require, to which, in every Point of View the proposed Canal appears to the Petitioners not only unnecessary and useless, but likely, in the Effect and Operation, to produce to far the greater Number of the Inhabitants serious Inconveniencies and Mischiefs **99**
>
> *Ibid.*

In 1791 the gentlemen of Hereford needn't have worried too much about any serious Inconveniences and Mischiefs. It was to be over half a century before these became a possible threat to the city. The petitioners' view of the Wye seems to be through rather rose-tinted spectacles. Only ten years later William Coxe was writing

> From Lidbrook large quantities of coal are sent to Ross and Hereford; and we passed several barges towed by ten or eleven men, which by great exertions are drawn to Hereford in two days. **99**
>
> *Coxe, William, An Historical Tour of in Monmouthshire (1801) p. 253*

Coxe also tells us these barges

> which on account of the shoals do not draw more than five or six inches of water. **99**
>
> *Ibid. p. 351*

These could hardly have carried a great tonnage of cargo.

The concerns about both the quality and quantity of the coal from Newent and the total inadequacy of the financial arrangements turned out to be very close to the truth. No doubt by the turn of the century the words "I told you so" were often being heard in the market places of Hereford and Ledbury.

There were, however, several (much briefer!) supportive petitions from Hereford, the market towns, several villages and from places as far away as Brecon and Hay-on-Wye. The Bill received its second reading on March 7th with 61 "Yeas" and five "Noes". The Act received Royal Assent on April 17th 1791.

Clearly the promotional propaganda was effective as by 1792 the finance authorised by the Act had been raised and engineering work began, starting from the Gloucester end.

But the Proprietors, clearly disappointed that Clowes had followed Whitworth's route, were concerned that the canal did not pass close enough to the mines at Newent, on which so much depended. They commissioned Hugh Henshull, Brindley's assistant and son-in-law to re-survey the line between Ledbury and Gloucester. Henshull, who also had considerable experience of building canal tunnels, but now perhaps under some pressure, told them what they wanted to hear – that taking the route via Newent tunnelling under the hills north of Oxenhall was not as impracticable as Clowes believed.

Meeting in the Swan Inn, Hereford, on the 8th of October 1792 the Committee made the fatal decision to recommend to the General Meeting that Henshull's revised line be adopted.

> "Mr Henshall's Report having been read agreed that it be recommended to the General Meeting to be held tomorrow, that the Work is immediately begun at Gloucester, Ledbury and at both ends of the tunnel on the Summit pound as pointed out in Mr. Henshull's Report and that the variation and extension of the line pointed out by Mr. Henshull be also recommended.
>
> In consequence of Mr. Henshull's Report we are of the opinion that it will not be advisable to make the canal on a reduced scale."
>
> *Company Committee Minute Books: October 8th 1792*

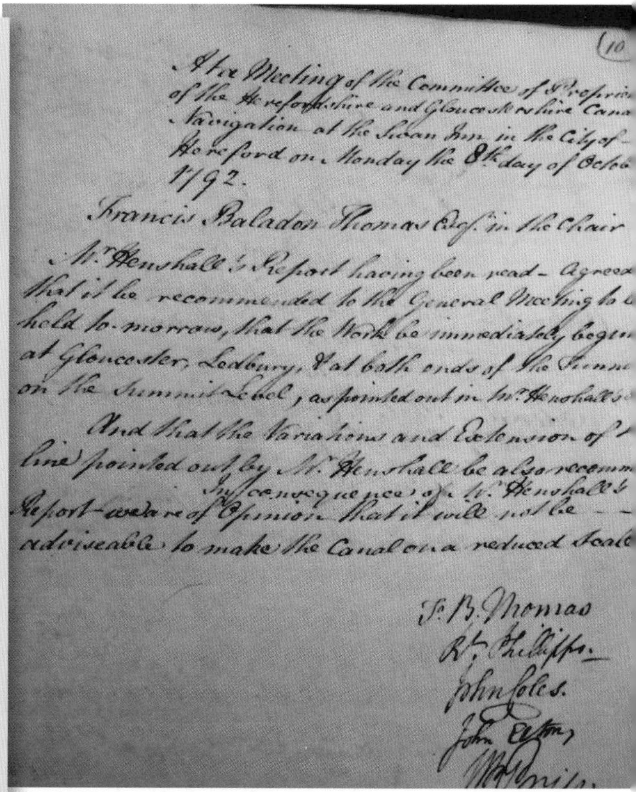
(10)
At a Meeting of the Committee of Propri... of the Herefordshire and Gloucestershire Cana... Navigation at the Swan Inn in the City of Hereford on Monday the 8th day of Octo... 1792.

Francis Baladon Thomas Esqr. in the Chair

Mr. Henshall's Report having been read – Agreed that it be recommended to the General Meeting to be held to-morrow, that the Work be immediately begun at Gloucester, Ledbury, & at both ends of the Tunnel on the Summit Level, as pointed out in Mr. Henshall's ...

And that the Variations and Extension of ... line pointed out by Mr. Henshall be also recommended.

In consequence of Mr. Henshall's Report – we are of Opinion that it will not be advisable to make the Canal on a reduced Scale

F. B. Thomas
Rd. Phillipps
John Coles.
John Eaton

Figure 11: The Great Mistake – Company Committee Minute Books, October 8th 1792. *(Author)*

Such was the importance of this resolution that the complete minute is reproduced in Figure 11. The die was cast and the Company was never truly to recover from this decision.

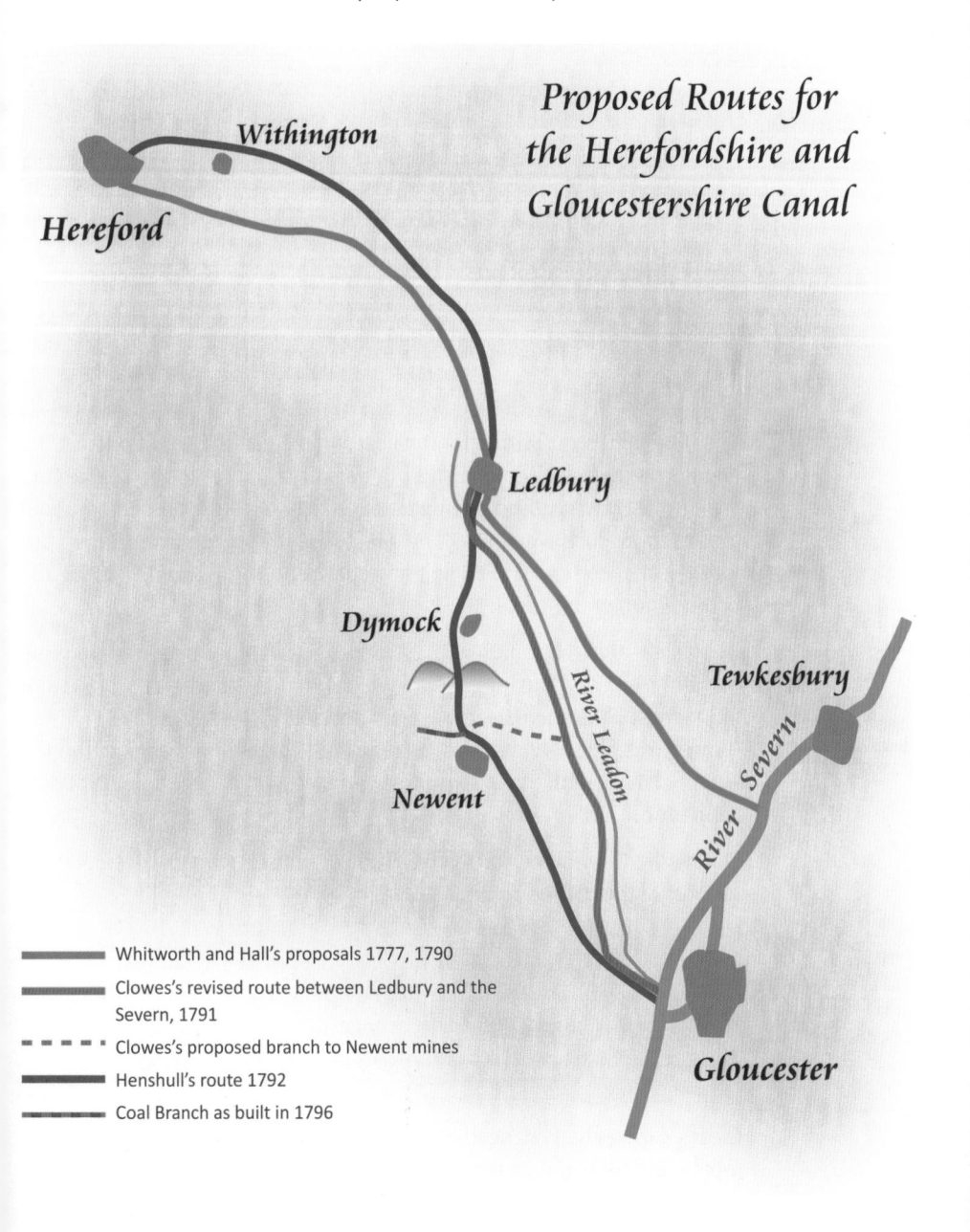

Figure 12: Proposed routes for the new canal. *(Author)*

On February 22nd 1793 Parliament heard the first reading of a Bill to alter the line of the canal from the route prescribed in the 1791 Act. The critical amendment read:

> 66 ... and that an Alteration in the Line of the said Canal, from or near Tilley's Green, in the Parish of Dymock, in the County of Gloucester, to or near to, Barbers Bridge, in the same County, so as to carry the Line of the said Canal through Newent, will not only render any Collateral Cut unnecessary, and thereby save many Acres of valuable Land from being taken for the Use of the said Canal, but will also be of great Advantage to the Counties of Hereford and Gloucester, and of public Utility, in as much as such Line will pass through a Country abounding with Coal and Lime Stone; 99
>
> *Journals of the House of Commons Volume 48 p. 252*

The new Bill also provided for the line of the canal to be extended at the Hereford end from Widemarsh to Bysters Gate, closer to the city centre, which must have caused even greater anxiety to those concerned about those serious Inconveniences and Mischiefs. It also contained provisions for the canal company to exploit any coal deposits discovered during the construction of the canal.

Skempton, AW: A Biographical Dictionary of Civil Engineers in Great Britain and Ireland 1500-1830 p. 142

It is likely that Henshull and Clowes had together reconsidered the Newent route and the long tunnel which would be necessary. They were old friends, Henshull having been a witness at Clowes' wedding in 1762. Clowes was probably the most experienced canal tunnel engineer in the country having worked on some of the longest built at that time, including Sapperton, Dudley and Lappal.

During the Committee stage it was Clowes himself who gave evidence in support of the revised route:

> 66 Mr. Josiah Clowes, an Engineer, being examined, said, That Surveys and Levels have been taken, to ascertain the Practicability of making the Deviations and Extension before-mentioned, and as described in the Petition, and the same are found to be highly practicable and eligible. 99
>
> *Journals of the House of Commons Volume 48 p. 454*

Clearly Clowes had changed his mind about the difficulties of the Newent route – or had had it changed for him. Parliament accepted his evidence, ordered the Bill to be read a third time and went on to debate a more important matter, namely the duty on beer costing more than six shillings a barrel.

On the 11th July 1793 Royal Assent was granted to enable construction of the canal along the revised route but it is likely that work had already commenced at Gloucester on the original route.

The Company Minute Book tells us by June 1792 John Swan had agreed to provide bricks and by October planks and wheelbarrows were being provided by the Company (presumably to save the workmen using their own!) and a workshop was to be constructed at Over.

> 66 Ordered – That Planks and Wheelbarrows be provided for the use of the Workmen at the expense of the Company and that Mr. Price procure the same. 99
>
> *Company Committee Minute Books: October 15th 1792*

> 66 Ordered – that a Workshop for the Carpenters and Wheelbarrow Makers be immediately built in the Ground adjoining Leaden between Over Mill and Vineyard Hill. 99
>
> *Company Committee Minute Books: November 8th 1792*

By December the Company was ready to set up its office in Gloucester, prior to which the Committee had met at the Bell Inn and the George Coffee House in Gloucester and at the Swan Inn in Hereford:

> 66 Agreed with Mr. Paul Walker to take his house late in the occupation of Mr. Greatwood on Foreign Bridge in Gloucester from Christmas next for the use of a Clerk and the Committee at £20 per annum rent.
>
> Ordered – that necessary furniture by provided by Mr. Price for the above house, and that a Board with the Words "Herefordshire and Gloucestershire Canal Navigation Office" painted thereon be placed over the Door of the said House. 99
>
> *Company Committee Minute Books: December 6th 1792*

Having agreed their new headquarters, the Committee got down to organising the first part of the canal to be cut:

> 66 Ordered – That Advertisements be inserted into the Hereford, Gloucester, Worcester and Birmingham Papers for Persons to contract for cutting the Canal and forming the Towing Path through that part of the parishes of Lassington and Rudford where the line is set out. 99
>
> *Ibid.*

The Hereford and Gloucester Canal was on its way.

Gloucester to Ledbury

Work along the level section of the canal between the junction with the Severn and Rudford began well enough. Clowes' original plan took the canal over the Western Channel of the Severn on an aqueduct and across Alney Island before locking into the Severn's Eastern Channel a short distance above Gloucester Docks. The idea of an aqueduct did not go down at all well with the local landowners who could see this as a likely cause of damaging flooding if the flow of the river was obstructed. The plan was changed to lock into the Western Channel and cross the Island on the level. The linking channel was excavated in 1793 using an earth-moving machine patented by the engineer John Carne in 1784.

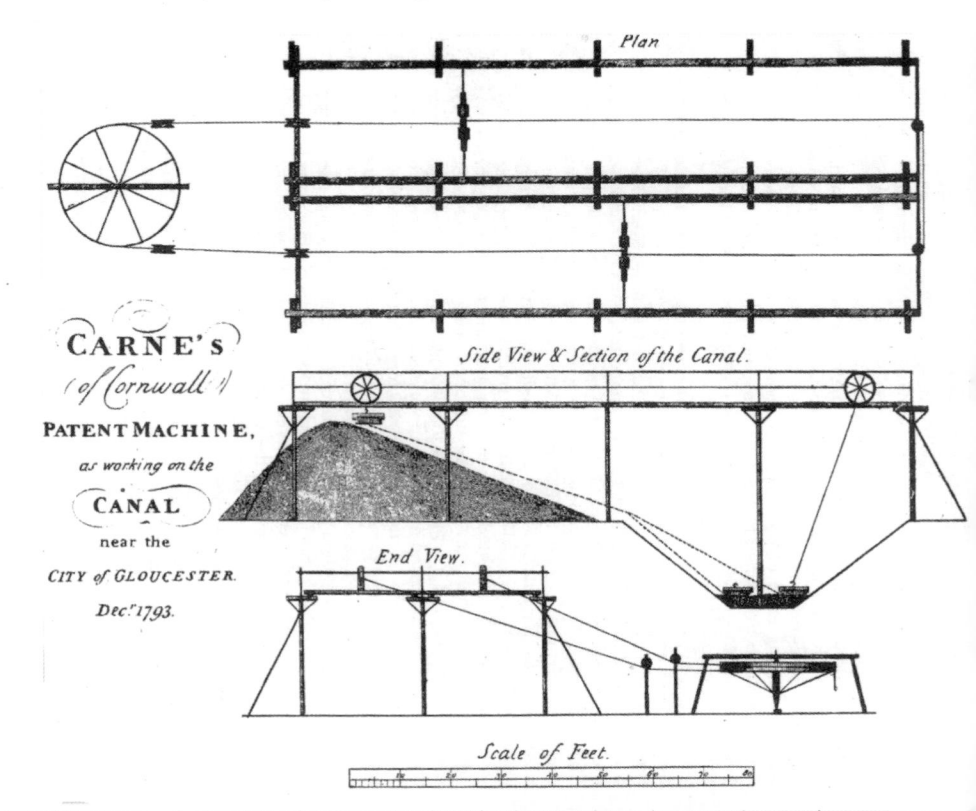

Figure 13: Carne's Patent Earth Moving Machine *(Railway and Canal Historical Society)*

While showing essentially a horse gin and primitive dragline, Carne's drawing is not entirely straightforward, with inconsistency in detail, possibly a deliberate ploy on Carne's part to prevent others copying his idea!

Under the direction of Peter Cross-Rudkin a working model was recently built at Coventry University. It took several attempts before a successful working machine could be made and it is possible that the bucket was filled by navvies and the machine was just used to dispose of the spoil. Almost certainly the machine was not quite as useful as it was cracked up to be. We know only that it was used on Alney Island and at Dymock and though Carne was involved with other canals there is little evidence that his machine was used elsewhere. The main disadvantage of the machine was that it had to be dismantled and re-erected at least every 40 feet along the canal and would have taken up a much greater width than the canal itself.

Peter Cross-Rudkin: Personal Communication

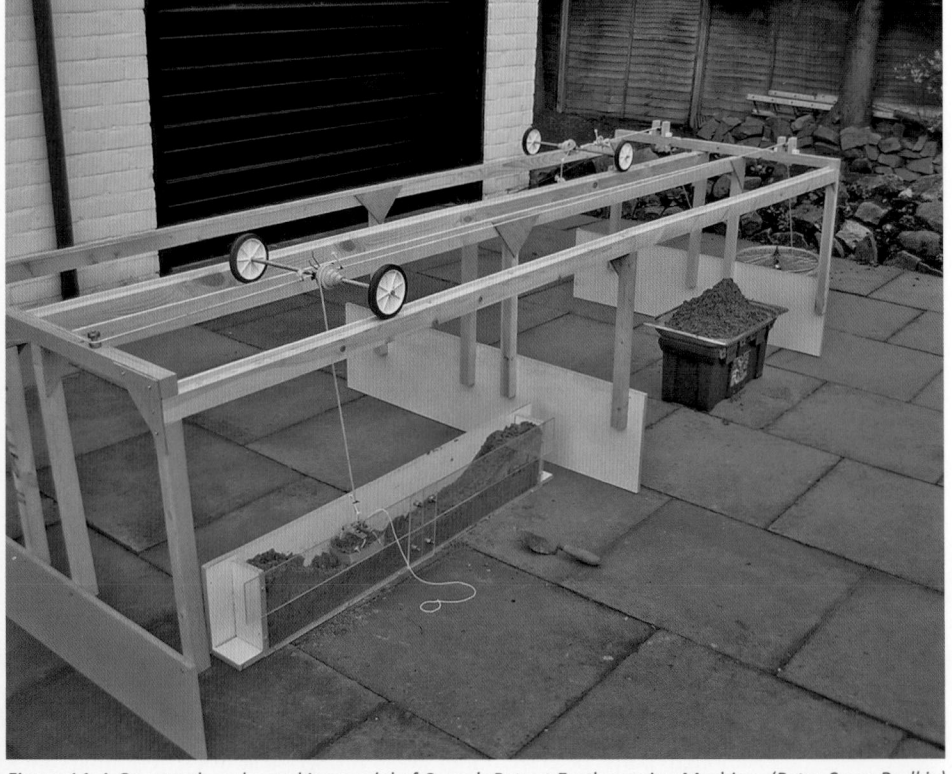

Figure 14: A One-tenth scale working model of Carne's Patent Earth-moving Machine. *(Peter Cross-Rudkin)*

It is not clear whether the cut across Alney Island was ever completed and it is likely that access to the canal was via the Lower Parting. Excavation and building of the canal between Over and Newent was going well including the construction of the eight locks. Clowes supervised the building process but, as he was involved with half a dozen other canal projects, he could hardly have devoted much time to it and William Maysey was appointed to take day to day charge of operations, a position he held for the next 30 years.

> 66 Ordered – That William Maysey be employed as a Clerk or Superintendent of the works; to be allowed a Salary after the rate of 50 Guineas per annum, & the use of Apartments in the House taken of Mr. Walker – Also to provide him Fire & Candles, & to allow him his travelling expenses whenever he is sent from home or the Canal concern – his time to commence from 1st December instant. 99
>
> *Company Committee Minute Books: December 12th 1792*

Work was also in progress between Dymock and the northern end of the long Oxenhall Tunnel and Carne's machine was moved to work here. Work also began on the tunnel and cuttings beyond Ledbury at Ashperton.

While all of this work was going on the Company was also getting side-tracked into speculative mining operations around Newent. Small deposits of poor quality coal were found but this only seemed to encourage further explorations. The details of these operations need not be retold here, suffice to say that far too much of the available capital was wasted in the vain hope of finding sufficient deposits which would justify the expense of the canal.

In December 1794 Clowes died at his home at Middlewich at the age of 59 and Robert Whitworth returned to Gloucestershire to take his place as engineer with the responsibility of driving a canal through a landscape he himself had originally thought it better to avoid.

By the end of October 1795 the canal was open from Over to Oxenhall, a distance of seven miles which, given the twelve locks and numerous bridges constructed, was no small achievement. Work had also progressed on the Oxenhall Tunnel but Whitworth's and Clowes' initial reluctance to take this route was beginning to be fully justified. Springs in the hill regularly flooded the workings and it was necessary to install two steam engines to pump enough water out to allow work to continue.

Although parts of the tunnel was through soft rock requiring brick lining much of it had to be driven, by hand with some assistance from

gunpowder, through solid rock. By 1797 nearly a third of the projected cost of the whole canal had now been spent on this tunnel alone.

In 1796, still believing that there were sufficient deposits of coal nearby, the Committee approved the construction of a branch canal running from above the top lock at Oxenhall to Hill House Colliery, a distance of about $1\frac{1}{2}$ miles. It was to prove extremely short-lived.

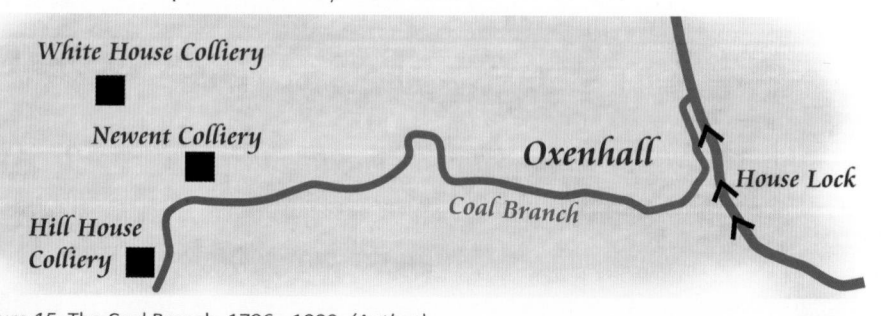

Figure 15: The Coal Branch, 1796 - 1800. *(Author)*

The Company of Proprietors of the Herefordshire and Gloucestershire Canal Navigation

No 116 One Hundred Pounds Share

Samuel Carless of the City of Hereford Mercer

is or was the original Proprietor of the Share No 116 and in right thereof intitled to one seven Hundred and Fiftieth part of the Profits and Advantages that may arise from the said Undertaking

Given under the Common Seal of the said Company the 20th day of August 1793.

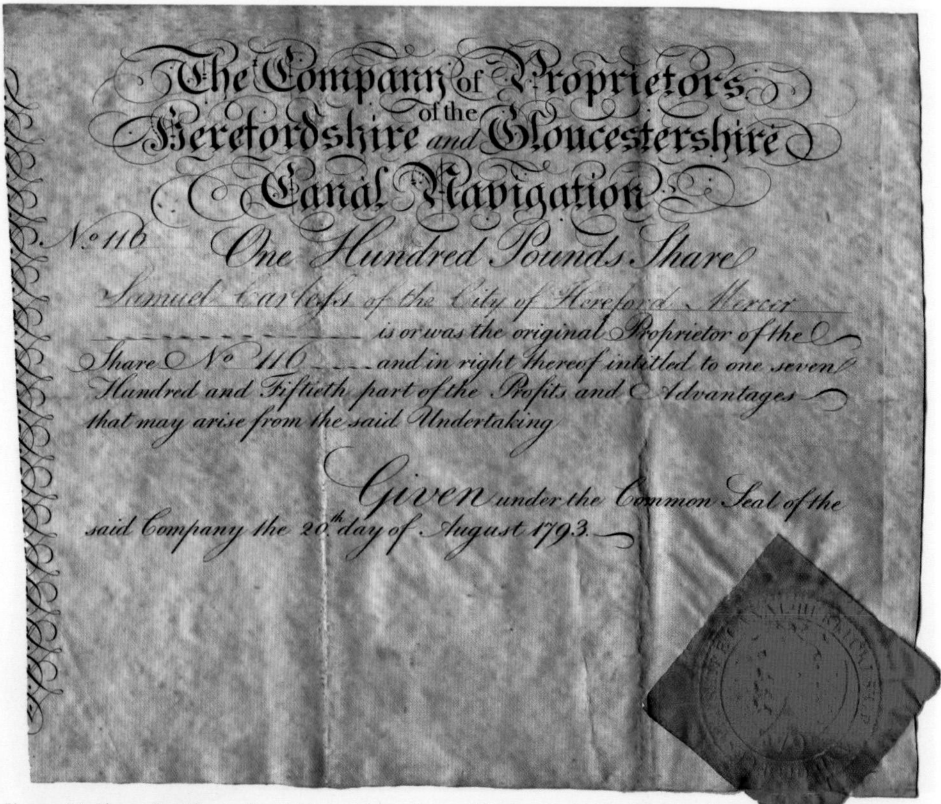

Figure 16: Share Certificate No. 116, issued to Samuel Carless in 1793. *(Nigel Jefferies)*

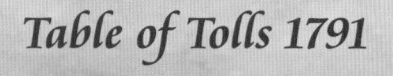

Table of Tolls 1791

For coal, two-pence per ton per mile.

For dung and other manure, bricks,
lime-stone, and other stone (except block-stone),
and clay, one penny per ton per mile.

For corn, grain, meal, etc. (except hops and wool),
from Hereford, or from Ledbury to the junction with
the Severn, three shillings and sixpence per ton.

For the same goods from any other part of
the canal or collateral cut, to the Severn,
two-pence halfpenny per ton per mile.

For corn, grain, meal, block-stone, hops, wool,
etc. not specified, three-pence per ton per mile.

Goods passing between Hereford and Ledbury pay
tonnage for half a mile less than the actual distance.

— — — ❖❖❖ — — —

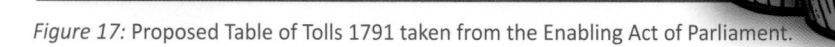

Figure 17: Proposed Table of Tolls 1791 taken from the Enabling Act of Parliament.

Further capital was raised and at last, in March 1798, the canal reached Ledbury. John Phillips describes the opening of the canal in some detail:

66 The Herefordshire and Gloucestershire canal from Gloucester to Ledbury is complete! "The opening of this navigation took place on the 30th of March, when several of the proprietors and gentlemen of the committee, embarked at the junction of the coal branch near Newent, in the first vessel freighted with merchandise consigned to Ledbury, which was followed by three others laden with coal. They passed through the Tunnel at Oxenhall which is 2192 yards in length, in the space of 52 minutes, and were met at the extremity by several gentlemen, and entertained with a cold collation at the Boyce, the seat of Mr. Moggeridge, one of the proprietors of the valuable coal mines recently opened at Oxenhall. Both ends of the tunnel, as well as the banks of the canal, were lined with spectators, who hailed the boats with reiterated acclamations. It is supposed that upwards of 2000 persons were present on their arrival at Ledbury, (about 9 miles) which they reached in 4 hours. A dinner was provided on the occasion, at the George inn, where the greatest conviviality prevailed, and many appropriate toasts were drank. The advantages which must result from this inland navigation to Ledbury and the adjoining country are incalculable. In the article of coal the inhabitants of this district will reap an important benefit by the immediate reduction in price of at least 10s.per ton. Coals of the first quality are now delivered at the wharf, close to Ledbury, at 13s/6d whereas the former price was 24s per ton. 99

Phillips, John: A General History of Inland Navigation 4th edition 1803 p. 587-8

It is highly improbable that this "first quality" coal came from the Newent pits. Far more likely, it was coal shipped up the Severn from Lydney. Perversely, now that coal could reach Ledbury from further afield it reduced the need to rely on local coal from Newent.

The wharf at Ledbury was located on the Ross Road still a mile from the town centre.

There were now problems in Gloucester. The cut across Alney Island was suffering badly from the silt brought up by the tide and Whitworth began building a dam across the Severn at Over to prevent this. Understandably, the local landowners were even more upset about this than they had been about the aqueduct and the Company was ordered to remove it.

Hadfield, Charles: The Canals of South Wales and the Border p. 201

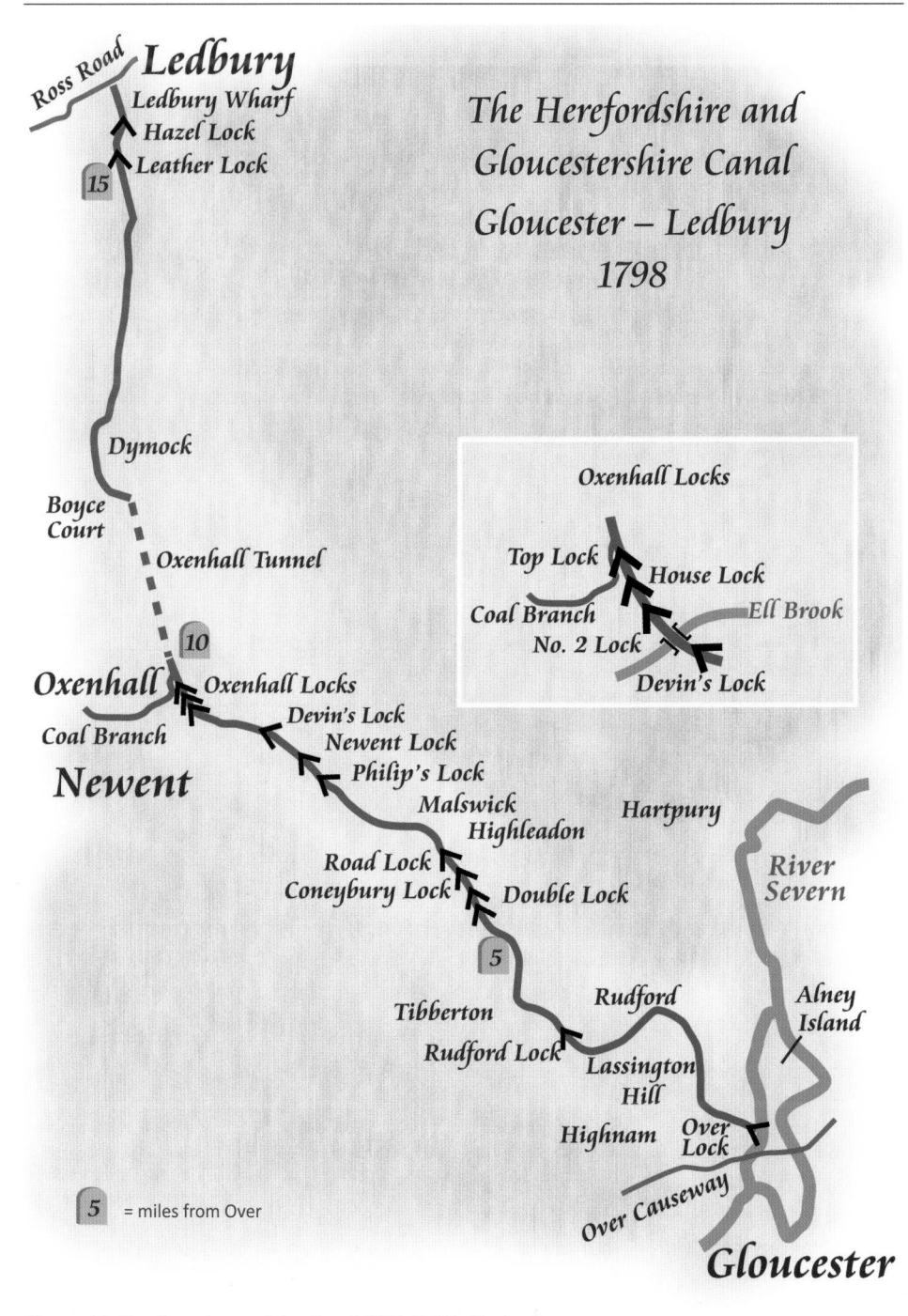

The Herefordshire and
Gloucestershire Canal
Gloucester – Ledbury
1798

Figure 18: The first phase of the Canal 1792-1798. *(Author)*

And so things stood for over 30 years. Despite costing far more than the estimate for the whole project, the canal was only half built. Hereford was still some 16 miles away. Because the main source of water, the River Frome, had not been reached there was a chronic shortage of water, at least on the section between Ledbury and Newent.

As little further construction was being undertaken the Company Minutes reflect the day to day issues which arose in the life of the canal:

" Ordered – That John Bovary inform the Boat Owners & the Captains that the Committee do insist that their Horses be muzzled otherwise they must pay the damage which is continually done to the parish by the Horses feeding upon it. "

Company Committee Minute Books: July 13th 1799

The Company laid off some of its staff which enabled expenses to be slightly less than income, but things were obviously not going as well as had been hoped. The "valuable coal mines at Oxenhall" proved as disappointing as all the others. Traffic along the branch which had been built to serve them had ceased altogether by 1800.

" The Committee likewise with pleasure observe the expense of the Company's establishment being reduced from £500 to £280 per annum & a further reduction of £150 about to take place at Midsummer, the Monies arising from the Tonnage have been & will in a still greater degree be applicable to the liquidation of the debts of the Company but they are at the same time by no means prepared to say when the finances will be in a sufficiently flourishing state to flatter the Company with a prospect of a dividend even on the loan of £4000, much less on the original Capital.

As to the Colliery at Oxenhall the Committee are sorry that the proceedings of that Concern entirely enveloped in mystery; whenever any intercourse takes place between the Committee and the proprietors they express themselves highly satisfied with the undertaking, at the same time little appears to be doing – "

Company Committee Minute Books: July 13th 1799

The canal was operated by a minimum of staff and it appears that the Committee never actually met between 1800 and 1812, the minutes simply recording a series of adjournments.

The canal received a boost to its trade in 1810 when the 2nd Baron Somers began the building of Eastnor Castle. 4000 tons of sandstone, quarried in the Forest of Dean were transported by canal to Ledbury and thence by mule to the castle.

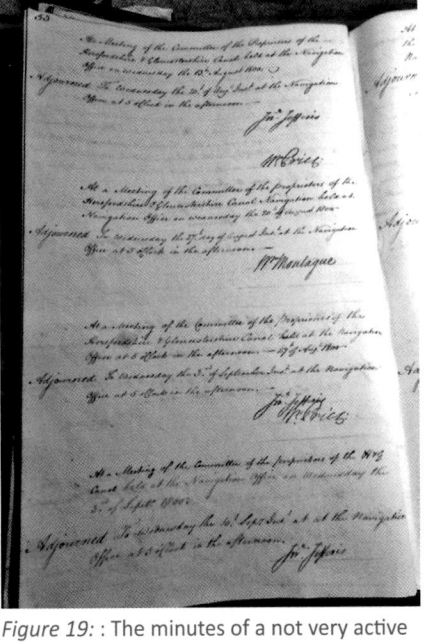

In 1812 the Committee did get round to having a meeting – no doubt much to the relief of lock keeper Thomas Hatchett who was able to point out that he had not been properly paid for the last 13 years. Mr. Hatchett had been appointed in April 1798 as Wharfinger at Newent at an annual salary of 26 guineas and must also have been given the job as a lock-keeper.

66 Tho's Hatchett having applied for some remuneration for attendance as Lock-keeper for thirteen years last, it was resolved that he be paid Twenty Pounds on that account, & that his wages in future shall be as such as Wharfinger & Lock-Keeper 99

Company Committee Minute Books:
November 12th 1812

Figure 19: : The minutes of a not very active committee! *(Author)*

It also enabled the Company to tackle a problem in Dymock :

66 Mr. Thurston of Dymock represented to the Committee that persons riding or driving cattle etc. frequently trespassed on the towing path, in order to evade the turnpike, whereby great damage was done to that path and fences. Resolved, that notice be given by putting up boards in proper places, declaring the determination of the Company to prosecute persons so offending for the trespass so committed & also information laid before the Comms of the Turnpike for such evasion & that Mr. Maysey be directed to take the proper steps against the future offenders. 99

Ibid.

While the company employed lock-keepers and lengthsmen there appears to have been no accommodation provided for them and, if Mr. Hatchett is anything to go by, sometimes their employees had more than one job. It is clear that the company was being run on a shoestring.

This meeting in 1812 seems to signal the first signs of recovery and Maysey had reported that the company was in credit to the tune of £1,200.

The minutes of the Committee held on 21st April 1814 illustrate some more of the day to day issues faced in running the canal.

" It appearing that considerable damage has been done to the works by
boats passing through the Locks in the night.

Resolved, That measures be taken to prevent the passing of boats
between the hours of seven in the evening and five in the morning
during the Summer months and between five in the evening and seven
in the morning during the winter except at the time of Spring Tides.

Mr. Maysey states that about 20 oak trees of about 15 inches girth will
be wanting for Lock gates.

Ordered, that he take proper means to procure the same. It being
represented that the Bridge, called Yewtree Bridge in the Tything of
Malswick in the Parish of Newent is, at present, in a very inconvenient
and dangerous state.

Ordered, that Mr. Maysey examine the site of it with accuracy
and report to the Committee what would be the expense of
raising the parapet walls and Coping of the same, and improving
the approach to the bridge by lessening the declivity –   "

Company Committee Minute Books: April 21st 1814

By June 1817 the Company felt confident enough to contemplate
extending the canal:

" Resolved, that Mr. Ralph Walker be employed as Engineer to
survey the line of Canal from Moat Meadow to Monkhide
Mill, immediately, and, estimate the expense thereof or in
case he shall be engaged, that his Nephew Mr. J Walker, or
other competent Person be applied to for the same Purpose. "

Company Committee Minute Books: June 11th 1817

Mr Ralph Walker was not otherwise engaged and was appointed as
engineer, though nothing seems to have been done about the extension
and in August the Committee ordered that "the canal from Ledbury to
Over be thoroughly repaired" and to "obtain an estimate for the expense
of making a wharf at Over with a house for the Clerk." The Committee
approved the building of the house in the following January.

*Company
Committee Minute
Books: August
30th 1817.*

Ralph Walker was not without stature as a civil engineer, having worked
with John Rennie and William Jessop in the building of the East India
and Surrey Commercial Docks in London, but there is no record of him
actually designing anything for the Hereford and Gloucester Canal. He
died in 1824.

After not meeting for six years, on May 13th 1827, at the Feathers Hotel in Ledbury with John Biddulph in the Chair, the Committee now made one of its best decisions:

> “The clerk having frequently represented the infirm state of his health, and the committee considering the necessity of appointing a successor.
>
> Resolved, That Mr. Stephen Ballard be appointed as such upon at a salary of £60 a year, up to the 1st of January 1828 untill which time the present clerk shall continue his salary and appointment on condition that he renders every possible assistance and affords the requisite information to his successor.”
>
> *Company Committee Minute Book: May 19th 1827*

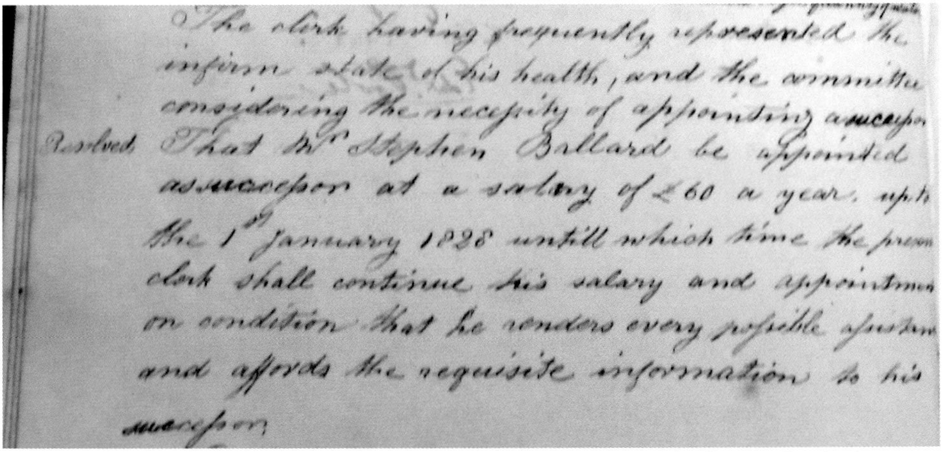
The clerk having frequently represented the infirm state of his health, and the committee considering the necessity of appointing a successor
Resolved That Mr Stephen Ballard be appointed as successor at a salary of £60 a year, up to the 1st January 1828 untill which time the present clerk shall continue his salary and appointment on condition that he renders every possible assistance and affords the requisite information to his successor

Figure20: A great decision – the appointment of Stephen Ballard on May 13th 1827. *(Author)*

John Biddulph was the owner of Ledbury Park and of land through which the canal ran and it was almost certainly Biddulph who persuaded the Committee in August to appoint a bright young man from Malvern Link as Company Clerk to succeed William Maysey. Stephen Ballard had a great interest in horticulture and geometry, but without sufficient capital to fulfil his dream of starting his own company. Frustrated by this, he had turned to the building trade and for two years was apprenticed to a Cheltenham Builder, Henry Lucy, working mostly as a carpenter. When Lucy went out of business the far-sighted Biddulph, perhaps knowing something of Ballard's talents, grasped the opportunity this presented.

The appointment of a man of 23 with no experience at all of transport management or engineering to this post looks like another disastrous decision on the part of the Company, but it was undoubtedly the best choice it ever made. He was given a salary of £60 per annum "with house and travelling expenses".

From the outset Ballard believed that the only future for the canal lay in its extension to Hereford. Apart from the increase in trade, the extension was needed to secure an adequate water supply for the rest of the canal.

In 1828 he was given a £20 bonus for his "zeal and activity" and particularly for his plans, in which he was assisted by the young Robert Stephenson, to bring a water supply from Canon Frome Mill. Ironically, this scheme was never implemented. If it had been it would have been the first seven miles of the canal to Hereford.

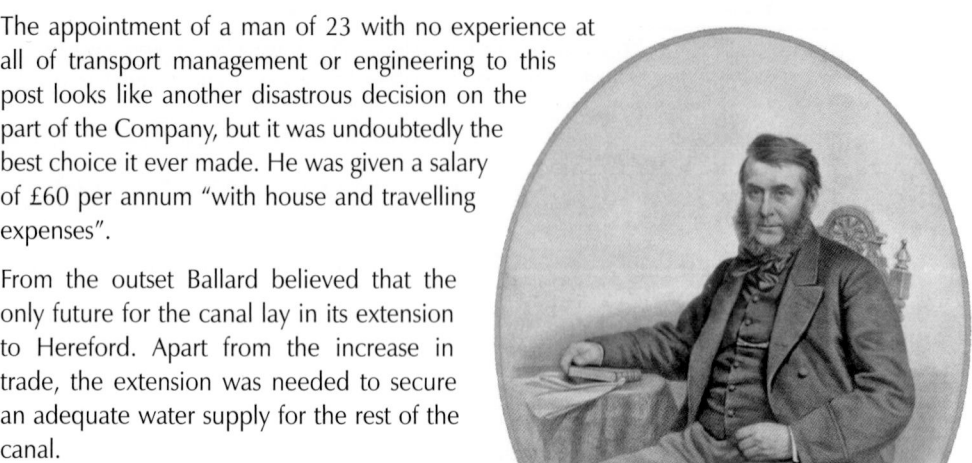

Figure 21: Stephen Ballard
(By kind permision of Lyn Ballard)

Ballard used the first years with the Company well. There being little need for his services on a day-to-day basis he travelled widely, visiting the Shropshire and Ellesmere Canals and the canals around Manchester. He made copious notes and sketches, no doubt all the while planning the completion of his own canal.

By 1830 the argument seems to have been won and the Company was buying land to complete the canal to Hereford. By September Ballard was able to report to the committee:

> 66 I beg leave to inform you that the new Lock at the Wharf is complete excepting the gates, that the new cutting as far as the Little Marcle Road is completed and that the Bridge to carry the Little Marcle road over the canal is now in progress. 99
>
> *Ballard, Stephen: Letter to the Committee September 2nd, 1830*

In December 1831 Ballard reported that, up to 1827 the canal had to close for three or four months every year through lack of water, but supplies had been improved and since then the only stoppage had been for six weeks that summer. At Ledbury, there was now:

> 66 on the Wharf an excellent carpenters workshop, a Warehouse, a Stable a drying shed for timber, and inclosed timber yard, the machine house is enlarged and now contains six rooms and a new bason has been made which is a great convenience to the traders in unloading their Coal. 99
>
> *Ballard, Stephen: Diary entry for December 27th 1831*

The Ledbury wharf had also been enlarged and several locks had been fitted with new gates. The average income had risen from £552 per annum prior to 1827 to £1452 since.

On May 20th 1832, with 27 tons of stone aboard, the canal's repair boat passed through the wharf lock to the stone yard above, and probably to the gas works beyond the Little Marcle Road, but the canal was extended no further.

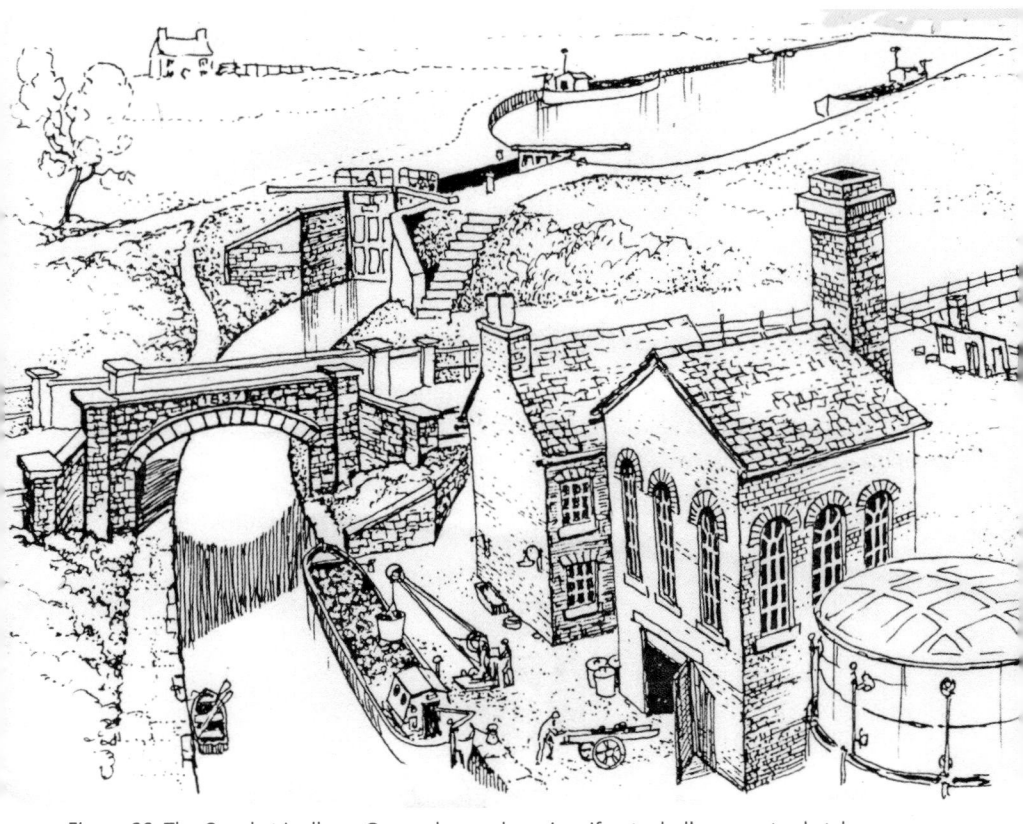

Figure 22: The Canal at Ledbury Gasworks – a charming, if not wholly accurate sketch.
(From a private collection)

In 1837 Ballard began to prepare plans in earnest, making revisions to the route authorised by Parliament in 1793. These revisions required a further Act, but this would also enable further capital to be raised. The estimated cost of completion now stood at £75,000. Various alternative routes into Hereford were considered including locking into the Wye below Hereford to save costs. Another proposed using the Lugg with the optimistic thought of traffic from the Leominster Canal. The various options are shown in Figure 23.

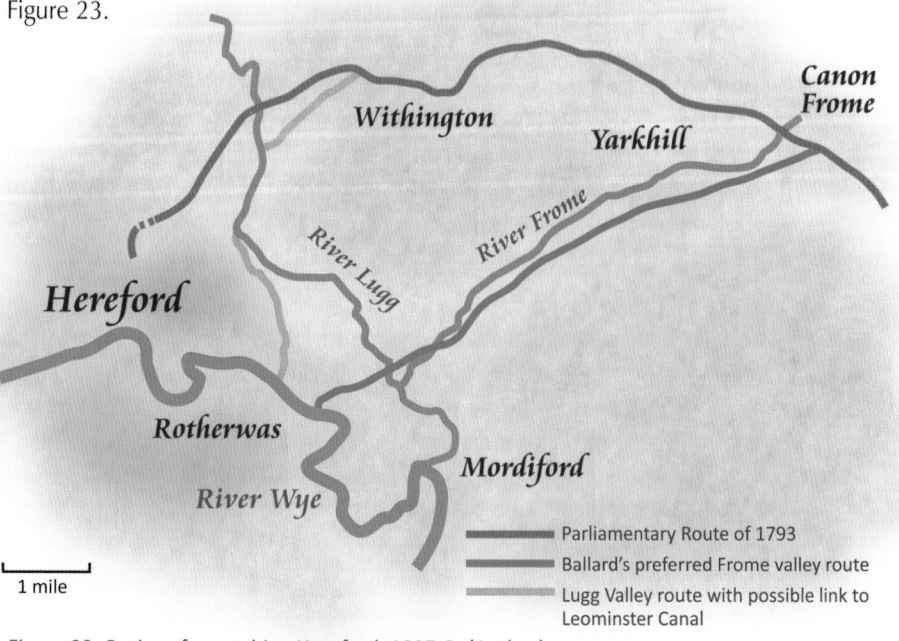

Figure 23: Options for reaching Hereford, 1837-8. *(Author)*

Ballard had been referred to as "Clerk and Engineer" since early in 1832, but in 1838 the Committee called upon James Walker, the late Ralph Walker's nephew and President of the Institution of Civil Engineers, to advise them on the route of the proposed extension to Hereford. Ballard had already explored a number of options and on Saturday September 28th, after breakfast with Walker at the Gloucester Canal Office, drove to Priors' Court and together they walked thence along the line to Hereford. Ballard coped better than Walker –

> At Hereford with Mr. Walker, slept at the Green Dragon. Went to a barber's shop and shaved myself. It is a disagreeable thing to be in a strange town on Sunday with no one to speak to and nothing to do, I do not mind being in the country by myself. 8 o'clock and Mr Walker not up yet.
>
> *Ballard, Stephen: Diary entry for September 30th 1838*

I don't think Stephen Ballard and James Walker got on particularly well, a couple of weeks later he writes -

> 66 Called on Mr. Walker, did not like his behaviour. 99
>
> *Ballard, Stephen: Dairy entry for October 16th 1838*

Ballard's strong preference was for the route through the Frome Valley, but on October 1st Walker was called before the Committee and persuaded it to go with the line authorised by Parliament in 1793, but incorporating some of Ballard's suggestions. The River Lugg option was probably only considered because it is possible that the Leominster Canal company was prepared to contribute to the cost of improving the Lugg. Their canal had only been opened between Leominster and Mamble the year before and the company was already considering making their connection with the Severn via a tramway instead of canal.

Hadfield, Charles: The Canals of South Wales and the Border p. 196

Ballard's time was now being spent in surveying the line of the extension to Hereford, but he was also surveying the River Lugg, no doubt with a view of a possible connection with the canal. He was also working on a flood protection scheme for the Wye below Hereford and on a scheme for the Bishop of Hereford's length of river bank in the palace gardens. Furthermore, he was working for the Llanelly Railway, with which he was less than impressed, as his diary reveals:

> 66 At Office work of Lugg Survey. Received £50 through Mr. B from the Llanelly Railway Company which sum I agreed to take instead of £79, the amount of my bill. I hope the lesson I have learned from the rascals comprising this committee will be of service to me in making any agreement with any other Committee or Company, for I have been used by them in a most shameful manner. 99
>
> *Ballard, Stephen: Diary entry for May 3rd 1838*

A new Bill for the extension of the canal was laid before Parliament on February 20th 1839. Its passage was not entirely straightforward. Ballard records an early difficulty in his diary:

> 66 Hubert Edy went to the House of Commons, he said Lord Shaftesbury opposed the Act. The old arbitrary rascal would give no reason for this unreasonable proceeding and we were informed that there would be no chance of success if we were to attempt to get an act passed without his approval. Thus it is this one man, an hereditary legislator, has the power to stop a public work without assigning any reason for it. 99
>
> *Ballard, Stephen: Diary entry for March 25th 1839*

The old arbitrary rascal must have been won round, for the Bill then suffered a slight technical hitch at its Select Committee stage when it was reported that, although the Bill related to the whole length of the canal, no advertisement had been placed in a Gloucester newspaper. However, as the money to be raised under the Act was to be used for works exclusively in Herefordshire and two advertisements had been placed in "a Hereford paper", the Hereford and Gloucester Times, the Bill was allowed to proceed subject to "giving Notices forthwith for three successive weeks in some newspaper of the county of Gloucester".

This would have been the 6th Earl. His son was the great reformer for whom Ballard would surely have had the highest admiration.

Journals of the House of Commons Volume 94 pp. 77, 92

This achieved, a new Act was obtained on May 31st 1839 authorising the raising of £50,000 by mortgage and £45,000 by shares. It appears that there were no objections from the Gentlemen of Hereford this time – they probably thought it would never happen.

Ballard was now spending much of his time negotiating with landowners, an experience he did not enjoy. Many of them he found unreasonable:

> 66 If the whole of an engineer's work was as disagreeable as arranging with landowners, I should not follow up the business. Nothing satisfies them. 99
>
> *Ballard, Stephen: Diary entry for December 4th 1839*

The company published a glowing prospectus waxing lyrically on the anticipated income once Hereford had been reached. It proposed that a link to the Leominster Canal could be "effected at trifling expense" yielding an annual income of at least £8,000 and even suggested a seven mile branch to Bromyard "is very probable, a cursory survey showing that there are no apparent difficulties"

Company Prospectus: "Completion of the Herefordshire and Gloucestershire Canal", 1839

The anonymous writer of "Hints of Ledbury" as far back as 1831 tells us that:

> 66 The advantages that will accrue from completion of the canal to Hereford are great. The deficiency of water, that fatal obstacle, will be supplied from many and permanent sources, whereby constant traffic on the canal will be afforded hitherto so limited, and that to the most unfavourable part of the year. The communication with Hereford will cause a vast addition of business, and the heavy goods of all kinds to and from Ledbury, will be conveyed at probably one half of the present rates of carriage. 99
>
> *A Native Inhabitant (of Ledbury): Hints of Ledbury. 1831 pp. 97- 103*

COMPLETION OF THE HEREFORDSHIRE AND GLOUCESTERSHIRE CANAL.

————

	Miles.
THIS Canal is navigable two-thirds of the year from the river Severn, at the Port of Gloucester, to near the town of Ledbury, in the county of Hereford, a distance of	$16\frac{1}{2}$
The remainder, from Ledbury to the city of Hereford, to be completed, is	$17\frac{3}{4}$
Making the total length of the Canal, viz. from the Severn, at the port of Gloucester, to the city of Hereford	$34\frac{1}{4}$

N. B.—When completed, the supply of water, for the whole length, will be abundant, even in the driest seasons.

COMMITTEE.

THE RIGHT HONOURABLE EARL SOMERS,	SAMUEL BAKER, ESQ.,
MAJOR-GEN. SIR J. K. MONEY, BART.,	J. M. SHIPTON, ESQ.,
E. T. FOLEY, ESQ., M. P.,	W. T. WASHBOURNE, ESQ.,
THE REV. K. E. MONEY,	EDWARD POOLE, ESQ.
JOHN BIDDULPH, ESQ.	T. SPENCER, ESQ.,
JOSEPH GIBBINS, ESQ.,	T. HANKINS, ESQ.,
ROBERT BIDDULPH, ESQ.,	Mr. T. BAYLIS,
THE REV. ARCHDEACON ONSLOW,	Mr. T. BALLARD,
GEORGE WATSON, ESQ.,	Mr. HUBERT EDY.

Capital already expended by the old Shareholders................................ £105,000

Capital now to be raised in 2250 preference shares of £20 each 45,000

Under the provisions of the acts relative to this Canal, and particularly by virtue of an act of the present session of parliament, intituled *"An Act for enabling the Company of Proprietors of the " Herefordshire and Gloucestershire Canal Navigation to raise a further sum of money, and for " amending the Acts relating thereto,"* and also by virtue of resolutions passed at the last General Assembly of the Company, the above-mentioned £45,000 will be raised upon the following

CONDITIONS:

1st.—2250 new or preference Shares to be issued. £20 to be paid for each share by calls of £2 per share at intervals of 3 months. The proprietors of the preference shares to receive, out of the revenue of the Canal, dividends to the amount of $7\frac{1}{2}$ per cent. per annum (to be reckoned from the time of payment of the calls) previous to the payment of any dividend to the old shareholders: such priority in payment to continue until the revenue of the Canal will enable the Company to declare on both new and old Shares a larger dividend than $7\frac{1}{2}$ per cent.; from which period an equal dividend shall from time to time be paid on all the shares in the Canal.

The new shareholders to be in every case entitled to a priority of $7\frac{1}{2}$ per cent per annum. The first call to be paid immediately on the new or preference share being entered in the Company's books.

And so it goes on for several pages. The writer even points to a bit of tax avoidance:

> 66 Every article excepting coal, paid a turnpike toll before it reached the town. By the canal coming within the borough, that tax will be avoided. 99
>
> *Ibid.*

If the Herefordshire and Gloucestershire Canal could have been built and operated on optimism alone it would surely have been one of the most successful in the country!

But, thanks largely to the enterprise and sheer hard work of Stephen Ballard and a new Committee which consisted entirely of local men most of whom lived in or around Ledbury, the canal was about to enter a new phase of its history.

◀ *Figure 24:* The first page of the Prospectus for the completion of the canal.

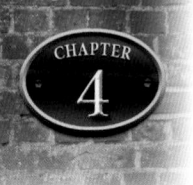

Ledbury to Hereford

Before the end of 1839 there was work going on at several places and Ballard saw his first glimpse of the excavations. His diary records on December 17th:

> 66 Went to Furnimore where the men were to start this morning on the first contract. The first I saw of the workmen was through a gap in the hedge, they were in the distance and I must say the appearance of them had an electrical effect on me, never shall I forget it. The appearance of the men at work seems to have made a lasting impression on my memory for I almost fancy I can see them now. They were got in a muddle and had lost much labour. 99
>
> *Ballard, Stephen: Diary entry for Dec 17th 1839*

During 1840 the four deep locks taking the canal from above the wharf lock outside the town were constructed and a new Ledbury Wharf built on or near Bye Street. George Wargent, writing in 1905 recalled:

> 66 At this time the Canal to Hereford was not made, and a railway not even dreamt of, green fields and stately oaks and elms were there instead. The making of the Canal to Herefordshire ... was talked of for some years before it was commenced, but like the Gloucester Railway it did come at last.
>
> When the Canal started there seemed to be a need for a public house near Bye Street Bridge and the present lodging house was licensed and a big trade was done among the canal people ...
>
> Directly after the canal to Hereford was made Mr Thomas Edy had Bridge House built, and it was known for some years as the 'The Bridge Inn' kept by Thomas Greenway and subsequently by Mr Goode during whose tenancy the licence was lost. A bowling-alley was attached to this inn as to many others in the town. 99
>
> *Wargent, George: Recollections of Ledbury. A series of personal articles written for the Ledbury Free Press & Hereford Advertiser. 1905 pp. 19, 21*

Ballard's diary records that by April 1840 there were 500 men working on the canal and he himself was working from dawn to dusk:

> 66 Commenced work on the Canal soon after 4am. and was tired by breakfast time but was hard at it until 9pm. S. Willcox was so tired that he had to remain at Ashperton. 99
>
> *Ballard, Stephen: Diary entry for May 29th 1840*

The first coal arrived at Bye Street on 22nd February 1841, personally supervised by Stephen Ballard. The census carried out on June 6th tells us that Richard Maddox was already living at the Wharf doing his accounting. By this time work was well advanced between Ledbury and the tunnel at Ashperton. Ballard had reduced Clowes' planned length of the tunnel itself by 920 yards to a mere 400 by making long, and quite spectacular cuttings, but the work was difficult and, like Oxenhall, required the use of gunpowder in some places. The tunnel was fully lined to provide stability and to keep spring water out. It also included a towpath – an unusual luxury. It was generally known at the time as "Walsopthorne Tunnel" because it was rather closer to the manor house of that name than to Ashperton village.

Census Returns, 1841

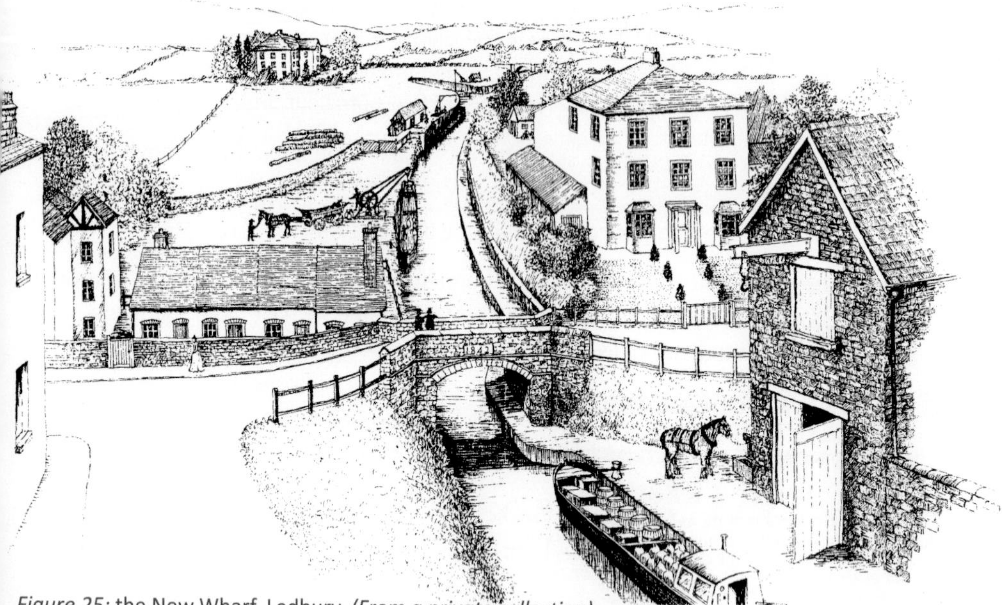

Figure 25: the New Wharf, Ledbury. *(From a private collection)*

1841 had been a busy year. On New Year's Eve Stephen Ballard writes:

> **“** This year I have been very much engaged. Not a single day, not even Sundays have I been disengaged from the work of the Canal. To look back to this time last year it appears an immense long time. **”**
>
> *Ballard, Stephen: Diary entry for December 31st 1841*

In 1842 the canal reached Canon Frome and on January 10th agreement was reached with John Hopton of Canon Frome Court for the right to

use all the water that flowed over a newly constructed weir and thence to the canal by a long feeder. This was a major achievement, virtually guaranteeing an adequate water supply to the canal all the year round.

The Canon Frome Wharf received its first goods the following year with, according to the Hereford Journal, salutary implications for the River Wye:

> **66** HEREFORD and GLOUCESTER CANAL.—On Wednesday last the spirited carriers Messrs. Bunting and Gibson, had their first boat-load of goods to Canon Frome Wharf. From that day may be dated the desertion of the river Wye as a navigation for the conveyance of foreign produce; the opening of the Berkely Canal in 1837. and now the extension of the Hereford and Gloucester Canal to within ten miles of Hereford, have given facilities that will, probably, for ever supersede the Wye as a navigation for the carriage of Bristol goods. It must he highly gratifying to the promoters of the canal to find their calculations of traffic are being fully borne out; and, in some instances sources of revenue have already sprang up that were not expected. **99**
>
> *Hereford Journal January 11th 1843*

They meant, of course, Bunning and Gibson!

Company Minute Book October 24th 1842

By 1842 there must have been sufficient traffic for there to be queues at the locks, necessitating the Committee to have "the following notice printed and delivered to the Lockkeepers and Traders on the Canal":

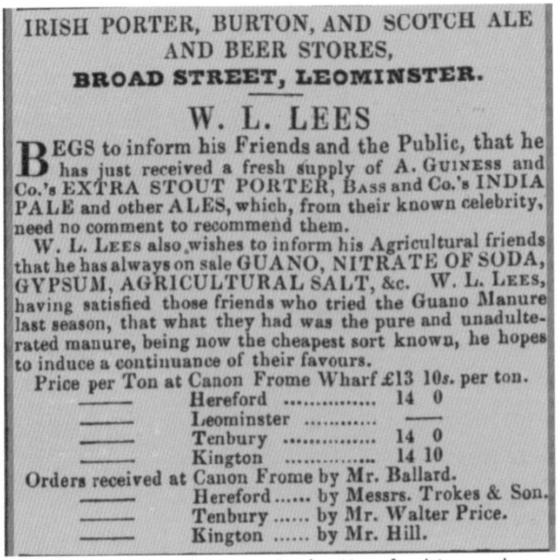

IRISH PORTER, BURTON, AND SCOTCH ALE AND BEER STORES,
BROAD STREET, LEOMINSTER.

W. L. LEES

BEGS to inform his Friends and the Public, that he has just received a fresh supply of A. GUINESS and Co.'s EXTRA STOUT PORTER, Bass and Co.'s INDIA PALE and other ALES, which, from their known celebrity, need no comment to recommend them.

W. L. LEES also wishes to inform his Agricultural friends that he has always on sale GUANO, NITRATE OF SODA, GYPSUM, AGRICULTURAL SALT, &c. W. L. LEES, having satisfied those friends who tried the Guano Manure last season, that what they had was the pure and unadulterated manure, being now the cheapest sort known, he hopes to induce a continuance of their favours.

Price per Ton at Canon Frome Wharf £13 10s. per ton.

Hereford	14	0
Leominster		—
Tenbury	14	0
Kington	14	10

Orders received at Canon Frome by Mr. Ballard.

Hereford	by Messrs. Trokes & Son.
Tenbury	by Mr. Walter Price.
Kington	by Mr. Hill.

Figure 26: Advertisement in the Hereford Journal March 22nd 1843 following the opening of Canon Frome Wharf.

66 Lockkeepers are directed to see that Boats carrying Grocery and other goods on regular days are not hindered in passing the locks and that all other Boats give way and wait at the discretion of the Lockkeepers to allow such regular carrying boats to pass first.

By Order

Stephen Ballard **99**

Figure 27: The first page of the agreement between the Company and Revd. John Hopton for the supply of water to the Canon Frome feeder. *(Colin Dymott and Herefordshire Archive Service)* ➤

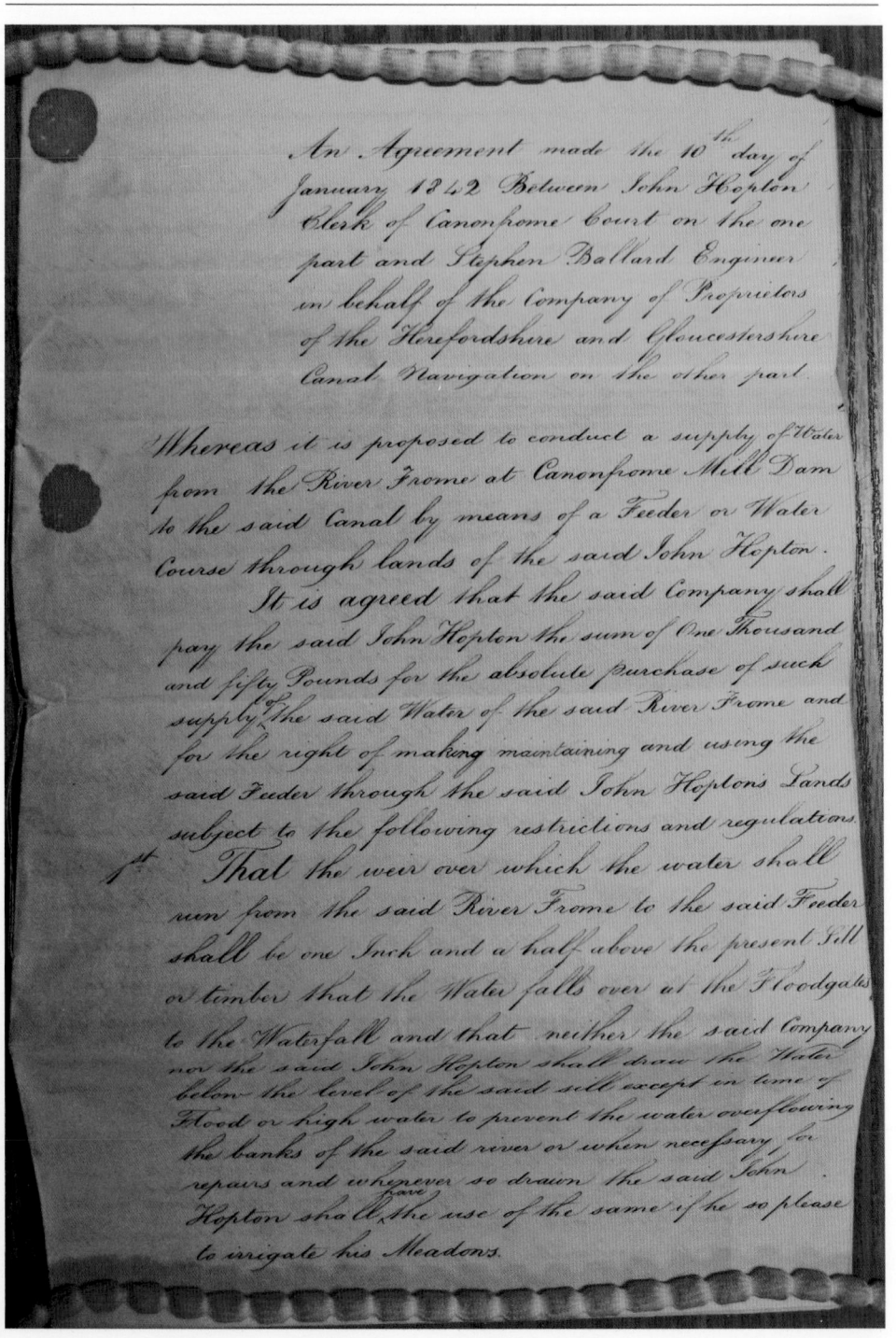

An Agreement made the 10th day of January 1842 Between John Hopton Clerk of Canonfrome Court on the one part and Stephen Ballard Engineer in behalf of the Company of Proprietors of the Herefordshire and Gloucestershire Canal Navigation on the other part.

Whereas it is proposed to conduct a supply of Water from the River Frome at Canonfrome Mill Dam to the said Canal by means of a Feeder or Water Course through lands of the said John Hopton.

It is agreed that the said Company shall pay the said John Hopton the sum of One Thousand and fifty Pounds for the absolute purchase of such supply of the said Water of the said River Frome and for the right of making maintaining and using the said Feeder through the said John Hopton's Lands subject to the following restrictions and regulations.

1st That the weir over which the water shall run from the said River Frome to the said Feeder shall be one Inch and a half above the present Sill or timber that the Water falls over at the Floodgates to the Waterfall and that neither the said Company nor the said John Hopton shall draw the Water below the level of the said sill except in time of Flood or high water to prevent the water overflowing the banks of the said river or when necessary for repairs and whenever so drawn the said John Hopton shall have the use of the same if he so please to irrigate his Meadows.

By 1844 a regular freight service was running between Ledbury and Birmingham using the Hereford and Gloucester Canal, the River Severn and the Worcester and Birmingham Canal.

The next length opened was to Withington on 26th February 1844 to great celebrations.

> 66 The completion of the Canal has been for some time regarded as an object of great importance to this city and county, and the circumstance of the work having been finished up to Withington about four miles only from Hereford, was therefore hailed with much satisfaction. A more suitable occasion indeed for paying a just tribute of respect and approval to Mr. Stephen Ballard, the talented engineer, for the manner in which he has conducted the work throughout the entire line, could scarcely have been chosen, and he was accordingly invited to a public dinner, which was given at the Hotel on Monday last. The interest felt on the occasion by all classes of citizens was intense, and the number and respectability of those who attended were beyond all expectation.
>
> In pursuance of the previous arrangement a procession of five boats left Ledbury at nine o'clock the same morning, the first containing a band of music, the next the committee and friends; one with goods belonging to Messrs. Bunning and Gibson; one the property of Messrs. Crowley, ditto; and one with salt from Droitwich. These boats were all decorated with union-jacks, flags, &c and had a very pleasing appearance. About twenty-seven other boats freighted with coal, &c. followed in the course of the day. The view from the wharf at Withington along the line of the Canal to the lock, was extremely picturesque, and the whole scene was peculiarly animating. On the wharf itself from fifty to sixty labourers were employed, and the whole preparations and arrangements were completed in a very short space of time.
>
> The procession reached the present terminus at half-past two o'clock, having been five hours on the way from Ledbury; and some delay then took place in advancing towards Hereford, in consequence of a very heavy shower of rain, the weather having been unpropitious all the morning with the exception of intervals when the sun burst forth in great splendour. Three hogsheads of cider were given to the workmen, and mirth and good humour universally prevailed. No accident of any consequence occurred, the only circumstance of this kind being that of a horse led by a respectable inhabitant of this city getting into the canal, where he was soon released without sustaining damage. 99
>
> *Hereford Journal, February 28th 1844*

The great and the good of Herefordshire then repaired to the Green Dragon Hotel for a night of dining and extravagantly optimistic speeches.

The euphoria surrounding the opening to Withington was to be short-lived. In the space of only a few months the tide turned. Ballard's diary takes on a depressing tone.

> 66 Received a letter from the Manager of the Gloucester Bank saying we could not overdraw our account any more. I wrote and told him we must for paying the men tomorrow, this gave me great annoyance and I spent a most miserable day.
>
> Paid men at tunnel today and discharged a great many.
>
> In extremely low spirits, vexed at the affairs of the Canal. The trade does not go on well, we have very little work to do to complete and the Railways are coming in from the north and south…Railways are everywhere and no funds to complete our little work without personal security. 99
>
> *Ballard, Stephen: Diary entries for March 28th – March 31st 1845*

Perhaps it was this state of affairs which led him to ask the Committee if he could be released:

> 66 Mr. S. Ballard having requested the opinion of the Committee as to the possibility of their dispensing with his services at present, and the Committee having taken the state of the works into their Consideration
>
> Resolved – that in the present unfinished state of the Canal the Committee do not consider that they would be justified in consenting to release Mr. Ballard unless a sufficient portion of his time could still be occasionally guaranteed for the General Superintendence of the Business of the Canal Company, and such is the opinion of the Committee as to Mr. Ballard's integrity of purpose on all occasions that they readily leave to himself the determination of this question. 99
>
> *Company Committee Minute Book: April 21st 1845*

Work continued and on May 22nd 1845 the basin at Hereford was filled with water for the first time. In contrast to the celebrations at Withington the event passed off unwitnessed and almost unnoticed. The Hereford

Times carried a brief and complimentary report of the engineering feat, but was only mildly enthusiastic as to its future benefits:

> 66 The Canal.—The Hereford and Gloucester Canal is now opened to this city, which will soon have a remarkably spacious basin, warehouses, &c, at Monkmoor. On Wednesday water was admitted through the tunnel at Holmer, a stupendous work, which we have before described, and boats can now come on to the city. It must have been a source of high satisfaction to Mr. Stephen Ballard, the engineer, to witness the triumph of this important undertaking before leaving for Lincolnshire, where some important works have been confided to his superintendence. The cuttings on the Hereford side of the tunnel are really tremendous, reminding us of some of the awful railway excavations in Derbyshire, and the whole work is one of great skill and extent. The tunnel has a towing-path, and like the aqueduct over the river Lugg exhibits all the evidences of durability for future ages. The advantage of the canal in the conveyance of Staffordshire coal and all kinds of produce, will soon be experienced by the inhabitants of this city and the surrounding neighbourhood. 99
>
> *Hereford Times, May 28th 1845*

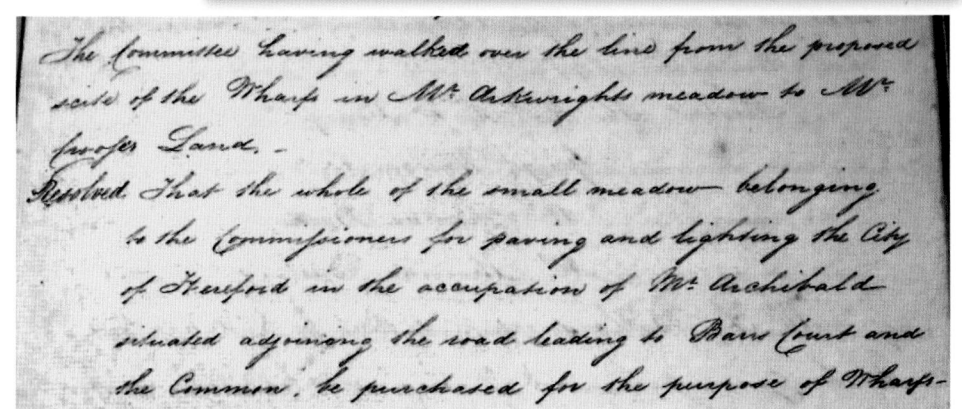

Figure 28: Extract from the Committee Minute Book for 25th October 1841 authorising the purchase of Mr. Arkwright's meadow in which to build the Hereford wharves. *(Author)*

The canal was complete. Ballard had given his all, probably knowing that the inevitable coming of the railways would surely make the whole project unviable. He left Herefordshire the same day to begin work on the Middle Level Drain in the fens. The words of his diary are now well enough known, but worth repeating in full here: →

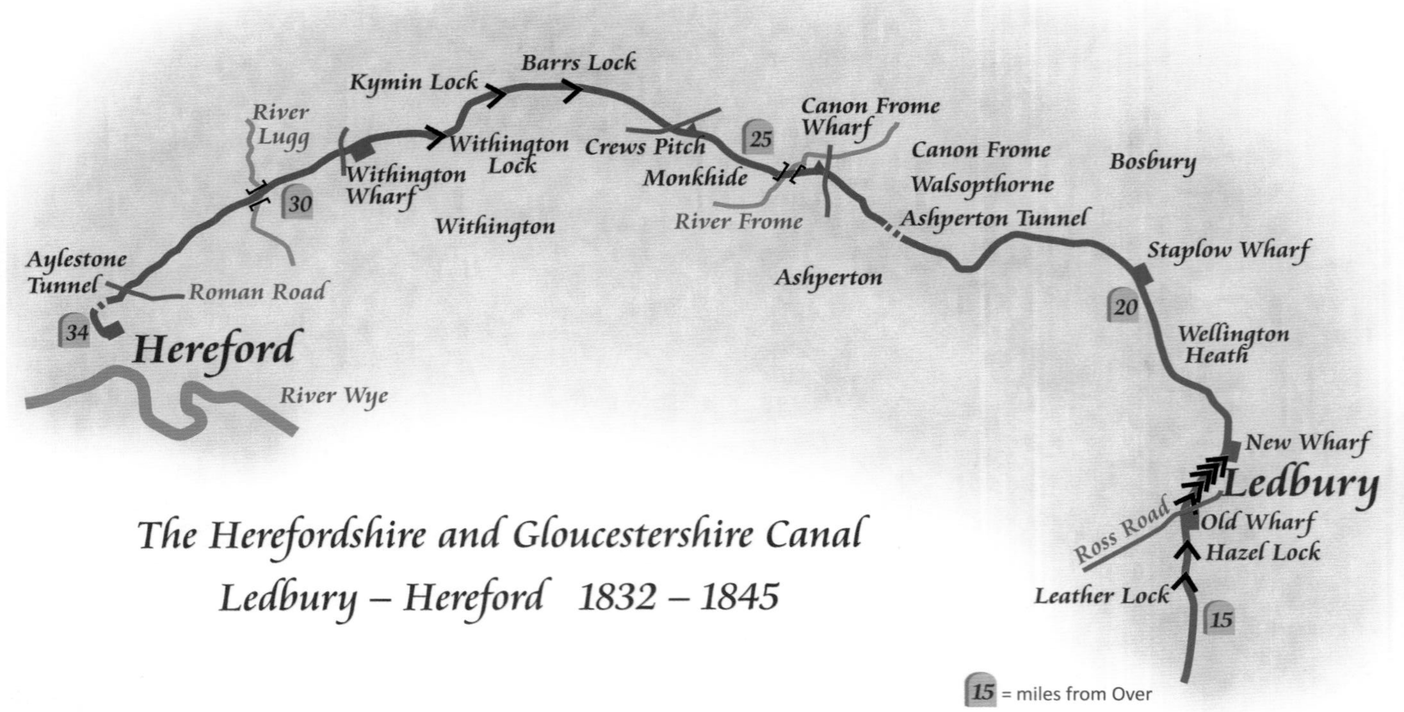

The Herefordshire and Gloucestershire Canal
Ledbury – Hereford 1832 – 1845

Aylestone
Tunnel
34
Hereford

River
Lugg
30
Withington
Wharf
Withington

Roman Road

River Wye

Kymin Lock

Barrs Lock

Withington
Lock
Crews Pitch

Monkhide
25
River Frome
Ashperton

Canon Frome
Wharf
Canon Frome
Walsopthorne
Bosbury

Ashperton Tunnel

20
Staplow Wharf
Wellington
Heath

Ross Road
Leather Lock
New Wharf
Ledbury
Old Wharf
Hazel Lock
15

15 = miles from Over

Figure 29: The second phase of the canal construction, 1832–1845. (Author)

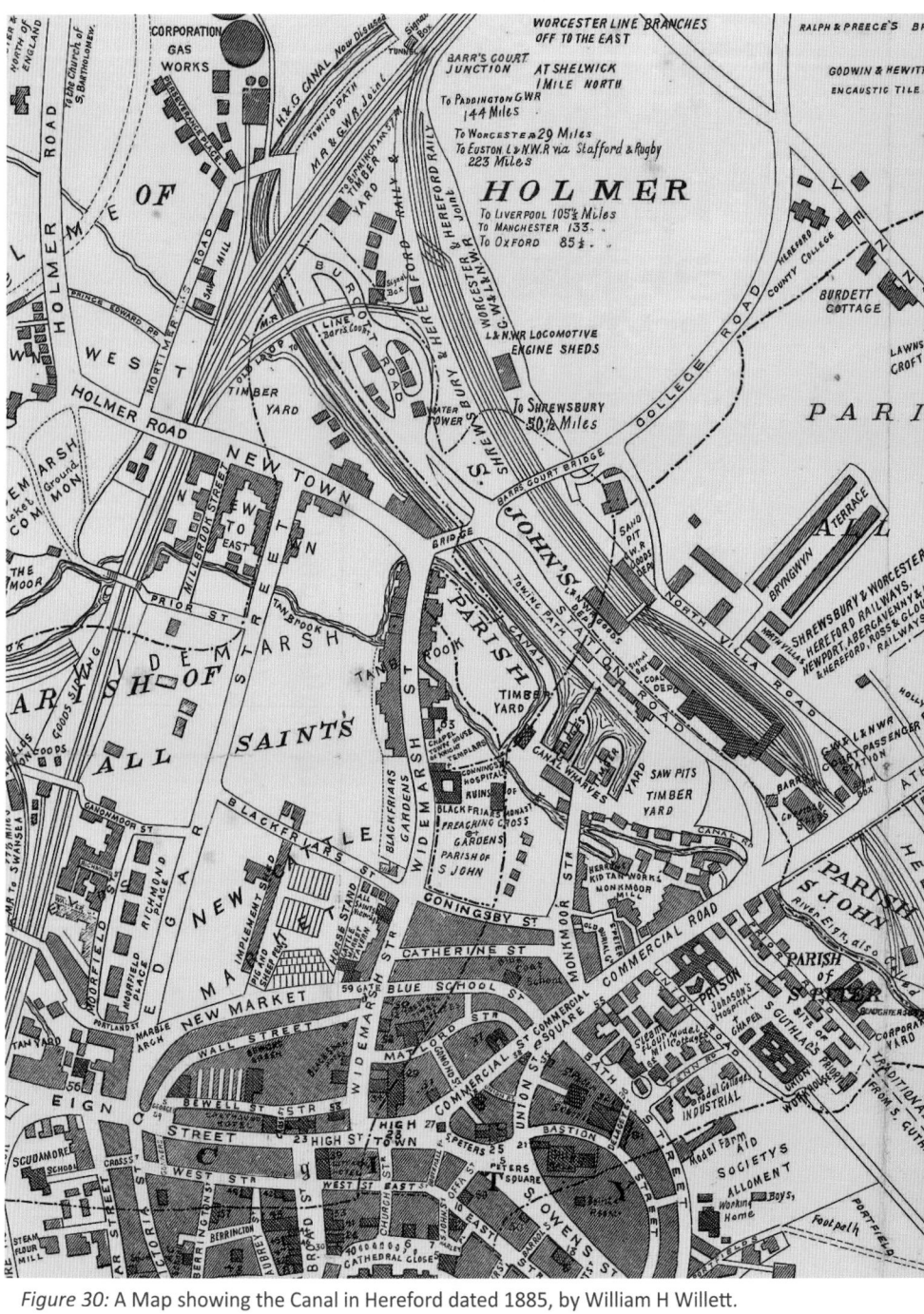

Figure 30: A Map showing the Canal in Hereford dated 1885, by William H Willett. The last goods were carried in 1883. *(Hereford City Library)*

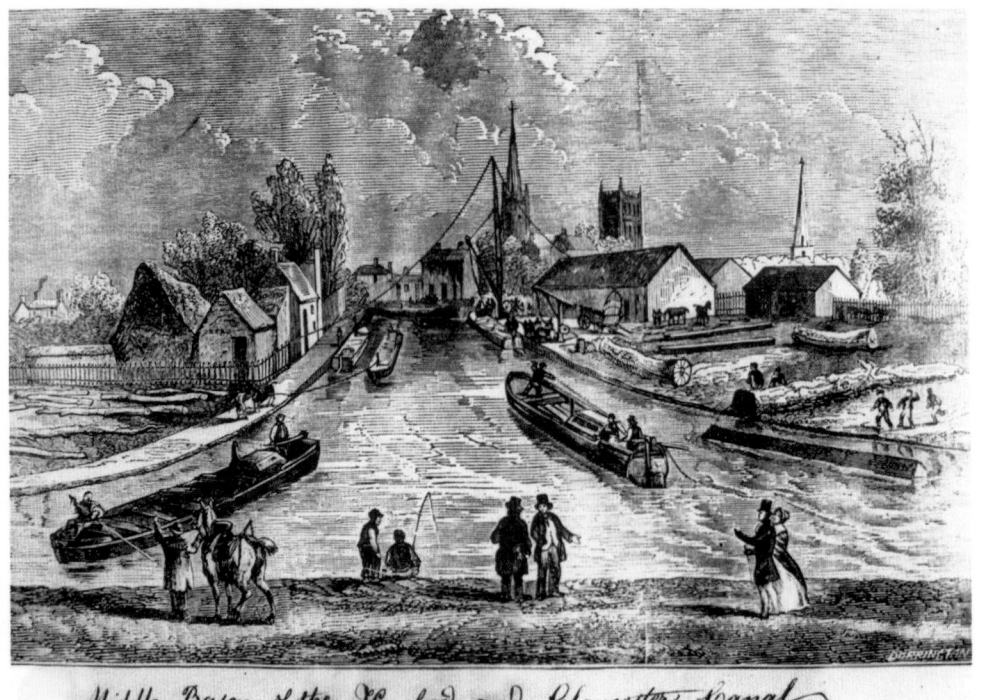

Middle Bason of the Hereford and Gloucester Canal.

Figure 31: One of the three Hereford Wharves, from an old etching. The only known illustration of the canal basins in Hereford. *(Hereford City Library)*

❝ Canal opened to Hereford. This morning had the satisfaction of seeing the water turned into the basin at Hereford. It was contrived that I should see it before I started for London.

I was greatly affected at leaving Withington, it was a fine morning and the country looked beautiful. I could not refrain from shedding tears. Near 18 years I have been employed on the canal and my spirits dropped when the hour arrived for my leaving it. Went from Gloucester to London by GWR. Bad headache. ❞

Ballard, Stephen: Diary entry for May 22nd 1845

The words "Bad headache" appear very frequently in Stephen Ballard's diary. This complaint clearly troubled him for most of the period covered by his diaries (1829-1853). At times he was so badly affected as to make it impossible for him to work. Before we allow Stephen Ballard to leave our story, though he will reappear very briefly later, a little more must be said about this exceptional man.

CHAPTER 5

An Exceptional Man

When first planning this book I decided that, as it was supposed to be about the canal and not about any individual person associated with it, I would limit my mention of Stephen Ballard to his involvement with the canal and say little about the man himself. But no one reading his diaries and other writings can fail to realise that there was far more to Stephen Ballard than just an excellent engineer. I have therefore added another chapter to my story.

Hurle, Pamela: Stephen Ballard 1804-1890 "One of Nature's Gentlemen", Aspect Design 2010 The best account of his life to date can be found in Pamela Hurle's delightful 'interpretation' to which I would refer any reader who would know more about Stephen Ballard and I am grateful to Mrs. Hurle for her willingness to allow me to share some of her extensive knowledge and enthusiasm with my readers.

We are fortunate to have the benefit of Stephen Ballard's diaries which he kept for much of his working life. Now held in the Hereford Records Office, these were written in Odells Shorthand, one of five different systems introduced in 1832 and were subsequently transcribed by his son, another Stephen.

Stephen Ballard was born in 1804, significantly, in a house standing on Malvern Link Common. While his indifferent education ill-prepared him for life as an engineer, from his early childhood he developed a great love of the countryside surrounding his home which led him to teach himself botany. At the age of 18 he secured a position at Lea and Kennedy's nurseries in Hammersmith. This was followed by work on the Earl of Plymouth's estate near Bromsgrove and the offer of a post at the Royal Botanical Gardens at Kew. However, he wanted to set up his own business and the lack of capital he would need for this determined that he would look for a totally different profession.

In 1825 he was apprenticed to a well-established Cheltenham builder, Henry Lucy, a position into which he threw himself with great enthusiasm. When Lucy's business failed in 1827, Ballard found himself Clerk to the Hereford and Gloucester Canal Company.

Knowing little of civil engineering, he was sent by the company to see

some of the great engineering works currently in progress – both railways and canals. With a mind like a sponge, he soaked up concepts and solutions to problems and by the time he returned home he was ready to put his ideas into practice.

In engineering circles he is now better known for his work in building railways than for his association with the Hereford and Gloucester Canal. He was interested in all things new and is credited with a number of inventions including lock gates without any iron work, a 'scorcher' – a device pulled by a horse which threw flames on the ground to burn wheat stubble and a machine for wetting bricks. One of his most notable inventions was his ice-breaking boat, demonstrated in Ledbury in 1838 and for his account of which he was later awarded the Telford medal by the Institution of Civil Engineers, the highest prize awarded by the Institution for a paper or series of papers.

The Mechanic's Magazine, Museum, Register, Journal and Gazette, Volume 28 p336

Long pieces of timber, cased with Iron, were fixed on the front of the boat, these timbers project before the boat, and form an Inclined plane, sloping upwards from the under edge of the ice to near the middle of the boat. By these means, when the boat is drawn forwards, the ice is forced upwards Instead of downwards, as is the usual way of breaking; and It is found the Ice breaks remarkably easy when thus lifted from the water. The boat, with its apparatus, was drawn along the canal by two horses at a brisk pace, and the ice, which was in some places upwards of four Inches thick, was ploughed up with great facility... It is calculated that one horse will do as much work with a machine of this kind as four in the common way.

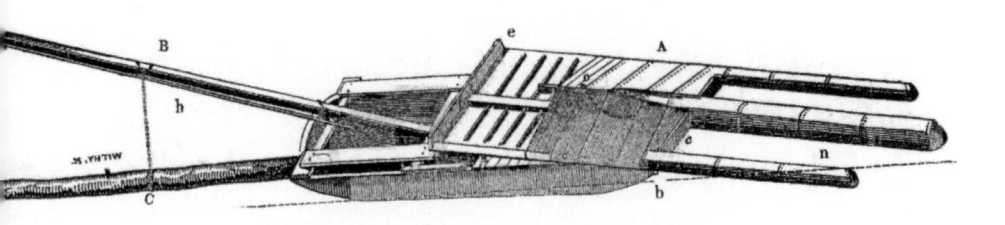

Figure 32: Ballard's Ice-Breaking Boat *(Mechanics Magazine, Museum, Register, Journal and Gazette)*

While working on the Hereford and Gloucester Canal he was constantly being approached by other companies and public bodies seeking to employ him. He was clearly a much respected engineer. After spending some years on engineering projects in the fens including the River Ouse and the Middle Level his work was almost exclusively on railway schemes.

In 1847 he began an association with Thomas Brassey who by that date had been responsible for building about a third of the railways in Britain. It proved to be a rewarding partnership for the next 20 years which took Ballard to India and Holland. Nearer to his boyhood home he worked on the Worcester to Hereford line which involved a long tunnel through the Malvern Hills. His later projects included lines between Evesham and Redditch and London and Bedford. His interest in railways continued right up until his death, only a few weeks before which he published the second edition of a pamphlet which argued the case for a cheaper form of railway which could be built to serve rural areas.

In the post-Beeching railway era his ideas make interesting reading:

66 A line suitable for a. rural district should be made for about £4,000 a mile. The gradients may be 1 in 25 and the curves of 4-chain radius; thus allowing the line for the most part, to be made on the surface of the ground, with very little cutting or earthwork. The speed of trains should be restricted to 15 miles an hour, thereby vastly reducing the wear and tear of the permanent way and rolling stock. Light tank engines would be sufficient; and as in most cases the line would be short, only one engine at a time would be on the line, thus avoiding collision and expenses in signalling. Light tank engines running only at moderate speed would allow of frequent stoppings for the accommodation of the district. The conductor of the train should act as general station-master, receive fares, and manage the traffic of the line; thus saving a great deal of the expense attending stations. 99

Ballard, Stephen: "Cheap Railways for Rural Districts", 1890 p.7

Though he became prosperous in middle to later life he always had a concern for the poor.

In 1839 he records in his diary:

66 Went from Bristol to Gloucester by coach. Walked to Newent and then coach to Ledbury. There was a poor woman from Stratford in the coach and as she seemed in distress I told the coachman I would pay her fare from Gloucester. 99

Ballard, Stephen: Diary entry for December 16th 1839

In 1840 he writes:

66 Payday. Holland has been at work for a month but on measuring up there is nothing to come to him. He was in great trouble and offered me his watch if I would lend him £4. I would not take it but advanced him the money which I expect he will never pay. 99

Ballard, Stephen: Diary entry for July 11th 1840

Cheap Railways for Rural Districts.

THOUGH a casual observer might suppose the entire face of this country to be covered with a network of railways, it is a fact that there are many places distant from existing lines that would be greatly benefited by their construction. Districts, though actually within a few miles of great railway centres, but yet distant from a line only three or four miles are, to all intents and purposes, commercially considered, lost parts of the country. They are approached only by crooked and, frequently, bad roads, while the aspect of everything about them indicates that they are an age behind places which fortunately have felt the beneficial and stimulating influence of railways, even though only for a few years.

Districts without Railways at great disadvantage.

People living in such districts, and not only feeling the want but seeing the advantages of railway accommodation, should know that the making of a line in the present day is a very different matter from what it was thirty years ago. The first railways were made in the best lines for traffic, such as Manchester and Liverpool, the London and Birmingham, the London and Bristol, and others between large and populous towns, where the prospect, almost the certainty, of profitable returns was sufficient to tempt capitalists to invest their money in this enterprise. The traffic on these well-chosen lines more than realised the anticipations of the promoters, and proved so profitable that they could

The first Railways placed in best lines for traffic, and provided by great Capitalists.

Figure 33: The opening page of Ballard's pamphlet "Cheap Railways for Rural Districts" *(Malvern, 1884)*

Ballard tantalisingly mentions an incident while the deep Ashperton Tunnel was under construction, about which I would love to know more details:

> 66 Boy fell down shaft No. 4, 60 feet deep. Was with him until 1am. 99
>
> *Ballard, Stephen: Diary entry for October 14th 1841*

His diaries also tell us something about his opinions. He frequently mentions his frustration with unreasonable landowners and he has little sympathy for members of the legal profession.

> 66 Went to Worcester to try and get Hill to reduce his bill (£34) of costs for defending father in the libel action. He would only take off £4. Said he had charged as low as he possibly could, which I do not believe. He is like other lawyers, will say and do anything for money. 99
>
> *Ballard, Stephen: Diary entry for June 13th 1839*

His view of race meetings was similarly uncompromising:

> 66 Ledbury races. Did not go near them as I considered that they ought not to be supported on account of the fighting and drunkenness which is encouraged there. 99
>
> *Ballard, Stephen: Diary entry for August 24th 1838*

He uses identical wording to describe the Hereford races!

While still a bachelor his views of women were interesting too:

> 66 Philip and his wife went to Ledbury to see the American Riders perform. I do think that the principal object of a woman's life is pleasure, they are always seeking it and most of them think of nothing else. 99
>
> *Ballard, Stephen: Diary entry for August 3rd 1842*

Perhaps this had changed by 1854 when Stephen married Maria Bird, the daughter of a farmer on whose land he had worked on the construction of the Great Northern Railway. They were, in some ways, an unlikely couple. At 25, Maria was half his age and, unlike her husband, totally devoid of any sense of humour. Their marriage was to last 36 happy years and brought eight children into the world, all of whom survived into adulthood. In 1855 the couple moved into the new centrally-heated home Ballard designed

on his Colwall estate. At the back of the house, adjacent to the kitchen was a large porch with seating for those who came begging for a bowl of soup. And come they did, for in a letter to the Daily News he writes:

> 66 Over 5800 basins of soup a year are given to the hungry poor at my back door. The plan adopted is this: a large stock pot is constantly in use on the kitchen fire range. Into this pot scraps of meat, bones, gravies and other edible scraps of provisions are put and then thoroughly stewed; thickening of rice, split peas with salt and pepper are added and the result is a savoury and nutritious soup....A very considerable amount of extra work is entailed on the cook, not only in making the soup but mainly in giving it away to the hungry applicants. This extra labour the cook cheerfully submits to, working people generally have a kind and charitable feeling for those who are in want. 99
>
> *The Daily News, February 1886 quoted in Hurle, Pamela: Stephen Ballard 1804-1890 "One of Nature's Gentlemen" p89*

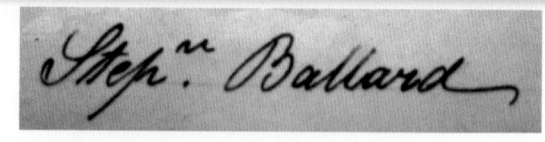

Figure 34: Stephen Ballard's signature from the Canon Frome Feeder Agreement.
(Colin Dymott and Hereford Archive Service)

His generosity towards the poor was not universally admired. In response to a remarkably modern argument he goes on:

> 66 Some objections are made to this method of helping the starving poor on account of the danger of encouraging regular tramps that never will work. Occasionally such idle impostors may be supplied but only a small proportion of the whole. Most of those supplied are working men, out of work and are worthy objects of charity. The fear of erring by encouraging an occasional idle tramp I think should not prevent the practice of saving food from waste now the very great proportion travelling are without doubt working men. 99
>
> *Ibid.*

Though he was not, it seems, as enthusiastic a church-goer as Maria and his children, his views are remarkably resonant with John Wesley's words "So wickedly, devilishly false is that common objection, 'They are poor only because they are idle'".

Wesley, John: Journal, February 8th 1753

He was a confirmed teetotaller and was opposed to capital punishment for any crime, even in 1836, the year of the last hangings in England for offences such as arson, burglary and rape, but still 32 years before the last public execution was carried out. There is no evidence that he changed his view after his older brother, Phillip, was murdered in 1887 during a burglary at his home in Hereford while his own daughter Ada was staying with him. James Jones and Alfie Scandrett were hanged in Hereford gaol the following year for the offence.

While he designed a number of public buildings in the area, perhaps his greatest legacy to the nation is found in the Malvern Hills themselves. The Hills had been part of a Royal Forest since the days of William the Conqueror but under Charles I this had become common land controlled by the Lord of the Manor. The law relating to commons is extremely complex and obscure and over the years this had enabled significant areas of the Hills to be taken into private ownership. Many poor people depended upon their common rights to graze sheep, pigs and cattle and to gather wood, nuts and berries.

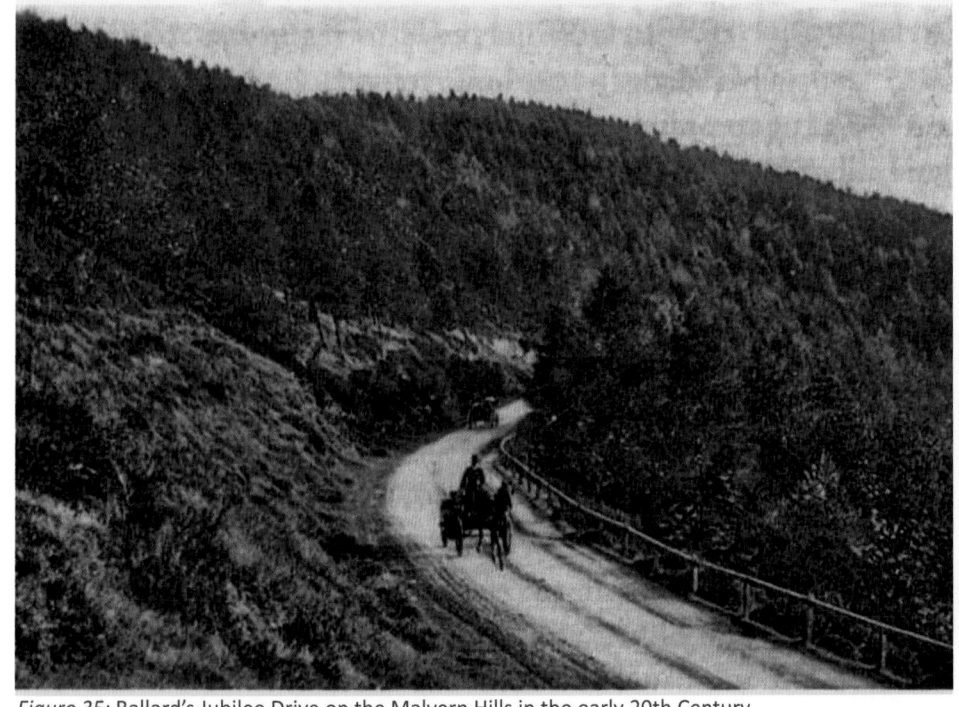

Figure 35: Ballard's Jubilee Drive on the Malvern Hills in the early 20th Century. *(Malvern Hill Conservators)*

During the 17th century protests among the poor became frequent, characterised by anonymous poems written at the time:

> They hang the man and flog the woman,
> Who steals the goose from off the common,
> Yet let the greater villain loose,
> That steals the common from the goose.

> The law locks up the man or woman
> Who steals the goose from off the common
> And geese will still a common lack
> Till they go and steal it back

By the middle of the 19th century this had become a serious issue, not only for the poor, but for the more affluent who saw their rights of access to the hills being steadily eroded and the condition of land itself deteriorating.

The main local culprit, in the eyes of many, including Stephen Ballard, was Lady Emily Foley whom he saw as stealing land from the poor. Lady Foley was no great admirer of Stephen Ballard either. She refused to travel by train through his Colwall Tunnel, preferring to travel by horse-drawn carriage to Great Malvern Station where she had a private waiting room, now Lady Foley's Tea Room.

Through letters to local newspapers and arranging and addressing public meetings Ballard was largely responsible for the Malvern Hills Act of 1844 which established the Malvern Hills Conservators and gave us the right of public access to the hills which we enjoy today. His last piece of engineering work was the design of the magnificent Jubilee Drive, running across the western flank of the Malvern Hills, opened in 1889 to celebrate Queen Victoria's 50th jubilee,

He died in 1890 at the age of 86 and was buried on his Colwall estate over his tunnel. We have much to thank him for.

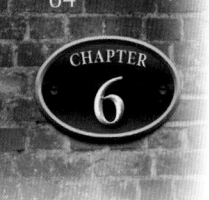

CHAPTER 6

Uncertain Times

The lack of interest shown by the people of Hereford to the arrival of the canal seems to have continued once the canal was fully operational. The canal had cost far more than Ballard had ever imagined and initially there was insufficient toll income to pay even the interest on the Company's loans. The threat of the railway hung over the whole enterprise with various schemes proposed, including one using the line of the canal itself, but they came to nothing.

A Table of Tolls

On the Hereford and Gloucester Canal.

TONNAGE.

PER TON PER MILE.

Corn, Grain, Meal and Salt	*Three halfpence.*
Stone, Bricks, Tiles, Slates, Lime, Manure, Clay, and other Soil	*One penny.*
Hay and other Fodder	*Three pence.*
Hops and Wool...	*Twopence halfpenny.*

Lath, per thousand, *one farthing* per mile.
Other Lading, not included above, 2*d.* per ton per mile.

WHARFAGE.

Timber, Hurdles, and Faggots, lying on the Wharf six months or less, 2½*d.* per ton.
Bark lying on the Wharf one month or less, 2½*d.* per ton.
Manure, Clay, and other Soil lying on the Wharf one month or less, 4*d.* per ton.
Lath lying on the Wharf six months or less, *one halfpenny* per 1000.
Hay and other Fodder lying on the Wharf one month or less, 1*d.* per ton.
Other Lading not included above, lying on the Wharf six months or less, 2*d.* per ton.

N.B.—40 feet of squared Timber ....
      50 feet of round Timber .... ⎰ Allowed to one ton.
      30 cwt. of Poles under 6 inches quarter girt ....⎱
      50 bushels Winchester measure of Corn, Grain, or Meal ⎰

Distance from the Severn

To	Barbers Bridge,......................	4 miles.
—	Newent,.............................	8½
—	The Boyce, ...	11½
—	Dymock Bridge, ...	12
—	Tilleys Green, ...	13½
—	Greenway,...........................	14
—	Ledbury Wharf, ...	16

STEPHEN BALLARD, CLERK

Canal Office, Ledbury.

Figure 36:
Table of Tolls.
(Eastnor Castle Archives)

Nevertheless, traffic gradually increased and the Company was able to meet its interest payments by 1847, but the promises of the early promoters of the canal were never realised. Even before the canal was open the proprietors had looked for ways to get rid of it. Initial interest was shown by the snappily titled Herefordshire, Gloucestershire, South Wales and Worcester Railway and by the Welsh Midland Railway, but like other attempts over the next few years, nothing actually happened.

Company Committee Minute Book: 23rd September 1845

The fears raised by the Gentlemen of Hereford in 1791 regarding the "serious Inconveniences and Mischiefs" which would result from the building of the canal were realised soon after it was completed. In 1849 the following letter appeared in the Hereford Times:

> 66 Sir,—Through the medium of your paper, I beg leave to call the attention of the police to the practice of bathing in the canal near the bridge at Widemarsh and close to the public road, where there are many persons continually passing. At about four o'clock on the afternoon of Friday last, as I was passing near the spot, my attention was attracted by seeing a crowd of persons on the bridge, and on looking to see what " puppet show" attracted their attention, I saw a naked fellow nearly grown to man's estate on the bank of the canal near to the bridge, exposing himself in the most indecent manner. Some music was being played in the street near the wharf, and this shameless fellow mounted some boards at a very short distance from the road and commenced dancing to the tune, a gentleman of the city, with a lady, being passing over the bridge at the time, the former cried shame that such a scene should be allowed. The fellow, having amused himself by dancing as long as he pleased, returned in a state of nudity, not by water, but along the towing-path to the wharf near the Commercial-road, where I suspect he had left his clothes. I thought the best accompaniment to his dance would have been the tune of a policeman's cane applied vigorously to his naked body; he might have been then made to "dance without a fiddle." Really, Sir, it is disgraceful that such things should be allowed so near a public thoroughfare, and I trust the police will give a sharp look out. 99
>
> *Hereford Times, June 27th, 1849. OBSERVATOR*

The Company struggled on. The Post Office Directory of 1856 gives only one coal agent at Hereford's Barr's Court Wharf – E. Pinkerton and one coal dealer, E. George. However Ledbury Wharf was full of coal dealers – B. Bill, J. Bill, Mrs A Davies, W. Pitt, T. Rees and E. Webb. There were others in Bye Street. and Bridge Street. J. Racster was a coal agent at Withington. Perhaps it is significant that two other coal merchants in

*Post Office
Directory for
Herefordshire 1856
p.116*

Ibid: p.61

Hereford are given as being "above Eign" suggesting that the Wye was still carrying a significant amount of coal.

Pickford and Co., Danks, Venn and Sanders and Henry Mounsell and Co. were the main carriers working 'by canal etc. to London and all parts'.

The boatmen had to work hard to make a living and there were suspicions that health and safety was not a high priority. By 1848 the order restricting the use of the canal to the hours of daylight had clearly been lifted and concerns were voiced by the Hereford Journal:

> ❝ At an inquest recently held, touching the death of Thomas Lanslett, late of Ledbury, in the county of Hereford, labourer, who was drowned during the night of 25th-26th January 1848, in the narrow tunnel on the Hereford and Gloucester Canal leading from Dymock towards Newent, and known as the "Oxenhall Tunnel", when helping John Beard to "leg" through the tunnel one of the "fly" boats belonging to Mr. Holloway of Withington, near Hereford, common carrier. The Jury with their verdict made the following presentment to the Coroner:– "The Jury unanimously consider great reforms are necessary, and ought to be insisted upon by the proprietors or acting committee of the Hereford and Gloucester Canal Company, in the working and managing thereof, by the removal of the present great risks thereon, and by a check to the flagrant desecrations of the Sabbath along the same;– Also that some change is required on the part of some of the carriers on the said canal as to the requirements from their servants, in regard to the number of hours of continuous work by night and day, and the constant violation of the entire Sabbath ❞
>
> *Hereford Journal: February 9th 1848*

There was another drowning in 1850, and again the Hereford Journal expressed its disquiet:

> ❝ It seems rather strange that there should be so many fatal accidents in the narrow Boat Canal between Gloucester and Ledbury while there are so few in the Ship Canal from that port to Sharpness Point. This fact would induce an opinion that there must be something radically wrong in the navigation or management, perhaps both, of the former. Some are inclined to attribute it to the construction, others to the working of it by day and by night, Sundays and week days, depriving the men of their necessary rest and sleep; while others suggest the use of improper cattle and tackle; it may be that all combine in a measure to occasion them. ❞
>
> *Ibid: February 20th 1850*

This particular drowning seems to have been caused by the behaviour of a notorious horse owned by a Mr. John Hodgetts who operated a fly-boat service. The animal seems to have had a will of its own which seldom coincided with that of the boatmen who had to work with him. He was much given to galloping backwards and forwards along the towpath, snapping the tow rope and escaping through towpath gates, which "he had learned to open", and thus over hedges and ditches until he could be caught. The coroner found that this horse had caused the death of John Evans, "a steady young man", by his unruly behaviour at 10pm on a windy February night.

Ibid

The Company also suffered from vandalism, especially it seems in Hereford between Burcott Row and the tunnel. In 1849 a boatman, Thomas Radbourn was hauled up before the magistrates for vandalising a bridge in Hereford, inflicting damage which was estimated to cost six shillings to repair. As Radbourn had to pay for the damage, the fine was relatively small, the total being £1.7s.10d. The Company must have thought he had got off lightly as it published a reminder to any would-be vandals informing them that:

> 66 … every such offender shall be guilty of a felony, and if convicted, shall be liable at the discretion of the Court to be transported across the seas for life, or for any term not less than seven years, or to be imprisoned for any term not exceeding four years: also to be once, twice or thrice whipped in addition, if the Court shall think it fit. 99
>
> *Hereford Journal, September 5th 1949*

In 1851 a remarkable case was brought before the Newent magistrates:

> 66 CAUTION TO CAPTAINS OF NARROWBOATS, – A case was heard the other day, at Newent, Gloucestershire, which should operate as a caution to captains of canal boats and others who are in the habit of impeding the free navigation of the canal. The proceedings were instituted by Mr. P. Ballard, the Clerk, of the Herefordshire and Gloucestershire Canal Company, and the case was heard before J.C. Thackwell, Esq., the Rev. H. L. Whatley, and R. F. Onslow, Esq. Mr. Edward Pritchard, of Hereford, appeared in support of the complaint, which was for impeding the navigation of the canal by remaining a longer time than was necessary in the tunnel at Oxenhall, and Mr. Poole of Gloucester, for the defendants. Those who are acquainted with this tunnel are well aware that it is a very low, awkward one—that it extends for a considerable distance, and that it is quite impossible for

two boats to pass each other within it. The roof, too, of the tunnel is but a few feet from the water, and the boats are propelled by "legging it", as the boatmen call it – that is, the men lie on their backs and, by pressing their feet against the roof and sides of the tunnel, thus propel it through. It may well be imagined that to be embowelled in such a place is both dreary and dangerous. It appears that one night just preceding the hearing of the complaint, a boat belonging to Mr. Collingborne, of Gloucester, entered the tunnel and made some unnecessary delay therein. Sometime afterwards, a boat of Mr. Smith of the Kerry Arms entered the tunnel. The two boats met about midway, and the captain of each boat refused to go back. Other boats entered the tunnel, and all of these were within it from 12 o'clock on the previous night till nearly the same hour on the following day, and thus all navigation was completely stopped. Three of the captains concerned in the blockade" were fined in the sum of £2 each and expenses. The situation of these obstinate parties could not be one of the most comfortable, remaining, as they did, for 12 hours in their dark, dreary, and subterraneous abode. 99

Hereford Times, May 24th 1851

Unfortunately the Hereford Times reporter had got things wrong and the embowelment in the dark, dreary, and subterraneous abode was for rather longer than he had imagined:

66 Stopping the Navigation on the Canal. - In consequence of our Reporter having misunderstood his informant, we represented in last week's paper, that, in the case heard at Newent, several boats remained within the Tunnel, at Oxenhall, from 12 o'clock one night till 12 o'clock the following day—a period of 12 hours ; whereas, the truth is, they remained in their dark, dreary, and subterraneous abode, from 12 o'clock on the Thursday night till 10 o'clock on the following Sunday morning—a period of 58 hours! Those who are acquainted with the Tunnel at Oxenhall will think it almost incredible that a number of human beings should, because neither party would give way to the other, choose to remain so long in such a situation. There is no towing-path through the tunnel ; but the men, as we have before said, lie on their backs, propel the boats through with their feet. Water is continually falling from the low roof, and, altogether, a more damp and dismal place cannot well be imagined. 99

Ibid: May 31st 1851

Two years later, in August 1853 it happened again, though the delay was a mere nine hours, the innocent party being forced back out of the tunnel

by the number of boats coming the other way:

> 66 Warning to Boatmen.– John Beard, a boatman, was summoned by Mr. P. Ballard, of Hereford, clerk to the Herefordshire and Gloucestershire canal company, for obstructing a boat in the tunnel of the Herefordshire and Gloucestershire canal. The defendant had been navigating his boat from Gloucester to Ledbury, and at the time when he entered the tunnel at the Newent end, he ought to have been out at the other end towards Ledbury. In consequence of his being so late he met a boat navigated by Samuel Boon, and there being room for only one boat to pass it a time, they stopped each other. Neither party would go back ; and there they lay for nine hours until other boats came up from Gloucester, entered the tunnel, and forced Boon, the complainant, out of the tunnel the way he went in. Mr. Pritchard, of Hereford, appeared in behalf of the canal company, and pressed for the full penalty, as it had become a matter of serious consequence to some parties waiting for goods. The case was proved by Samuel Boon and Richard Good, the lock keeper, and Beard was fined £4 ten shillings an hour being the full penalty.
>
> Thomas Fletcher was summoned by Mr. Ballard, for obstructing the navigation on the same canal by drawing off the water at the Oxenhall lock, by so doing causing the stoppage of boats in the tunnel for several hours for want of water. The case was proved by Richard Good, lock keeper at the Oxenhall double locks, and the defendant was fined £5. 99
>
> *Hereford Journal: August 13th 1853*

Beard's fine of four pounds ten an hour could hardly have been correct, amounting to over £40 if we count nine hours. This would be more than a boatman could earn by a journey from Hereford to Staffordshire and back. *Ibid: September 15th 1852*

On July 8th 1853, after over four hours' torrential rain overnight much of Herefordshire and mid Wales was indundated by some of the worst floods in living memory resulting in the loss of nine lives.

The canal between Oxenhall Tunnel and Dymock overflowed its banks and then the embankment near Dymock breached and water from the five mile pound cascaded into the already inundated fields below. It appears that the breach may have saved the lives of the crew of a Gibson's boat which had entered the tunnel as the water was rising dramatically only to be drawn out again as the canal level dropped equally quickly following the breach.

Another boat, fully-laden with timber, was in the tunnel at the time travelling from Newent. Meeting the deluge of water coming from the Dymock end of the tunnel, this boat was first forced backwards and then forwards again by the breach, finishing up aground three quarters of a mile from each end of the tunnel. The boatman and his wife were rescued by an empty boat which was able to reach them from the Oxenhall end. The Oxenhall lock-keeper, Mr. Goode, was astonished by the whole thing as he had seen no rain at all, first seeing a torrent of water overflowing the banks near the locks only to see it all disappear after the breach *Ibid. July 13th 1853* occurred.

In 1853 the railway line between Hereford and Shrewsbury opened, with the line to South Wales opening in 1854. During the early 1850s the various companies vying to link Hereford to Worcester were too busy fighting among themselves to take any interest in the struggling canal. The hopes that this line would utilise the route of the canal failed to be realised when a more direct route ignoring it altogether was approved in 1853, though the line wasn't opened fully until 1861. Stephen Ballard was one

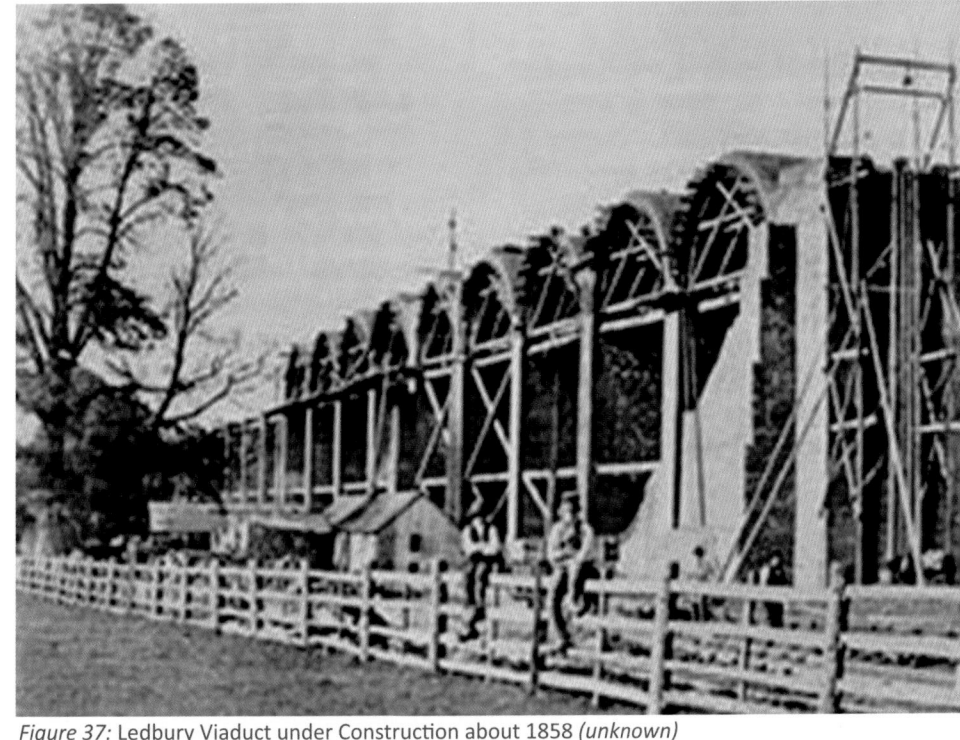

Figure 37: Ledbury Viaduct under Construction about 1858 *(unknown)*

of the contractors in its construction, his brother Robert supplying the bricks for the 31 arches of the Ledbury Viaduct.

In 1854 the Company did a deal with the newly opened Newport, Abergavenny and Hereford Railway to carry coal from Hereford to Newent at a discounted rate. Presumably the boats carrying this coal would meet those bringing coal from the Forest of Dean coming the other way!

Rescue, if it can be called that, came through the influence of the extraordinary William Philip Price. Dr. Price, owner of Tibberton Court, notable philanthropist and twice MP for Gloucester, was Chairman of the Canal Committee but also held influential positions connected with a number of other canals and railways. His business partner, Richard Potter had similar connections. He had been a member of the Great Western Board until 1856 and in 1860 became a Director of the West Midland Railway. When the West Midland and Great Western amalgamated in 1863 he returned to the GWR board and served as Chairman until 1865 when he was replaced by Sir Daniel Gooch.

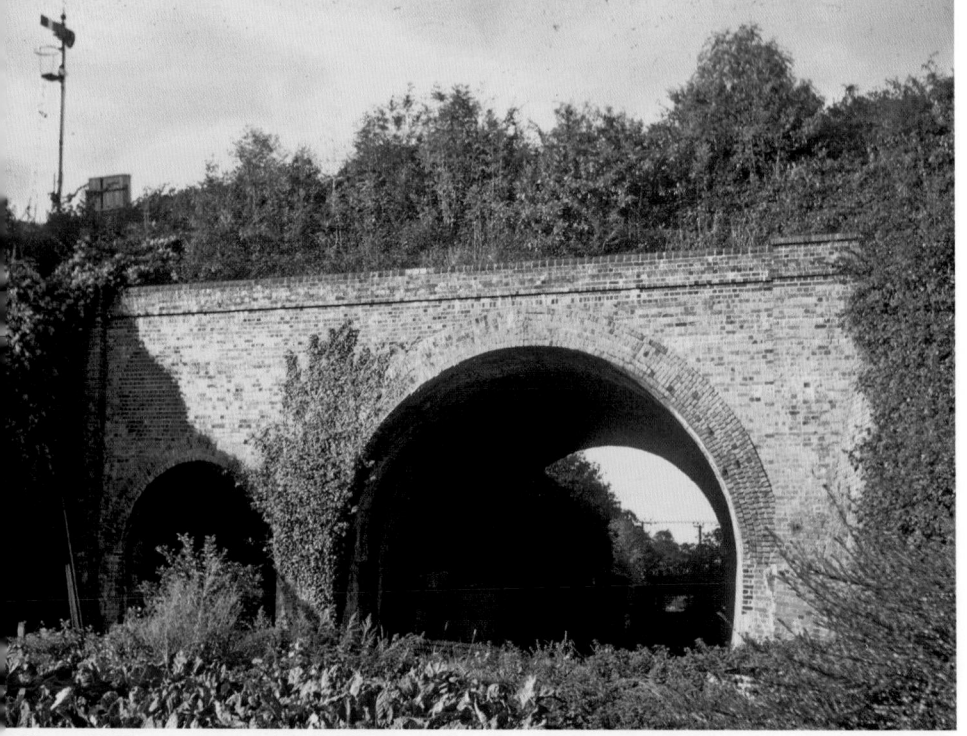

Figure 38: The separate arches for the towpath and canal taking Stephen Ballard's canal under his railway embankment *(Mike Potts)*.

Between them, on January 17th 1862 Price and Potter managed to broker an agreement with the Great Western and West Midland Railway Companies to lease the canal and to enable a railway line from Ledbury to Gloucester to be constructed on the route of the canal. The Memorandum of Agreement began as follows:

> ❝ The Canal to be bought by the Railway Companies for a perpetual rent charge of £5,000 per annum to commence from the 1st day of January 1862 payable half-yearly on the 15th day of July and the 15th day of January. The Canal and Railway Companies parties hereto bind themselves either one or both as may be decided upon to apply for an Act of Parliament to confirm this purchase and to convert the whole or a part of the Canal into a Railway in the same session of Parliament that a Bill shall be applied for to amalgamate the Great Western, and West Midland Railway Companies. ❞
>
> *Memorandum of Agreement between Herefordshire and Gloucestershire Canal Company and the Great Western and West Midlands Railway Companies: January 17th 1862*

The canal was to be run by a Joint Committee of members of the three companies until such time as a new Act of Parliament could be obtained transferring ownership.

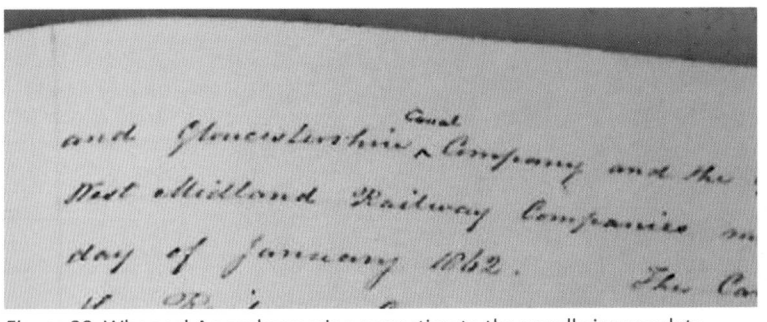

Figure 39: Whoops! An embarrassing correction to the usually immaculate Minute Book, October 28th 1862. *(Author)*

After it had absorbed the West Midland, the Great Western was in no hurry to obtain the new Act or to convert the canal to the railway and the Joint Committee had to remind the Great Western of the Agreement several times.

Matters were not formalised until the Great Western Railway (Canal Vesting) Act was passed in 1870. The official wording which appears in the London Gazette runs to several pages and deals with seven new

interconnecting railway lines. In relation to the section from Ledbury to Dymock we read the following :

> ❝ To authorize the Company to stop up and discontinue the navigation of that portion of the Hereford and Gloucester Canal, now vested in the Great Western Railway Company, which lies between Dymock and Ledbury; and to appropriate and utilize for title purposes of the intended railways, all or any part of the said canal between the places aforesaid, freed and discharged from all duties, liabilities, and responsibilities connected with that part of the said canal, and to enter into and give effect to agreements between the Company and the Great Western Railway Company for the sale and purchase of that part of the said canal, and to authorize the Great Western Railway Company to sell the same and to substitute stock, either with or without a preference or priority, of that Company for the canal rent charge of £5,000 per annum, now payable under the Great Western Railway (Hereford and Gloucester Canal Vesting) Act, 1870, to the Company of Proprietors of the Herefordshire and Gloucestershire Canal Navigation. ❞
>
> *London Gazette, November 26th 1872*

Similar provisions relate to the section of the Canal between Newent and Gloucester. Much of the line of the canal between Dymock and Newent, including the long tunnel at Oxenhall, was avoided by the railway, which explains why this part remains in water to the present day.

In tune with much of the canal's history, nothing was to happen for some years. Trade continued to decline. The Company had little money to spend on maintenance, never mind improvements, but benefited from works carried out by the Severn Commissioners. There had been concerns about water levels above the Lower Parting and access to Gloucester Docks for some years and in 1863 proposals were drawn up to raise the summer water levels by three feet.

A plan by W.B. Clegram, Superintendent and Engineer to the Gloucester and Berkeley Canal Co. (now the Gloucester and Sharpness Canal), was approved to construct:

> ❝ Two dams, one on the western or Maisemore branch of the river, and the other on the eastern branch between Gloucester and the Lower Parting, of such height as to raise the summer level 3ft about its present lowest form – to put a barge lock near the dam in the eastern part of the river to pass the river traffic below Gloucester – and to remove the existing shoals and complete the regulation of the channel between Gloucester and Tewkesbury, by the same means which have been so successfully used at the shoal at Deerhurst. ❞
>
> *Berrow's Worcester Journal, December 26th 1863*

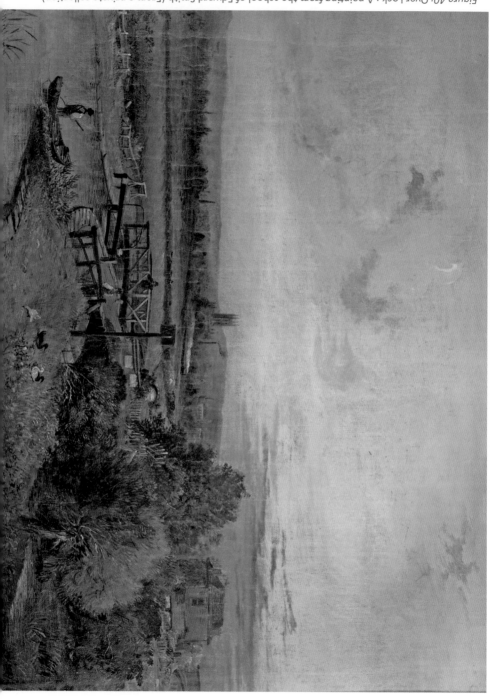

Figure 40: Over Lock : A painting from the school of Edward Smith (From a private collection)

The narrow Maisemore Lock and the much larger barge lock at Llanthony, which will feature later in our story, were opened in 1871.

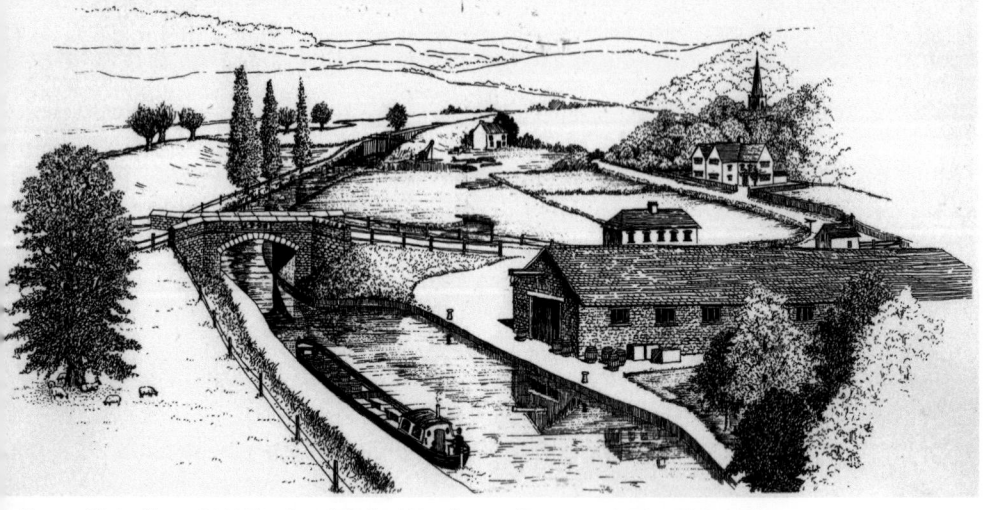

Figure 41: Ledbury Old Wharf and Cyder Warehouse (From a private collection)

A glimpse of the canal in Ledbury was given in the Ledbury Reporter in 1955 when it published some of the childhood memories of Mr. Ernest Bill, then aged 85. Ernest was a boy of 11 when the canal closed and he remembers helping to unload the very last cargo of timber to be carried along the canal. His father owned one of the three main canal carrying companies at the time in Ledbury. The principal cargoes, he recalled were corn, timber, coal, salt and 'various delicacies'. Cider and perry were loaded on to boats at the Old Wharf on the Ross Road having been stored in the Old Cyder warehouse. Ernest Bill also recalls the lighter fly boats "which used to ferry groceries from Gloucester to Hereford stopping at many villages on the way".

He also remembered the Ledbury boatmen:

> " Working hard, they earned plenty of money, and being lusty, cheerful fellows, they spent it lavishly. Hard working and hard drinking, they thought nothing of drinking a gallon or two of home brewed ale after the day's work.
>
> The canal provided employment for many men. For not only were there bargees, but crane men, lock men, loaders and a skilled band of "puddlers," who kept the waterway in order, repairing leaks and trimming banks.

In those days, the coal loaded into a barge was measured by displacement of water (the barge having been previously weighed), and Mr. Bill remembers an old story of a local barge owner who sent his newest barge to the official weighers fitted with a heavy oak bottom.

Having been measured it was returned to Ledbury, where he craftily removed the oak bottom and fitted a nice light deal one With this dodge be regularly 'gained' extra coal from the unsuspecting merchants! **"**

Ledbury Reporter, 1955

He would have been too young to have remembered the spectacular collision which occurred in 1873:

" Accident on the Canal.- An accident occurred on the Hereford and Gloucester Canal, near the town, on Friday evening, by which traffic will be stopped for a few weeks. A man in the employ of Messrs. Danks, the canal carriers, was towing a boat, and when near the lock at the Ledbury gasworks it was driven with such force against the gates that they were burst open. Some of the masonry was disturbed and one of the gates was torn away, and carried a considerable distance down the canal. The man in charge of the boat, who at the time was on the landing of the gates, about to open them, was thrown into the lock between the boat and the wall, and miraculously escaped unhurt. In consequence of the accident the water burst forth with such force that the new gasworks were for a time considerable flooded. **"**

Ross Gazette, September 4th 1873

This was by no means the first incident of its kind. In December 1851 a whole series of cases had been brought before the magistrates in Hereford.

" DAMAGING THE LOCKS on the Hereford and Gloucester Canal – A number of cases of this kind were called on for hearing, the greater number of which were disposed of and others we understand will be brought forward on a future occasion. Mr. K. Pritchard appeared on the part of the proprietors of the Hereford and Gloucester Canal accompanied by Mr. Philip Ballard, the company's clerk. Mr. Pritchard said the first charge they should bring before the bench would be against a person named Robert Smith, the owner of a boat plying on the said canal for having very improperly navigated the said water with his boat, by which he caused it to strike against the lock-gates at Withington. The erection of lock-gates or their repair was attended with

very considerable expense to the company, and it was therefore highly necessary that protection should be afforded it against the carelessness of the men plying on it in boats, and in order that other persons might be deterred from injuring the said lock-gates by improper conduct. The damage appeared to have been caused by the inattention of the defendant in passing through the lock. On a boat going through a lock it was the duty of the boatman to lay hold of a strap which is fastened to the boat and thrown over the lock on its passing through, and in order that the boat might take a proper course and prevent damage to the gates by any collision, the person in charge of the boat is not allowed to raise the boat's rudder until the upper gates have shut to. The defendant, Smith, having raised the rudder before the gates had closed they shut with great force, shattering it nearly to pieces, and for the loss thus sustained the company brought the present charge. The Act of Parliament appertaining to the case, before the court, provided that if any person should allow the boat under his care to strike against the bridges or locks of any such company, thereby doing any damage he shall be liable to be fined in the penalty of not less than 40/-. Mr. J. Davies, who appeared for the defendant, said that his client pleaded guilty to the charge, the Act of Parliament being so peremptory in such cases. However, he would ask them to deal in the most lenient manner with the case. Mr. Pritchard, on the part of the company, said that the Act of Parliament provided for the payment of the fine to the company, but Mr. Ballard would, on ascertaining the amount of damage done, make whatever allowance he possibly could to the defendant. The bench inflicted a fine of £2 with 9/6 expenses.

A SIMILAR CASE. -Noah Whitehouse of Gloucester owner of a boat plying on above-mentioned canal was summoned for a similar offence namely breaking the lock gates at Withington through neglect. After considerable hesitation this defendant admitted the offence and consented to be mulcted in a fine of 40s. Mr. Ballard said, in this case he could not hold out any hope of a mitigation as the damage, he feared, would amount to more than the fine. Defendant having to be summoned at Gloucester, amounted to £1.2s making a total of £3.2s.

ANOTHER LOCK-DAMAGING CASE. Two men named Perrins and Symonds, in charge of a boat the property of a person named Perks, were charged with having wilfully damaged one of the lock gates on the Hereford and Gloucester Canal. Symonds did not appear, having, it was stated, absconded on Saturday morning. The case was, however, gone into against Perrins; but it appearing from the evidence given that he did all he possibly could to avert injury done to the lock-gates, by holding the strap until his strength failed, with the view of preventing

the concussion that afterwards took place between the gates, it was agreed to abandon the case against him and proceed against Symonds, who had, contrary to the directions of Perrins, raised the rudder of the boat before it had passed the upper gates, - Symonds was fined £3 and expenses, and in default of payment, to be imprisoned for six weeks.

James Harper, a boatman, was then charged with having, through neglect, damaged one of the lock-gate. on the said Company's property. The defendant admitted the offence, and was fined £2 and 7/- expenses, Mr. Ballard saying that in that instance he would recommend a further mitigation by the Company. 🙶

Hereford Journal, December 10th, 1851

The reference to 'raising the rudder' in these reports is something of a mystery. David Blagrove suggests the following explanation:

🙶 The actual "raising" of the rudder was the withdrawal of the tiller on the rudder being swung over as the boat entered the lock. Dropping the boat down without doing this (in other words with the tiller at right angles to the lock walls) would result in a broken tiller or an unshipped rams head, or both. Insisting on withdrawing the tiller before opening the bottom paddles thus ensured that they would not be drawn until the top gate was properly closed. I suspect that the length of the locks was similar to those of the single-gate BCN locks, in which case a full-length boat has to swing its rudder over going downhill in order to get the bottom gate open.

I would hazard a guess that what really happened was that the boats concerned were travelling downhill, the steerer stepped ashore without removing the tiller and strapped in. Before he could get back aboard to take the stick out his mate had whipped the bottom paddles up and the top gate(s), assisted both by the "draw" of water and the way of the boat, came to with an almighty crash. Very naughty, but you should have seen horse boats working the BCN flights years ago. Banging and rattling paddles were the inevitable accompaniment of boats passing through. BCN gates though were built to withstand such treatment; even though it was frowned upon, everyone did it. Incidentally, on the Grand Junction, the District Engineer, Thomas Millner, ran his own system of justice in such matters. Boatmen reported for misusing locks or paddles were fined 5s by him and the money paid in to Northampton General Hospital! 🙹

Blagrove, David: Personal communication

Phillip Ballard reported two incidents to the Committee in 1869, one concerning another Danks's boat in a collision at Oxenhall. Quite what the steerer was doing at the time is a mystery, but the response is typical of a kindly Ballard.

> **"** I have to report that James Bayliss has been fined by the Magistrates at Ledbury £2.0.0 and expenses for ramming his boat against Staplow swing bridge, but it subsequently turned out he was insane, and is now in a Lunatic Asylum, the fines and expenses have not been paid. I am also sorry to report that a steerer of Messrs Danks's boats has been fined £2.0.0 and expenses for allowing his boat to strike the upper gates of Oxenhall No.2 Lock, but as it appears he was unavoidably absent from his boat at the time I returned him one pound of the fine. **"**
>
> *Company Committee Minute Book September 30th 1869*

By the 1870s trade on the Hereford and Gloucester Canal had declined to a trickle and the accounts we read of the state of the canal come from an unlikely source – tourist traffic!

In 1873 a party consisting of Mr. Farrant and three companions undertook a major holiday round trip from Oxford via Warwick, the Severn to Gloucester, Hereford, and the River Wye to Chepstow. Putting their boat on the roof of a train they crossed the Severn and by the Kennet and Avon canal and the Thames they returned to Oxford. All this in three weeks and in a rowing boat, occasionally assisted by a sail! Their trip on the Hereford and Gloucester Canal took two days and it seems to have rained most of the time.

They found the canal very narrow and full of weed but thought the entrance to Oxenhall was very pretty. Passing through the tunnel they took advantage of the acoustics with some merry singing. They met little traffic, except just outside Hereford when their mooring lines seem to have become entangled with the tow line of a passing boat.

Much more detail about the canal is given in the log of another holiday on the canal two years later. Mr. Howard Williams and his companions visited the canal in another rowing boat in 1875 and his account provides a rare detailed account of the state of the canal.

Williams, Howard: Extract from a boating log reproduced in Waterways World, November 1979, pp. 62-64

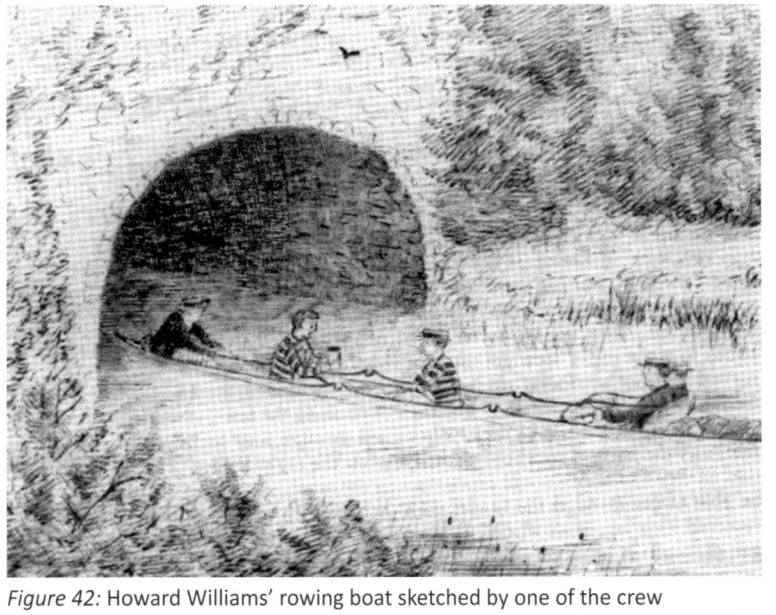

Figure 42: Howard Williams' rowing boat sketched by one of the crew
(Waterways World)

They too seemed to experience a lot of rain, but their first problem was to find the way in:

> " We saw on the map that a branch of the river about a mile above Gloucester led direct to Over, where we had to get into the Hereford & Gloucester Canal and we, of course, intended going along this branch, but some men that I spoke to told me that there were several weirs in it and no locks, so that we could not go that way but would have to follow the main stream, go through Gloucester and round Alney Island to Over. These men either knew nothing at all about it or else were most abominable liars, for the lock-keeper at Over afterwards told us that the branch was quite clear and was the usual route for barges.
>
> We very soon after this approached Gloucester ... The water here was very dirty and the streets that ran alongside the river equally so. We were very glad to get out of it and round the bend through a lock to Over. Here we went into a deep lock which leads to the canal. Fred and I climbed up the wall and went into the lock house while the other three took the boat through. I asked for our pass and the man made it out for me and wanted to charge 15/- but fortunately I had a letter with me which I had received in London from the Canal Company stating that the charge would be 10/-. This I triumphantly produced. So the man was done out of his expected bonus. "

The ambitious crew had hoped to reach Dymock that night but had not bargained for the state of the canal. While they found the countryside as beautiful as they had ever seen anywhere, reeds covered the water just leaving a few feet for a narrow boat to pass. From the towpath their boat was hidden by reeds six to eight feet high which made towing difficult to say the least.

They then encountered the Double Locks:

> ❝ It was an immense thing with about 30 feet fall and a pair of gates in the middle. None of us had ever come across such an affair as this before and we had no idea how to manage it. There was not a soul to be seen so we could get no information on the subject. We took the boat in, shut the rear gates and let down the sluices, then opened the middle gates and let in the water at the top sluices, but by some extraordinary means the water, as soon as it came in, rushed out again through some invisible exit and as there was a ledge across the middle of the lock we could not get sufficient in to float over. We experimented here for over half an hour. At last we made a tremendous effort and having let the water in with a rush, by means of pulling with boathooks and tugging at the sides, we managed to get over the ledge and float in the upper half of the lock. Our difficulty then was over, for we had only to shut the middle gates, when the upper half soon filled and we easily went through. This was the only lock of its kind that we came across during our tour and to this day I have no idea how it is worked. ❞

These were the double, or staircase, locks at Malswick, where the total rise was actually nearer 17' than 30'! With rain on and off adding to their discomfort they eventually reached Newent where clearly tourists were a novelty.

> ❝ We landed at a wharf close beside the bridge on which a large crowd soon assembled to see us disembark. We locked all the moveables up in a barn which the proprietor of the wharf kindly placed at our disposal and gave the boat in charge of some bargees who had their craft moored alongside. A mile beyond Newent there is a tunnel nearly two miles long, which we had to go through. We made enquiries of the bargees about the hours of going through and they told us that craft going in the direction of Hereford would have to go through between the hours of 6 and 9 and 12 and 3, both fore and after noon. ❞

The next morning, after negotiating four more locks, they tackled Oxenhall Tunnel but they found it less pretty than had Mr. Farrant two years before:

> ❝ The tunnel had not a very inviting aspect. It was very small and narrow and looked more like a sewer than anything else. It was so small that two craft going in opposite directions could not pass each other. That is the reason why there were specified times for going through. The bargees lie on their backs on the top of their barge and push along the roof with their hands and feet. We lit our lamp and entered at 7.25. George and Clarke sat in the stern, Tom and Fred pushed along on either side with boathooks and I knelt in the bow with the lamp. Very soon after we had got in the tunnel made a turn and we could see neither one end nor the other and were in complete darkness, with the exception of the glimmer from the lantern, which only made the darkness visible. It was a melancholy sort of place, not calculated to put one in the liveliest spirits, so I started a song, which revived us all, and we sang part-songs and choruses all the way through. It sounded very well, too, echoing and reverberating along the tunnel. ❞

Sadly, though clearly a tradition in the 1870s, the singing of part songs and choruses is no longer common practice while negotiating canal tunnels. After dodging a series of waterfalls in the tunnel they reached the end in only 35 minutes and began to enjoy the countryside again, despite the rain.

> ❝ Outside the tunnel the banks were again very beautiful, similar to the first 5 miles of the canal. Tom and George attempted to scull here, but the canal was so narrow and the water so covered with rushes that they soon gave up and Tom took the towline whilst Clarke went ahead and opened the gates and locks. Clarke was followed for some distance by a drove of little pigs. There must have been something very peculiar about him to attract pigs in the way he did. Once before at Heyford a similar thing happened. It was a fearfully dull and miserable day, a damp mist falling and occasionally rain. We passed through 7 locks before we reached Ledbury, where we landed, leaving the boat in charge of a lockman. It was raining at the time, so we walked up the town in full wet-weather costume, mackintoshes, leggings and sou'westers, and carrying the cans in our hands. The people rushed out to the shop doors to look at us and no doubt we did present a very curious appearance. ❞

After shopping in Ledbury, but unable to purchase any milk, they returned to their boat.

> 66 We stopped about an hour in Ledbury then went back to the lock where we had left our boat and which we found surrounded by a swarm of little children. We sculled on for about half a mile, hoping they would disperse, but about half a dozen of the dirty little enthusiasts were evidently bent on seeing us eat our lunch, for they would not go away, notwithstanding the most awful threats. We pulled up under a bridge for lunch and as they still hovered about, George made a rush after them. He caught one and held him over the water, threatening to drop him in unless he made off with his companions. 99

The rest of the journey to Hereford passed with little incident, though the towpath through Ashperton tunnel was virtually impassable due to six inches of mud and the crew were obliged to let Fred, who had been towing, join them in the boat which they then pushed through with boathooks.

Alfred Watkins, the noted antiquarian and discoverer of ley lines (if they actually exist) lived in Herefordshire all of his life. Writing in the early 1930s he recalls the canal just before it closed:

> 66 Early in 1881, hearing it was about to be closed (the embankment at the Ledbury Station end of the new Ledbury-Dymock railway having already started), I persuaded another young boating spark, (Ted George, whose father had founded a timber business at the Canal Wharf at Hereford), to come with me on a two days' final water-trip by canoe along the whole length to Gloucester. A very jolly trip it was, chasing down ducks who flew and flapped in terror at the strange invaders, diving through tunnels with a small boat's lamp, to give light, carefully balanced on the bow, and shouting songs to keep our spirits up in the case of that long weird tunnel (1¼ miles) at Oxenhall, where we could not see the other end and were paddling into the blackness of night, with the water washing the walls on both sides, for in this one the tow-path went over the top of the hill, and the canal-men had to leg their barges through by pushing with their feet against the roof. 99

Watkins, Alfred: Herefordshire in his own words and photographs, Logaston Press
2012, p88

When the Great Western actually got around to building their new line, construction began at Ledbury enabling materials to be transported by canal from the Severn. Due warning was given in June 1881, giving just 28 days for all "Barges, Boats and other craft to be removed accordingly".

John Masefield was born in Ledbury and the Canal Company issued its closure notice the day after his third birthday. Possibly he could remember the boat traffic which continued for a few years on the Hereford to Ledbury section. In 1922 he told Alfred Watkins that he regarded the canal as "a romantic highway to my childhood" and he describes the construction of the railway embankment on the line of the canal in his epic poem "The Widow in the Bye Street".

Masefield, John: The Widow in the Bye Street, Sidgwick and Jackson, London (1912)

In his autobiography "Grace Before Ploughing" Masefield recalls his childhood memories of the canal, the boats and the boat people. How much of the detail he actually remembered might be open to question, but clearly the canal was one of the delights of his childhood.

> " To my young mind, the most wonderful thing near my home was the canal, where barges passed all day long between Gloucester and Hereford.
>
> The canal that meant so much to me was a doomed concern at the time, though I did not know it. I saw its last prosperous years.
>
> To my young self it was the main wonder and delight in life. It crossed the fields directly below my home, and wherever it appeared it heightened Life.
>
> It seemed to urge the young soul to adventure on, away, away, to glorious Hereford; it seemed to tell of wonders, to try to get to which would be wonderful. It, in itself, was wonderful.
>
> In my memory, I cannot think why, all the barges are outward bound going from the south northward towards Hereford, in the two miles of flat valley offering there. I have no memory whatever of barges going towards Gloucester, except one which on the voyage south paused at Bosbury bridge to let another pass..."
>
> The barges were small and made from about two and a half to three miles in an hour ... The crews were either two men or a married couple. I have lively memories of the woman steering with her most becoming head-dress of a milkmaid's cap flapping on her cheeks, and the husband ahead minding the horse, and often singing, or knitting, or flinging words over his shoulder to the wife.
>
> Sometimes these glorious people begged the little boy to come aboard,

and showed me the marvellous cabin, bright as a new pin, with its bunks and gear, the most wonderful abodes on earth. I do not doubt that the crews had a hard life in the main, working cargo in port, and having the horse to groom, and the entire ship to keep clean, in addition to being either at the helm or minding the horse when under way. I suppose that a days tow would bring them to Ledbury from Gloucester, and that another days tow would bring them to Hereford. They would then have (as I suppose) to work to discharge the cargo, then to clean the hold, and take in whatever was going east. The work must have been often pretty hard, but never hard for long, and always varied in scene and company, and never exhausting…

In a very severe winter, the frost might stop navigation for a time. The frozen reaches then made good skating. I sometimes met a man who had skated from Ledbury to Hereford and back, about twenty-five miles, in the course of one winter day. He said that it was an easy run, but that he had not trusted the ice under some of the bridges. 99

Masefield, John: Grace Before Ploughing, Heinemann: London 1966 by permission of the Society of Authors

The Ledbury Free Press reported the draining of the canal in 1881 and solved the mystery of the whereabouts of the missing head of the town pump:

66 The past week will be memorable in the annals of Ledbury consequent upon the closing of the canal between this town and Gloucester. The operation of the letting off of water from the Hereford road bridge commenced on Monday last, and the canal is now cleared as far as the leather-mill lock. Among the many secrets laid bare by the removal of the water, not the least noteworthy is the recovery of the head (of the) town pump, the loss of which was recorded in these columns a few years ago. 99

Ledbury Free Press: July 12,1881

By 1883 all traffic had, at least officially, ceased. The Hereford to Ledbury section, now isolated from the rest of the canal network carried some local traffic for a year or two but for the next hundred years little would be heard of this canal.

For the Company though, financially at least, these were the Golden Years. Until the eventual nationalisation of the Great Western in 1945 the proprietors received their annual rent of £5,000. The Company had no boats, no salaries and no maintenance – in fact, no costs at all. The good Dr. Price had struck an excellent deal.

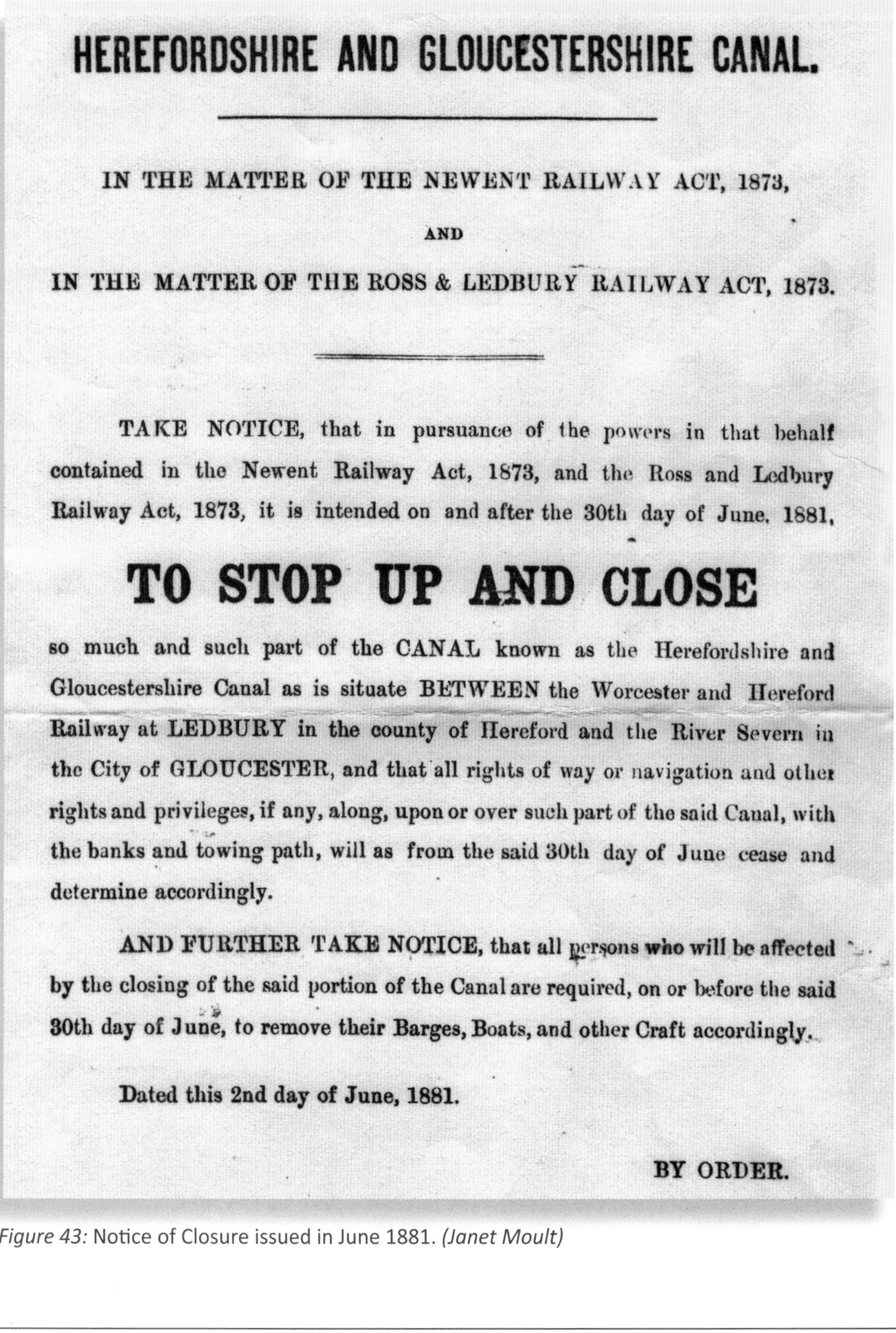

HEREFORDSHIRE AND GLOUCESTERSHIRE CANAL.

IN THE MATTER OF THE NEWENT RAILWAY ACT, 1873,

AND

IN THE MATTER OF THE ROSS & LEDBURY RAILWAY ACT, 1873.

TAKE NOTICE, that in pursuance of the powers in that behalf contained in the Newent Railway Act, 1873, and the Ross and Ledbury Railway Act, 1873, it is intended on and after the 30th day of June, 1881,

TO STOP UP AND CLOSE

so much and such part of the CANAL known as the Herefordshire and Gloucestershire Canal as is situate BETWEEN the Worcester and Hereford Railway at LEDBURY in the county of Hereford and the River Severn in the City of GLOUCESTER, and that all rights of way or navigation and other rights and privileges, if any, along, upon or over such part of the said Canal, with the banks and towing path, will as from the said 30th day of June cease and determine accordingly.

AND FURTHER TAKE NOTICE, that all persons who will be affected by the closing of the said portion of the Canal are required, on or before the said 30th day of June, to remove their Barges, Boats, and other Craft accordingly.

Dated this 2nd day of June, 1881.

BY ORDER.

Figure 43: Notice of Closure issued in June 1881. *(Janet Moult)*

Dark Ages

Once the canal had been closed and most of the line between Ledbury and Gloucester obliterated, the canal rapidly passed from public awareness. Between Hereford and Ledbury much of the canal was infilled and embankments levelled and ploughed up, but considerable lengths remained holding some water, especially either side of Ashperton Tunnel. During the Second World War it was proposed that Aylestone Tunnel might be used as an air-raid shelter, but, still being full of water, this was not pursued.

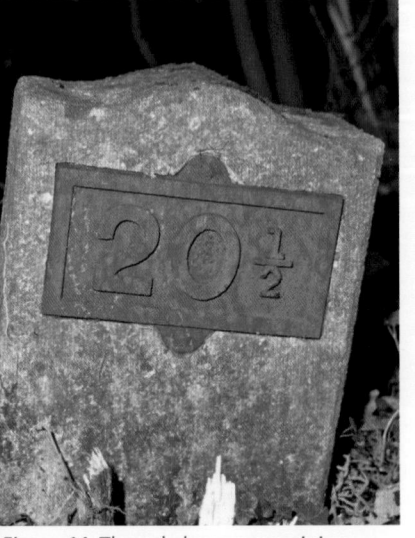

Figure 44: The sole known remaining intact original milepost. *(Mike Potts)*

One by one the simple milestones which marked the route disappeared, only one is now known to be complete with its plate remaining in its original position. At least one other stone remains in situ with its plate removed for safe keeping, but possibly others survive in the more remote and inaccessible parts of the towpath. Two others have been moved by their owners to protect them.

Road improvements required the culverting of some of the old stone canal bridges, but a surprising number survived. It is likely that much of the stonework from locks and bridges was taken away to be given a new life elsewhere. It certainly disappeared.

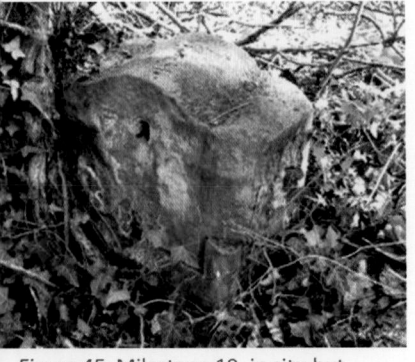

Figure 45: Milestone 19, in situ but lacking its metal plate. *(Brian Fox)*

Very few photographic records survive from these years, but some have been preserved to give us a glimpse of the canal as it faded from memory.

The canal crossed two rivers of some consequence, the Lugg and the Frome, both on substantial aqueducts.

There are varying opinions as to when the low stone-arched Lugg Aqueduct was demolished. A widespread belief that it was blown up by the Home Guard during World War II is contradicted

by recollections that it was still standing in the 1950s. The Lugg Drainage Board is unable to confirm either view. It was almost certainly demolished to reduce flooding and it is said that when the Lugg is running very low the bases of the piers are visible under the water, but in recent years I have been unable to confirm this.

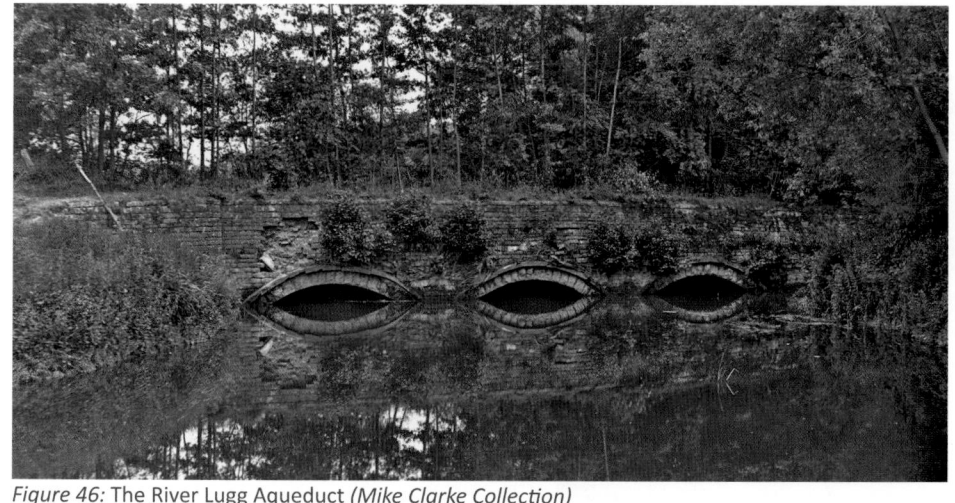

Figure 46: The River Lugg Aqueduct *(Mike Clarke Collection)*

The River Lugg floods frequently in winter and the design of the original aqueduct, with approach embankments across the flood plain, must have impeded the flow of water considerably as the photograph below shows. Trees can be seen growing through the stonework.

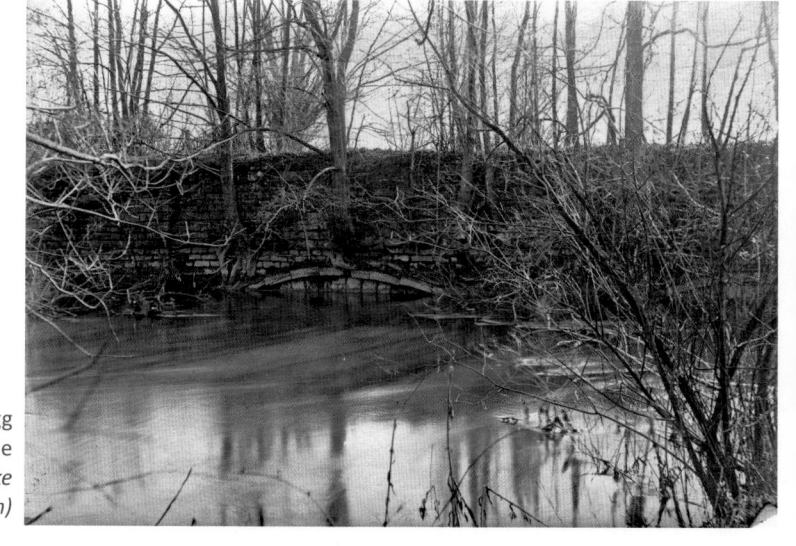

Figure 47: The Lugg Aqueduct with the river in flood *(Mike Clarke Collection)*

The Frome aqueduct has also disappeared and photographs exist which almost certainly show it being demolished, though the exact date for this demolition too is still something of a mystery.

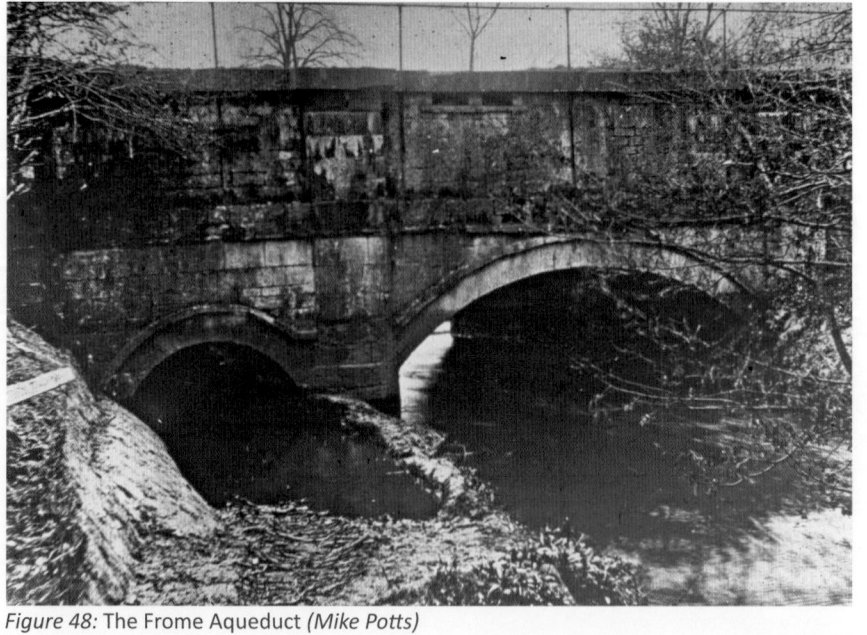

Figure 48: The Frome Aqueduct *(Mike Potts)*

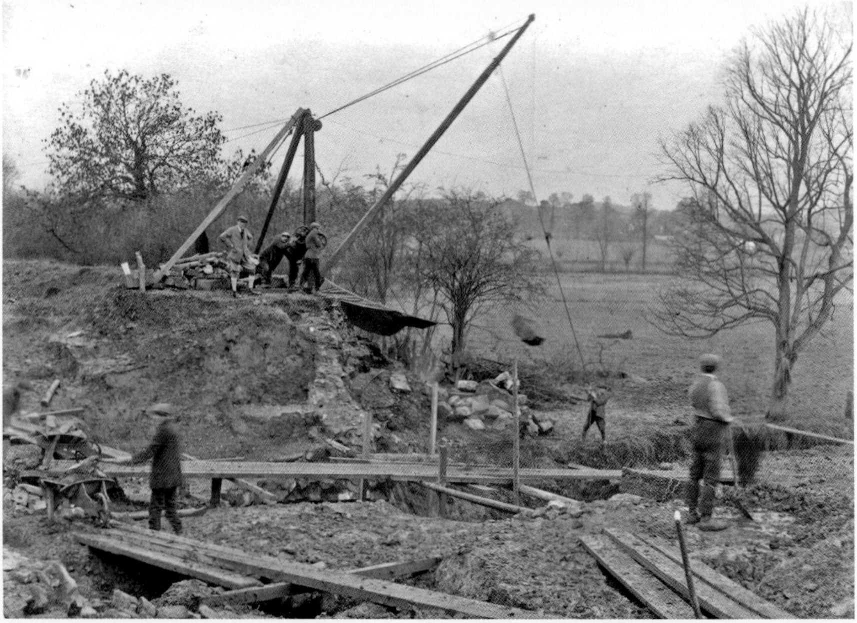

Figure 49: The Frome Aqueduct under demolition *(Mike Clarke Collection)*

Gradually almost all signs of the canal in Hereford disappeared. The basins were not filled in until the 1950s and there are local people who still remember canoeing in them. The canal offices were demolished in 1983.

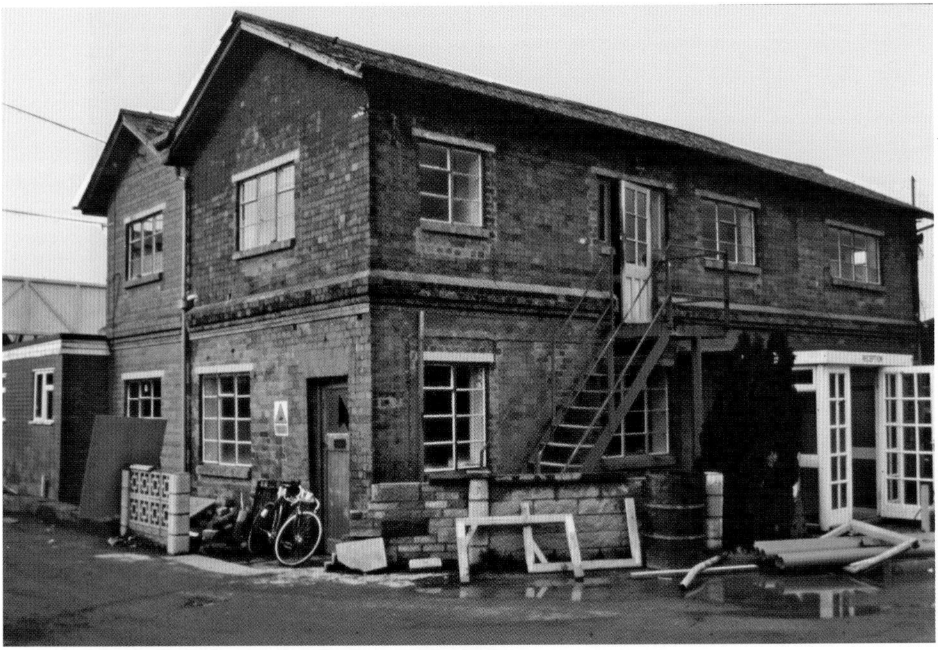

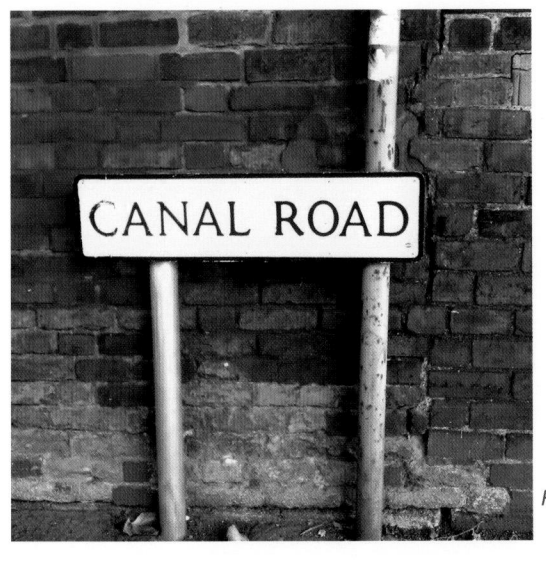

Figure 50: The Canal Offices in Hereford, demolished in 1983 *(Mike Potts)*

CANAL ROAD

Once these had gone, only Widemarsh Street bridge and the sign in Canal Road bore visible evidence of the existence of the canal. Ironically, when the canal was open, what is now called Canal Road was part of the present Monkmoor Street. Originally, Canal Road led to the wharves from the corner of Station Road near its junction with Commercial Road. (See Fig.30)

Figure 51: A rather ironic road sign in Hereford *(Author)*

In Gloucestershire most of the canal line was quickly obliterated by the building of the Ledbury-Gloucester railway. The exception to this was the section beginning south of Dymock, which avoided the Oxenhall tunnel to rejoin the canal line just north of Newent. Here the canal survived largely intact, much of it in water. Only two bridges survived from the first phase of the canal built from 1793 to 1798, Cold Harbour Bridge, just south of Oxenhall Tunnel and Boyce Court Bridge to the north of it. On the Ledbury to Hereford part of the canal more bridges survived, several road bridges still carrying traffic today. Other bridges were replaced by culverts or demolished completely.

All three tunnels survived, though the portals of the Oxenhall Tunnel suffered badly. The northern portal was intact until the 1930s but by the 1960s had almost entirely disappeared. The two shorter tunnels survived almost undamaged, a tribute to Ballard's engineering work.

A few glimpses of the canal from the early years of the last century are to found in old post cards, most of which feature the section of the canal between Dymock and Ledbury. Very few postcards of the canal in Herefordshire have survived if, indeed, many were ever produced.

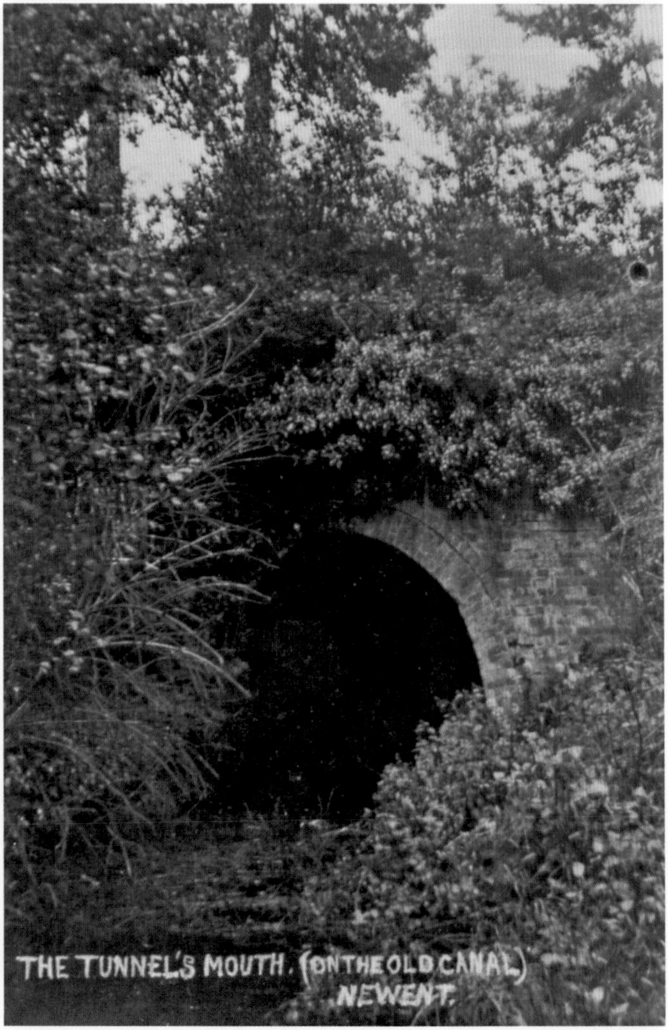

THE TUNNEL'S MOUTH. (ON THE OLD CANAL) NEWENT.

Figure 52: The South Portal of Oxenhall Tunnel from an old photograph *(Mike Potts)*

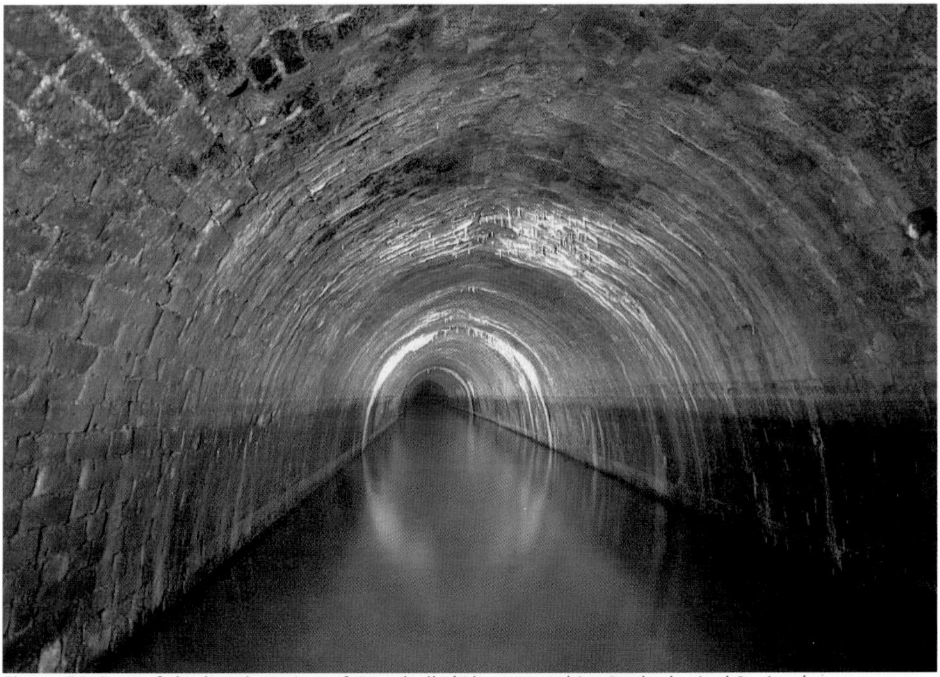

Figure 53: Part of the lined section of Oxenhall. *(Gloucestershire Speleological Society)*

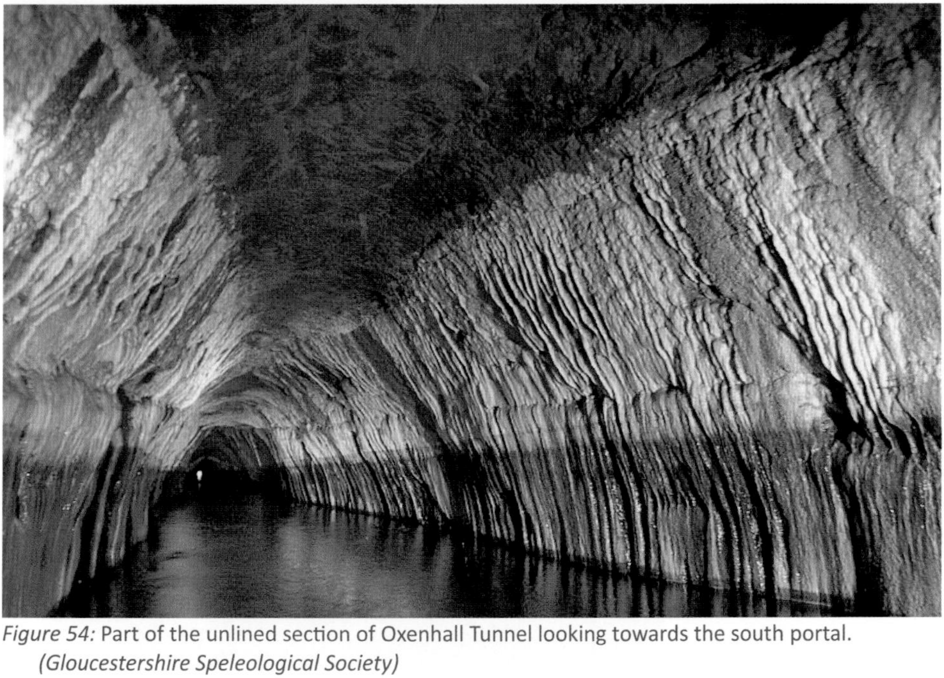

Figure 54: Part of the unlined section of Oxenhall Tunnel looking towards the south portal. *(Gloucestershire Speleological Society)*

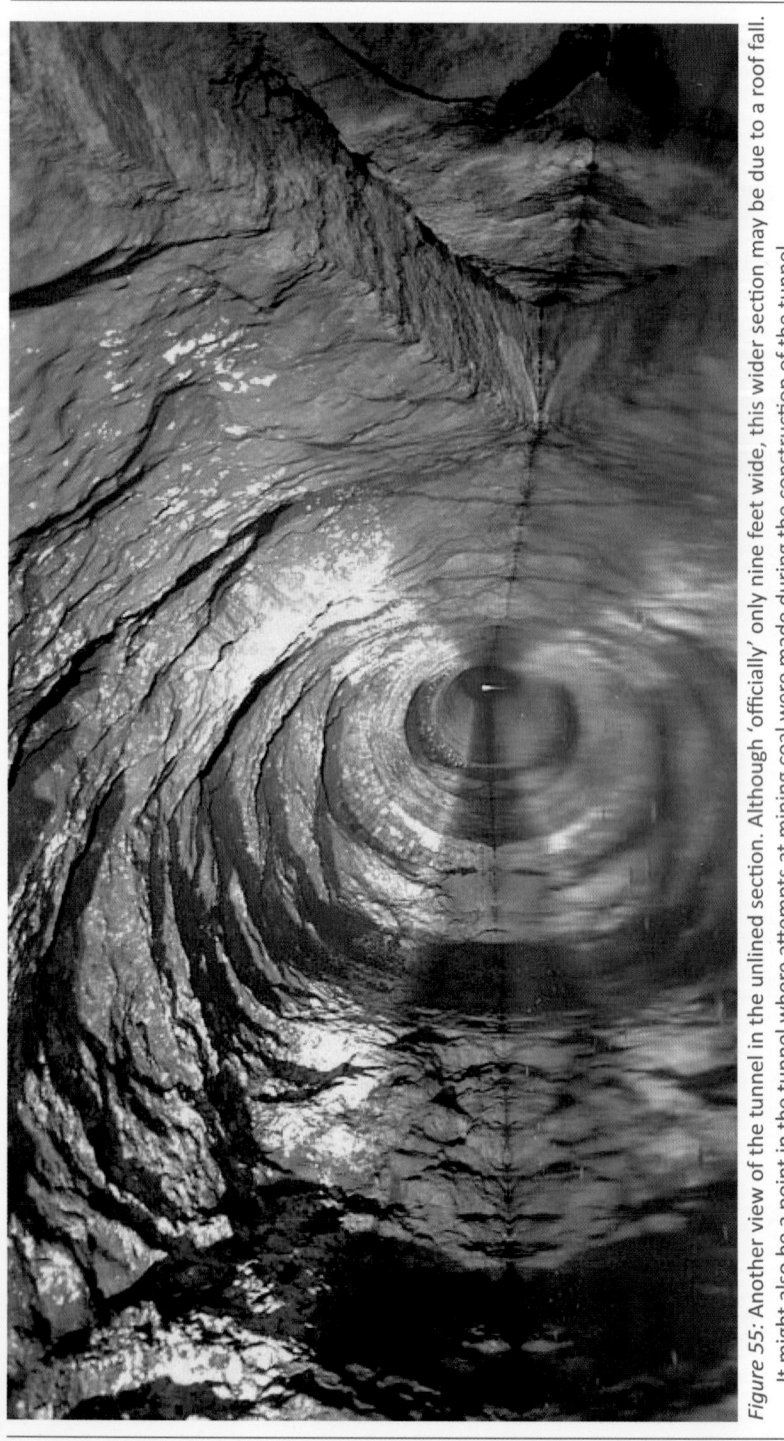

Figure 55: Another view of the tunnel in the unlined section. Although 'officially' only nine feet wide, this wider section may be due to a roof fall. It might also be a point in the tunnel where attempts at mining coal were made during the construction of the tunnel *(Gloucestershire Speleological Society)*

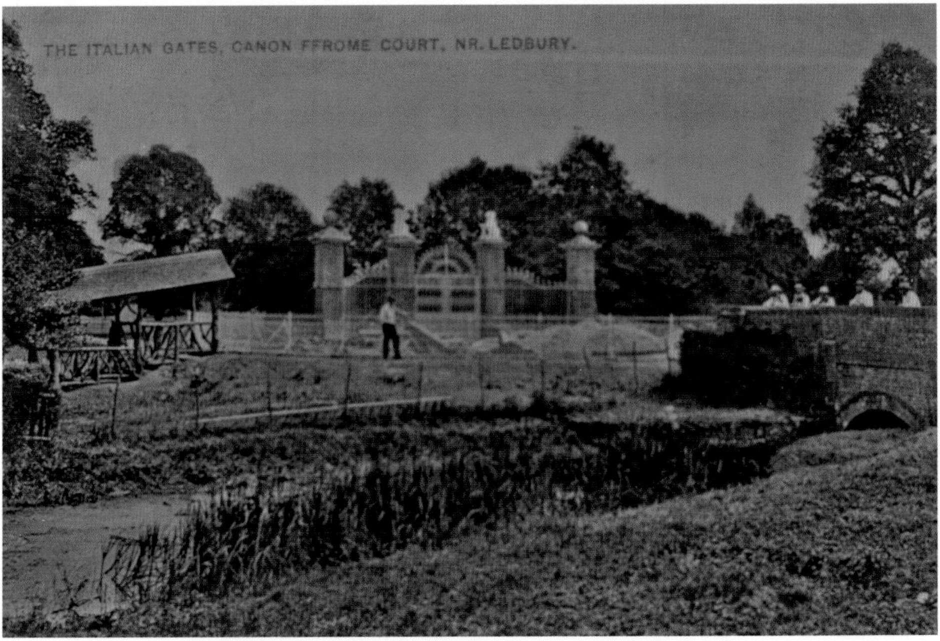

Figure 56: The canal at Canon Frome Court from an old post card *(Mike Potts)*

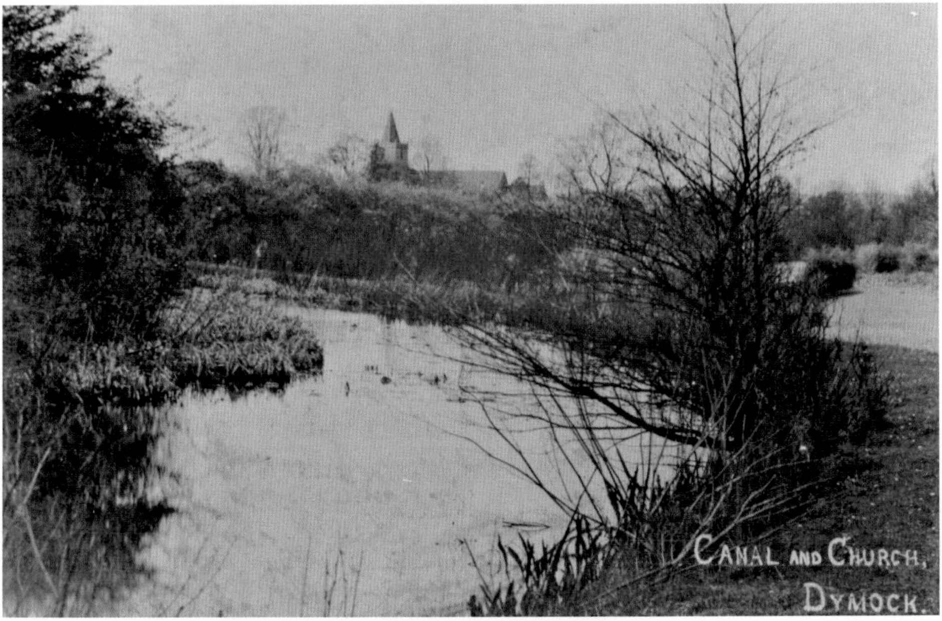

Figure 57: The Canal at Dymock from an old postcard *(Mike Potts)*

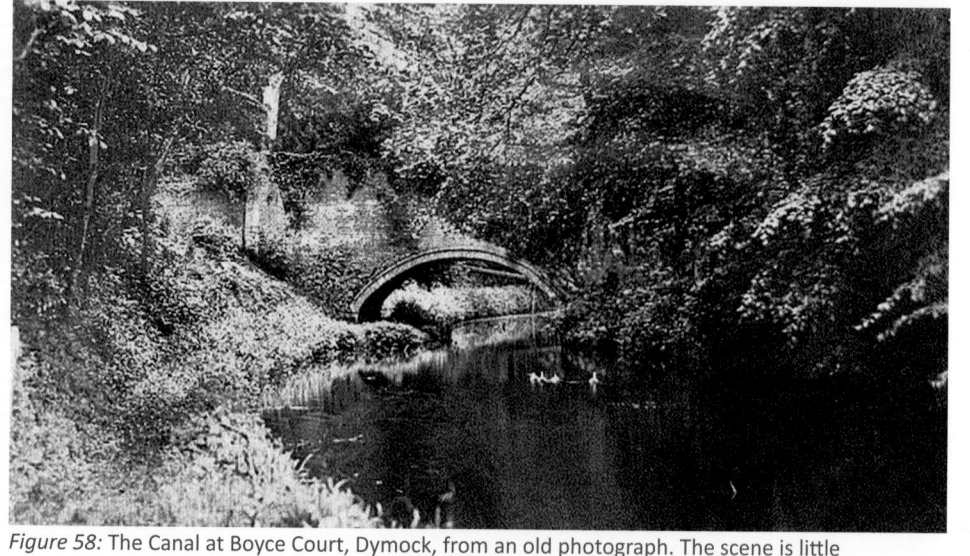

Figure 58: The Canal at Boyce Court, Dymock, from an old photograph. The scene is little changed today *(Source Unknown)*

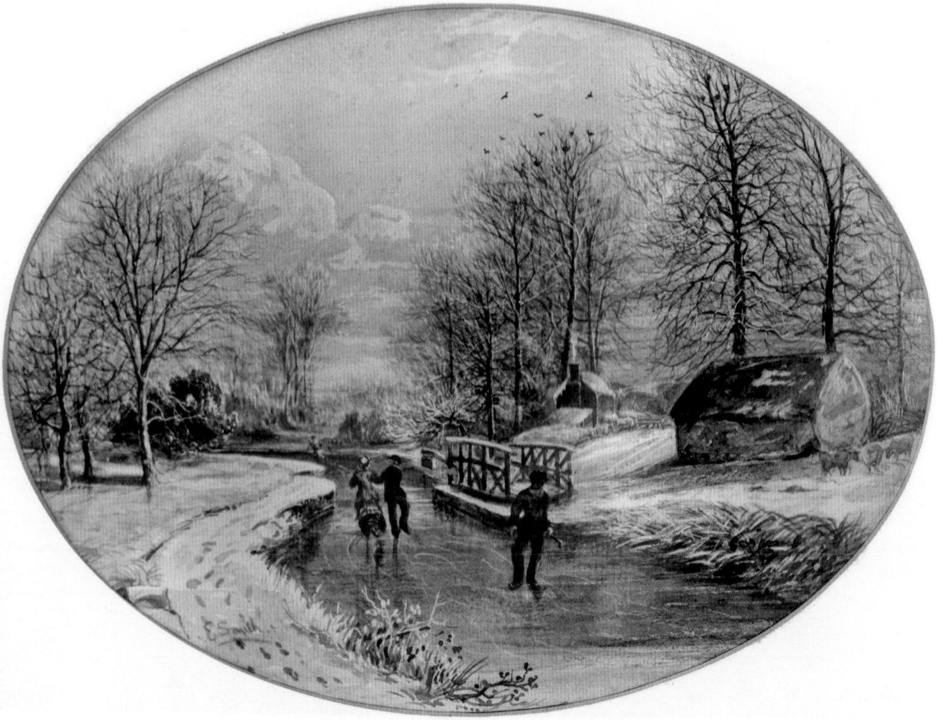

Figure 59: Skating on the Canal at Newent *(Mike Potts)*

A significant number of buildings associated with the canal have survived to the present day, mostly restored quite independently of the canal, and these will be described in Chapter 15. They include a fine cluster around the wharf at Withington, although the wharf itself is represented only by a few coping stones along its edge. The wharfhouse itself survived, though somewhat altered, and until relatively recently the words "William Bird – Wharfinger" could clearly be made out on the wall. It was this fading inscription which inspired the name of the Hereford and Gloucester Canal Trust's magazine. Another wharf building once bore the word SALT on its end wall, just visible when photographed in the 1960s. A similar inscription was once to be seen on the side of a wharf building at Canon Frome Wharf where an old warehouse also survived together with the support of the wharf crane.

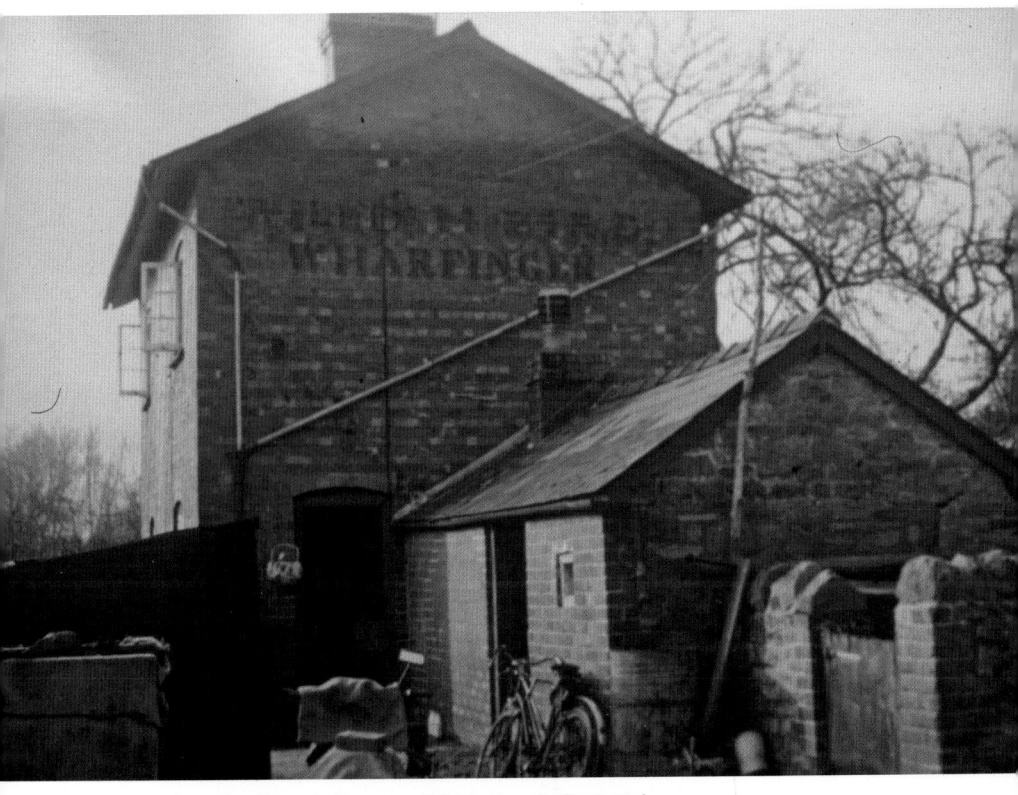

Figure 60: The Wharfinger's House at Withington *(Mike Potts)*

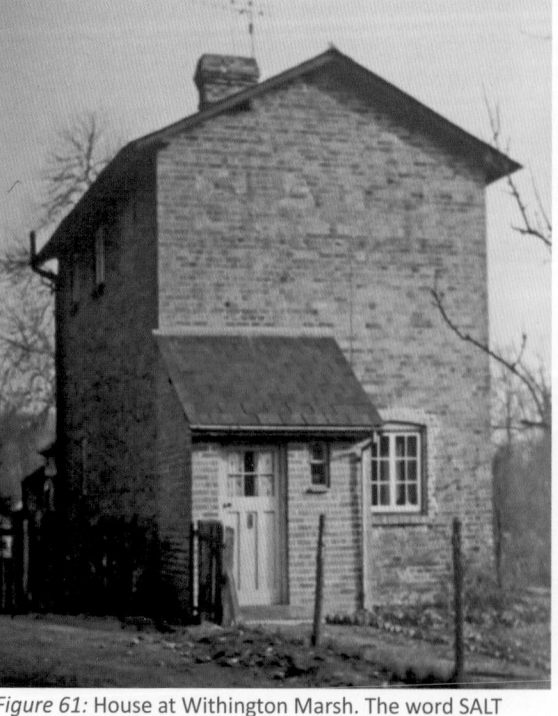

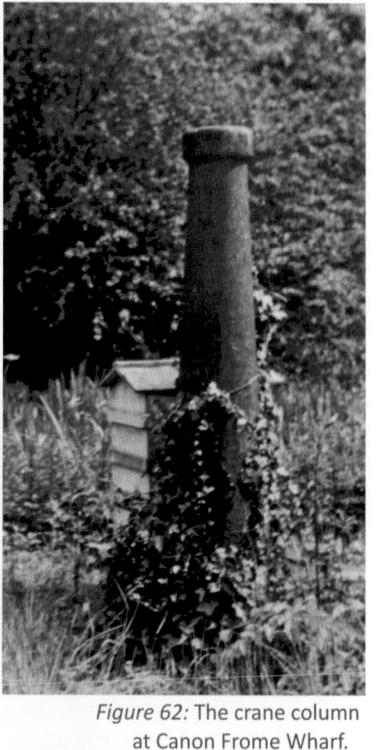

Figure 61: House at Withington Marsh. The word SALT is just discernible on the end wall. *(Mike Potts)*

Figure 62: The crane column at Canon Frome Wharf. In July 1854 Stephen Ballard reported that the crane at Canon Frome Wharf needed replacing as it was "in a decayed and dangerous state" *(Mike Potts)*

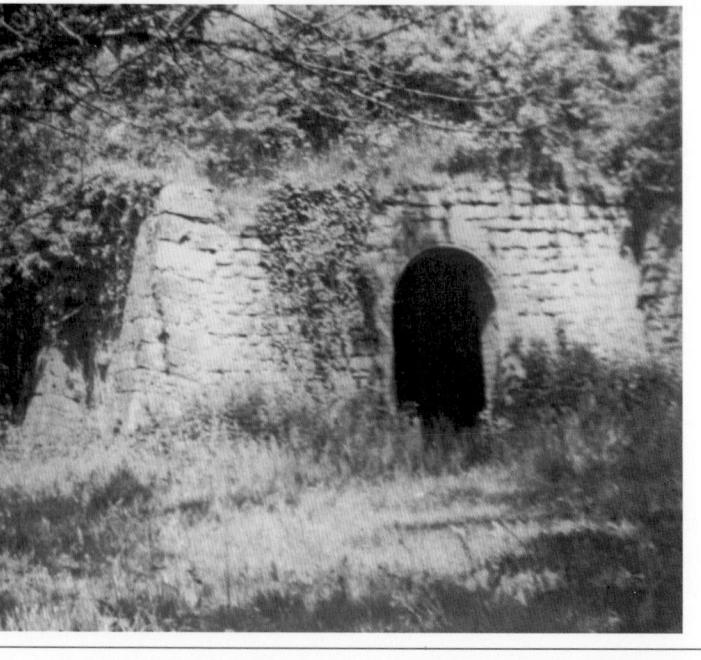

Figure 63: An old warehouse at Canon Frome Wharf *(Mike Potts)*

There is nothing now visible of the various wharves which served the canal in Ledbury, indeed there is some mystery as to exactly where they were. It has long been thought that the Old Wharf was on the Newent side of the Ross Road, on the site now occupied by the Countrywide store. A long building believed to be navvies' accommodation dating from the time of the building of the canal was demolished to make way for the developments on this site.

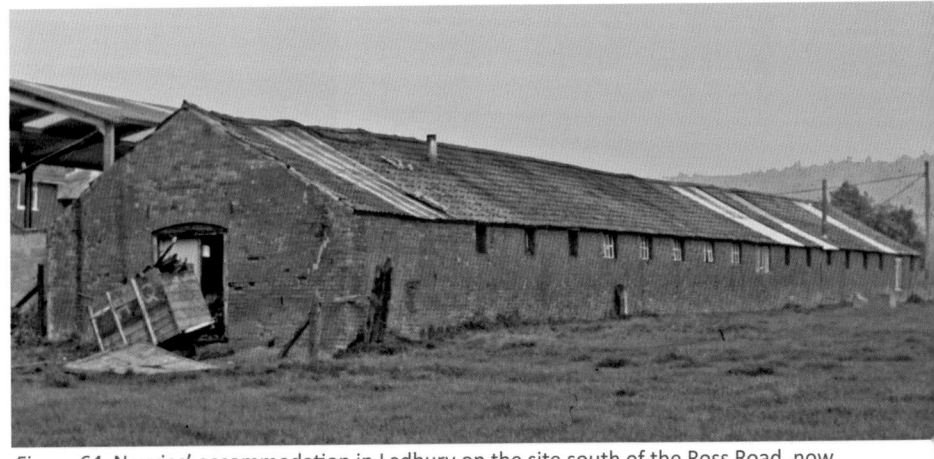

Figure 64: Navvies' accommodation in Ledbury on the site south of the Ross Road, now demolished. *(Mike Potts)*

It is known that the first coal arrived in Ledbury in March 1798, probably at this wharf, but the Minute Books tell us that it was not until August that Mr. Biddulph was paid "£272 for the purchase of his land taken into the Canal, Towing Path, Wharf and Bason at Moat Meadow near Ledbury". Moat Meadow is on the Ledbury side of the Ross Road and it is likely that this became the main wharf area as shown in maps of the early 19th century.

A wharf cottage stood here on New Street a few yards towards Ledbury on the opposite side of the road to the Biddulph Arms, now the Full Pitcher. In the early 1960s this was still owned by British Railways and Robin Stiles, who purchased the lock cottage at Oxenhall from them, rescued some plans for providing bathroom accommodation for this cottage from a skip. While this building has long gone, the plans give us some idea of the sparse accommodation provided by these old canal cottages.

The pair of cottages which still stand on the South side of the Ross Road may have been part of the wharf there though they are said to date from before the time of the canal.

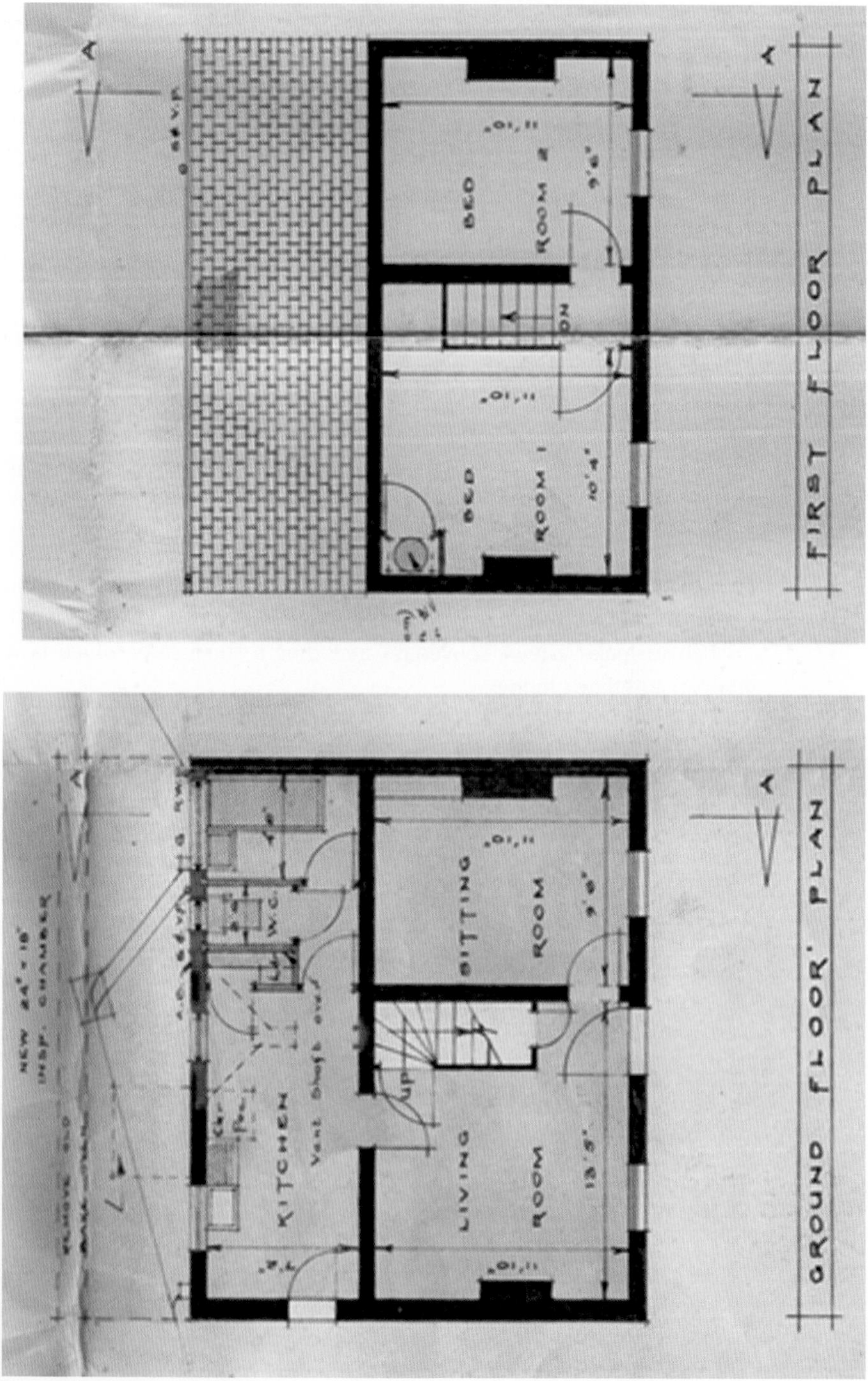

Figure 65: Ledbury Wharf Cottage - Plans for installation of a bathroom *(Robin Stiles)*

Most of the 22 locks on the canal completely disappeared, the stone having been incorporated into later buildings and in all probability used by the railway on the Ledbury – Gloucester branch line. The lock at Withington was infilled and probably remains intact in the garden of the lock cottage. There are scant remains at Kymin Lock and some masonry at Over Lock, now buried, but little else. The exception is at Oxenhall where House Lock survived relatively intact, though in a crumbling state. It was listed in 1989 the Official Listing describing it thus:

> **❝** Lock. c.1795. Designed by Stephen Ballard; engineer, for trustees of the Hereford and Gloucester Canal. Built of limestone ashlar with later brick repairs and stone coping. The gates have decayed. 75 x 8 ft. This is the last surviving lock on the Hereford and Gloucester Canal. **❞**
>
> *English Heritage: List entry number 1248345*

While the lock cottage is certainly Ballard's work, the lock is not, having been built some nine years before he was born. The gates though, had unquestionably decayed. By 1989 a few fragments were all that remained, enough to make a few "souvenirs" including a small stool which now graces the author's lounge.

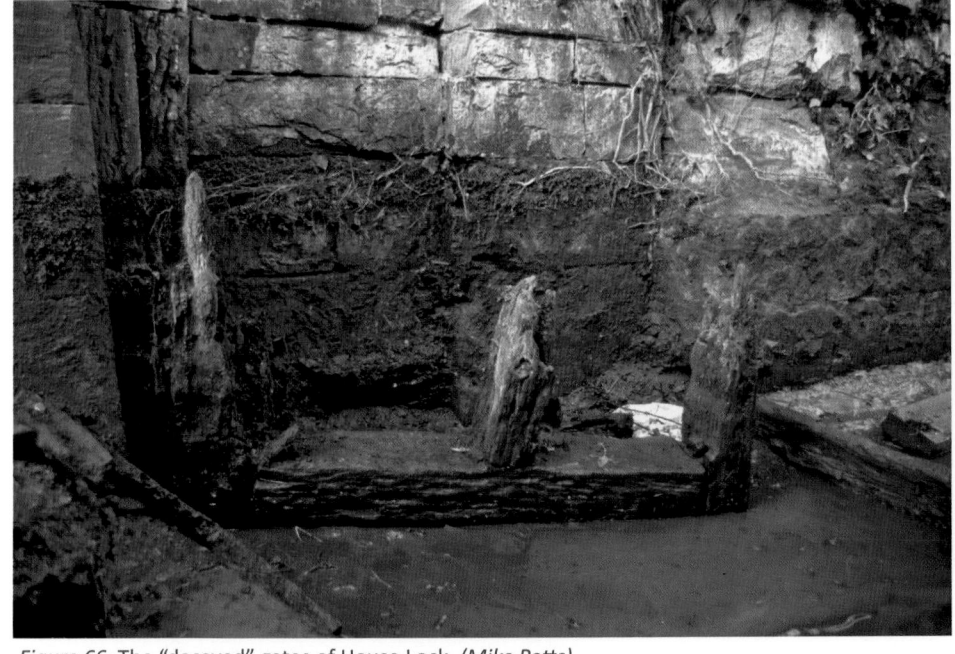

Figure 66: The "decayed" gates of House Lock. *(Mike Potts)*

Around 1880 Alfred Watkins photographed a lock on the canal, which has generally been supposed to be House Lock at Oxenhall. It certainly looks very much like it and, after careful restoration by Trust volunteers, there is no other now in such a good a state of preservation.

In recent years, the location of the photograph has been questioned, notably by the Oxenhall restoration Site Leader, who points to evidence that the location might be Rudford or Coneybury lock.

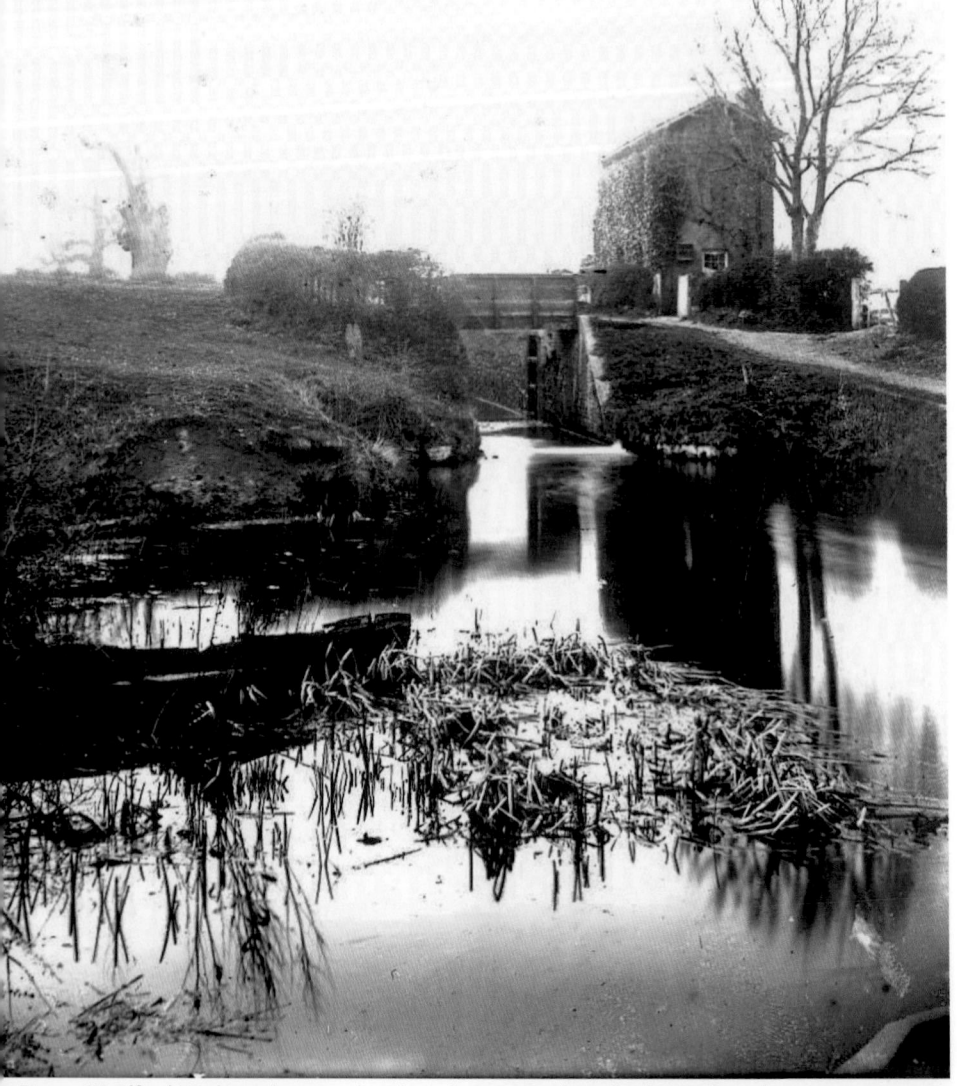

Figure 67: Alfred Watkins photograph, taken about 1880. *(Hereford City Library)*

The two locks on the River Severn used by boats to reach the Hereford and Gloucester Canal have both survived to the present day. The lock at Maisemore with its lock house was sold by British Waterways in the 1980s to a private owner, but the barge lock and its lock houses at Llanthony was retained, albeit in a steadily deteriorating condition.

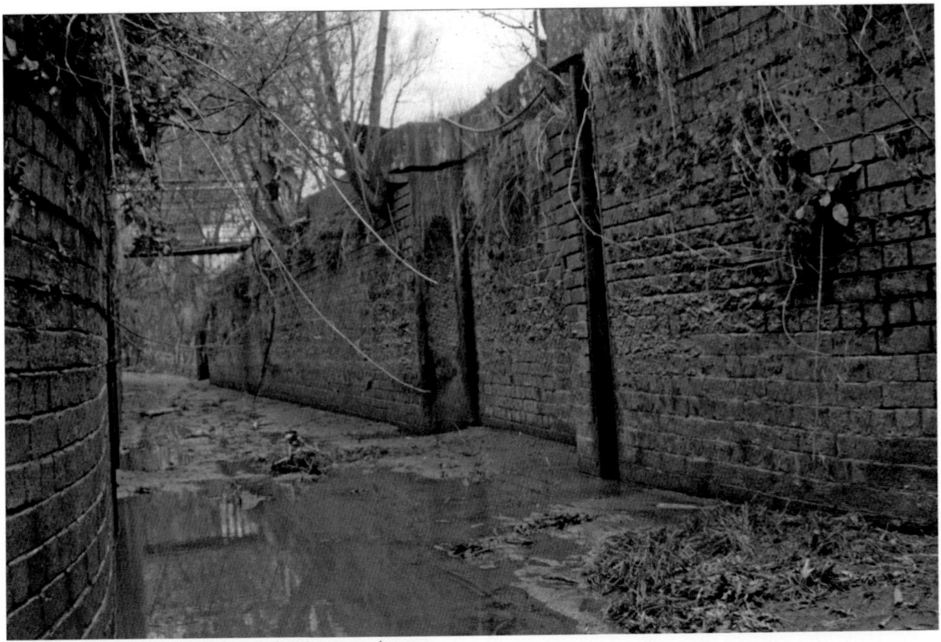

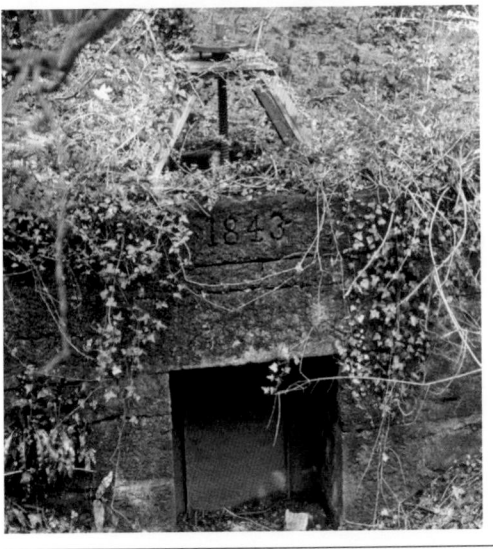

Figure 68: Maisemore Lock *(Mike Potts)*

Other, smaller artefacts lived on, sometimes buried in the accumulated silt or hidden in undergrowth. The sluice controlling the water from the Canon Frome feeder still exists, and in 2012 with the permission of Mr. Gilbert the landowner, a Trust volunteer organised an investigation of the feeder itself, assisted by members of the Gloucestershire Speleological Society. Most of the feeder runs underground through a 4' high tunnel built of local stone, and not brick as was previously thought.

Figure 69: The Sluice for the Canon Frome feeder. *(Mike Potts)*

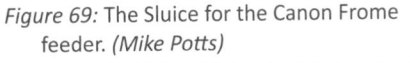

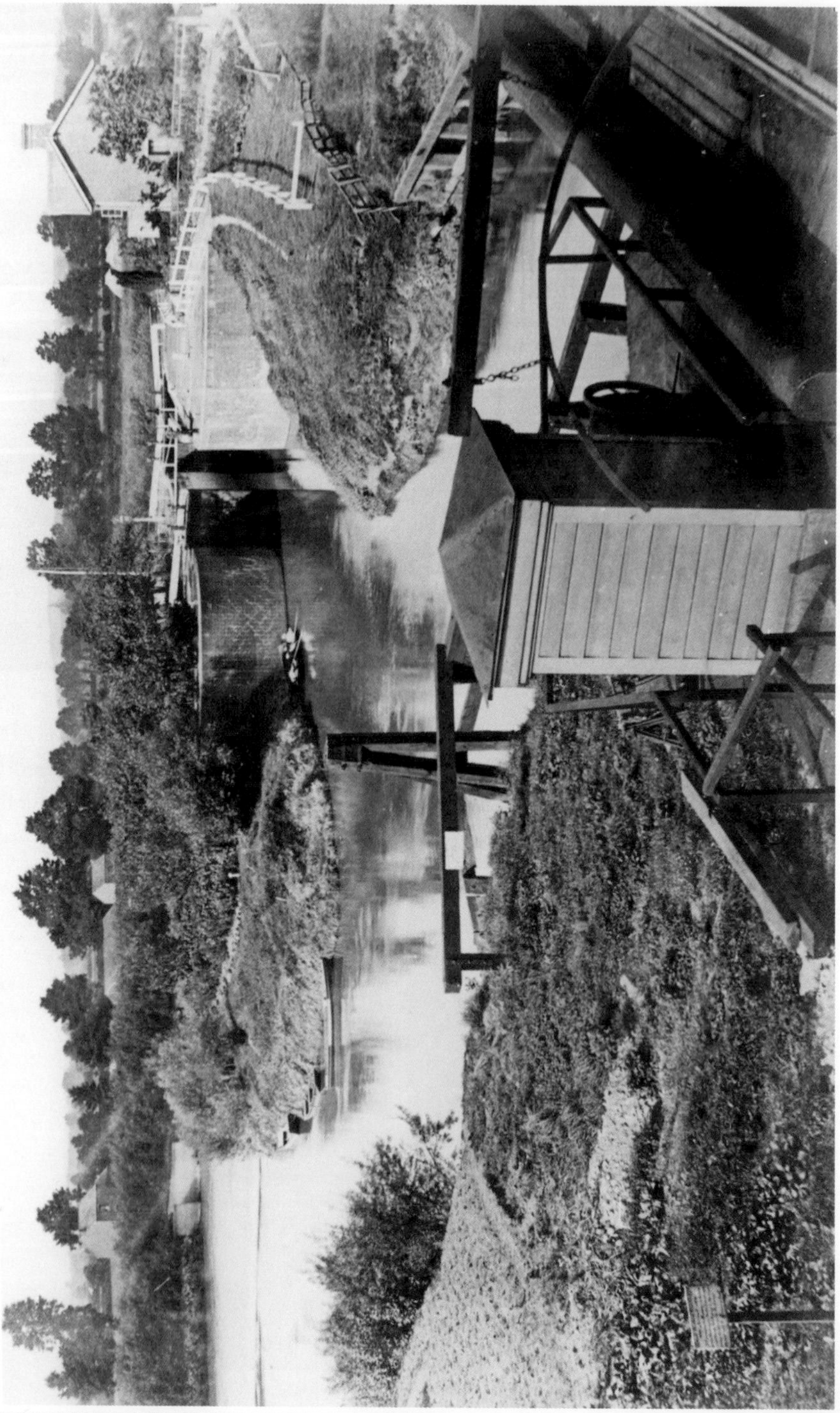

Figure 70: Llanthony Lock in the 1950s. (Canal and River Trust)

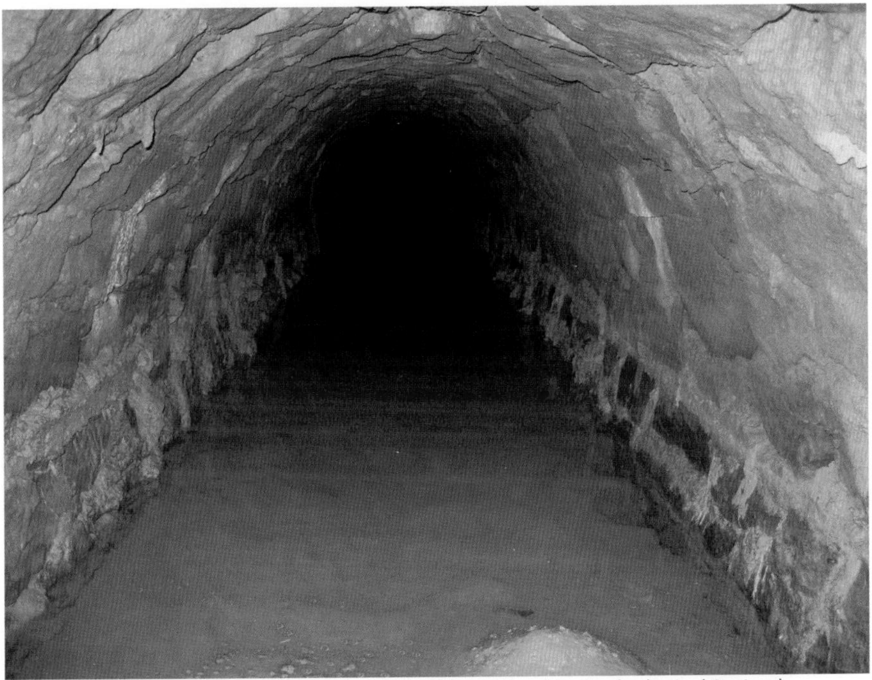

Figure 71: The Canon Frome feeder in 2012. *(Gloucestershire Speleological Society)*

Perhaps even more remarkable is the drainage "plug" at Oxenhall. This not only survived but did so in a state which allowed it to be opened by its leather strap - and were it not for the silted channel below, to fulfil the purpose for which it was designed!

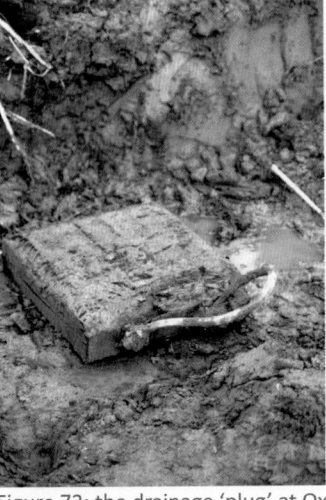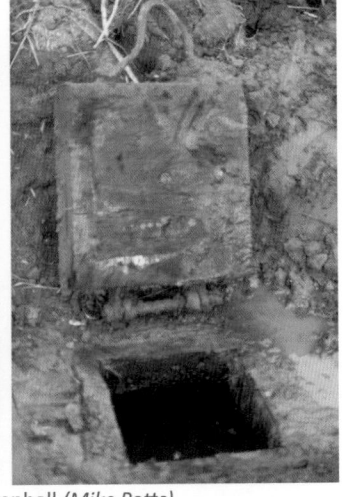

Figure 72: the drainage 'plug' at Oxenhall *(Mike Potts)*

Where the canal ran along embankments stop gates were fitted to ensure water loss was minimised should a breach occur. These are marked on old Ordnance Survey maps as "Lock" and remarkably one of these survived at least until the mid 1980s. On the Prior's Court embankment, near Staplow the unmistakable bulky timbers of a stop gate still in position across the canal, unused for over 100 years, were discovered by members of the Hereford and Gloucester Canal Society – the story of which must shortly be told.

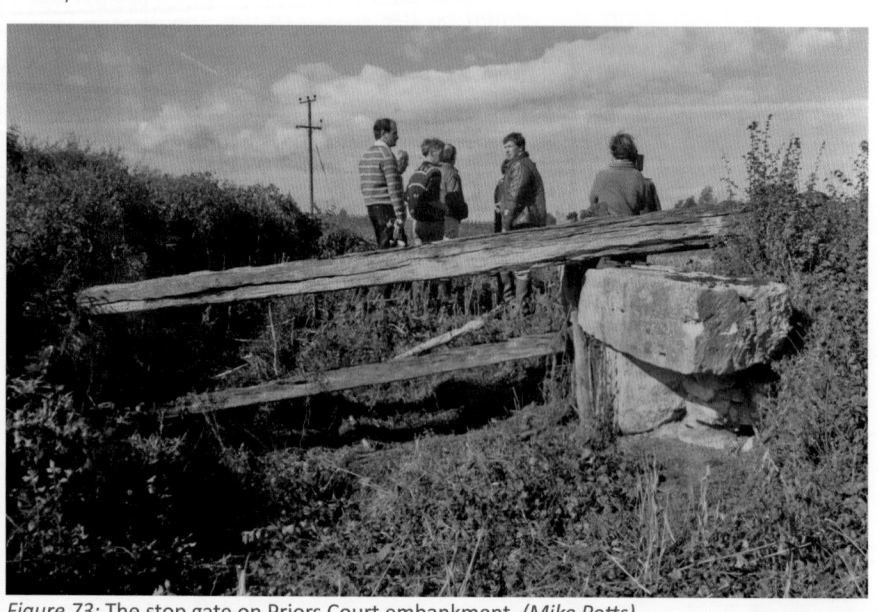

Figure 73: The stop gate on Priors Court embankment. *(Mike Potts)*

Some documents from the working days of the canal have also been preserved, notably Stephen Ballard's diaries and the Minute Books of the Committee and General Assembly of the Company. Share Registers and other documents and maps are held in the National Archives at Kew and in the Records Offices at Hereford and Gloucester.

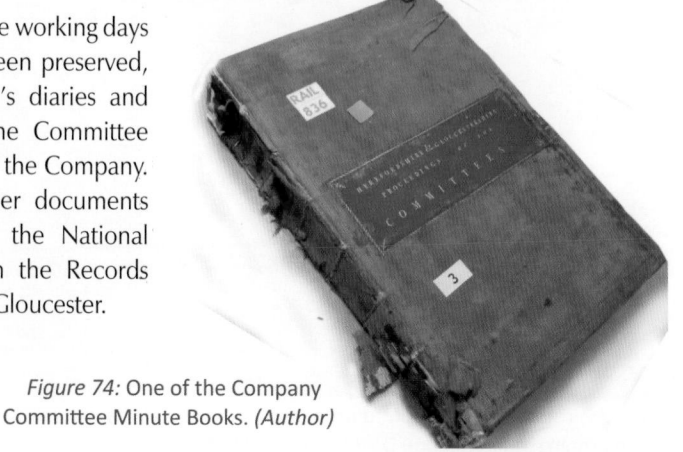

Figure 74: One of the Company Committee Minute Books. *(Author)*

A New Beginning

Bick, David: The
Hereford and
Gloucester Canal,
Oakwood Press,
Third Edition
2003 p.65

The canal was to sleep for 100 years and it awoke slowly. In 1979 David Bick proposed the restoration of a four hundred yard stretch of the canal near Newent Lake and work was actually started, but was soon abandoned on the advice of the Inland Waterways Protection Society.

After a number of letters and articles appeared in local papers a meeting was convened on 13th April 1983 at which the Herefordshire and Gloucestershire Canal Society was inaugurated. The meeting was held at the Red Cross Hall in Hereford, only two hundred yards or so from the site of the terminal Canal Basins. A committee was formed and a number of visits organised to inspect the scant remains of the canal and its associated buildings, the first being to the area around Withington Wharf.

It was agreed that, where possible, cast aluminium plaques should be fixed to some of the important remaining structures, the first being to Widemarsh Bridge in Hereford.

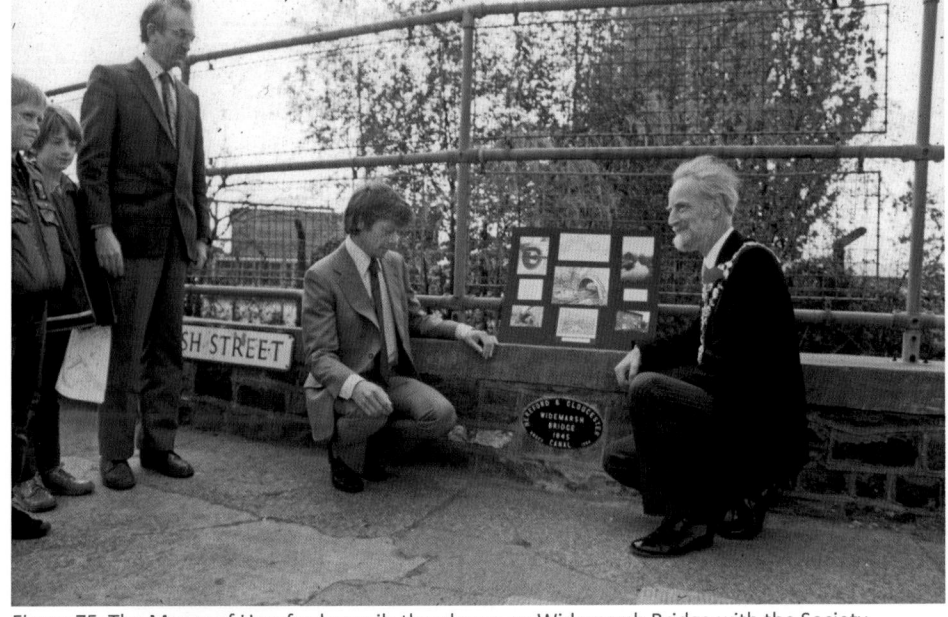

Figure 75: The Mayor of Hereford unveils the plaque on Widemarsh Bridge with the Society Chairman (squatting) and David Bick. *(Mike Potts)*

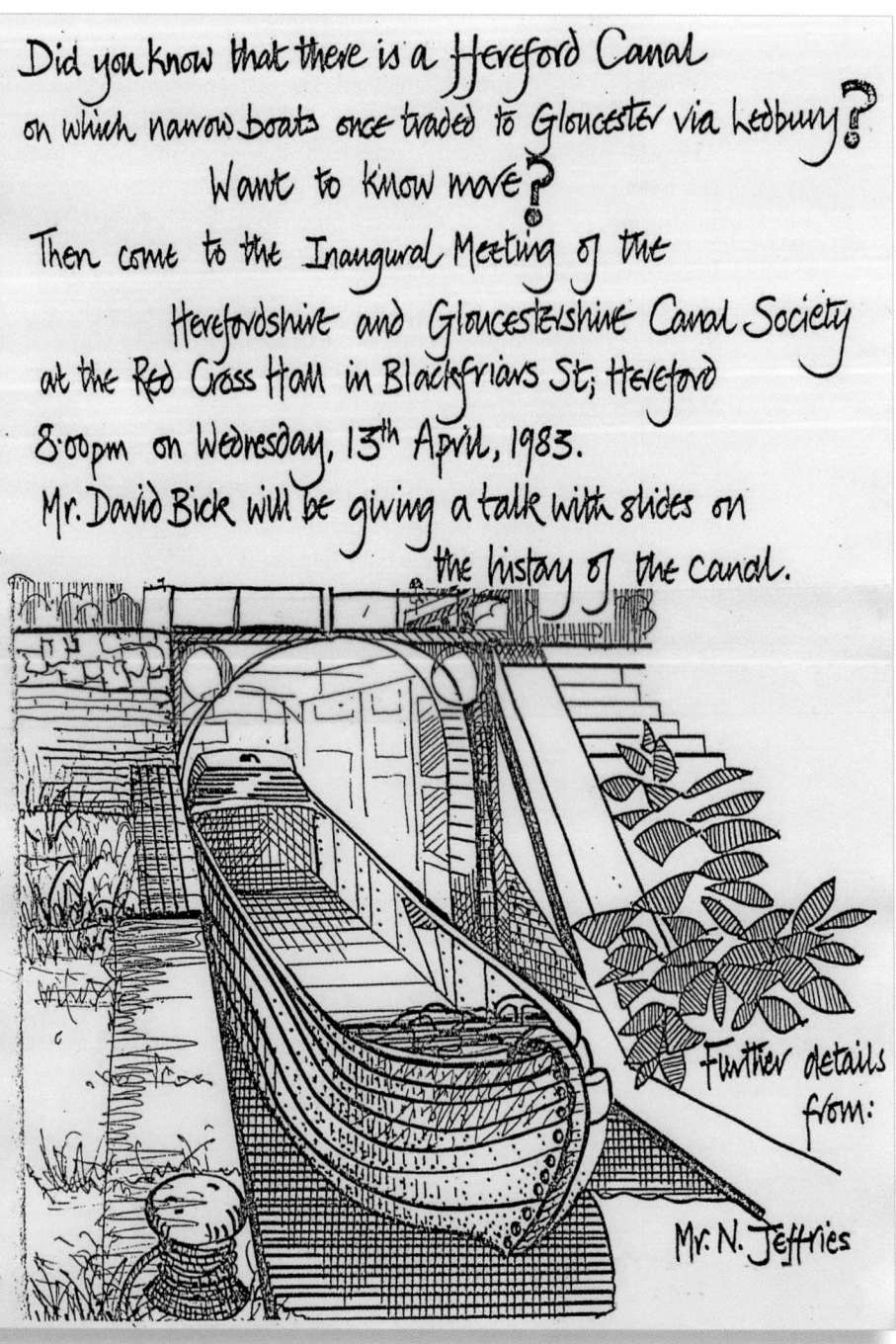

Figure 76: Poster advertising the inaugural meeting of the Herefordshire and Gloucestershire Canal Society – complete with mis-spelling of Nigel Jefferies name! *(Mike Potts)*

There was at this stage no idea of restoring any more than a few short lengths of the canal to show what it might have looked like and if possible, to protect such structures as remained. The first working party descended upon a stretch of the canal adjacent to the main A4103 Hereford to Worcester road at Monkhide, some eight miles by canal from Hereford. This length was owned by Major Robert Barnes a member of the Society and through his mother, a relation of Stephen Ballard himself.

The stretch included the famous Skew Bridge, possibly the most skewed brick-built bridge built over any canal in Britain. Almost obliterated by ivy and undergrowth, the bridge was exposed, the canal excavated and towpath reinstated. Protection for the bridge was gained by the securing of Grade II listing in January 1986.

Regular working parties met over the next four years and by 1987 the canal had been cleared from the Hereford-Worcester Road, to Skew Bridge. This was only a partial restoration as the full width of the canal was not excavated and the towpath remained considerably higher than the original level, but it demonstrated what could be done.

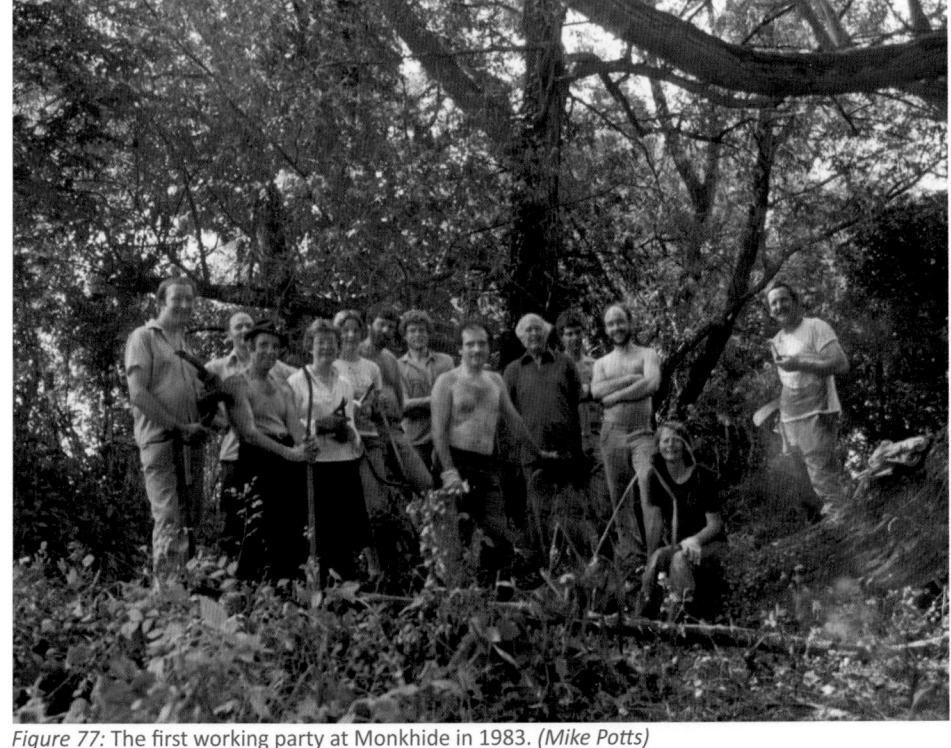

Figure 77: The first working party at Monkhide in 1983. *(Mike Potts)*

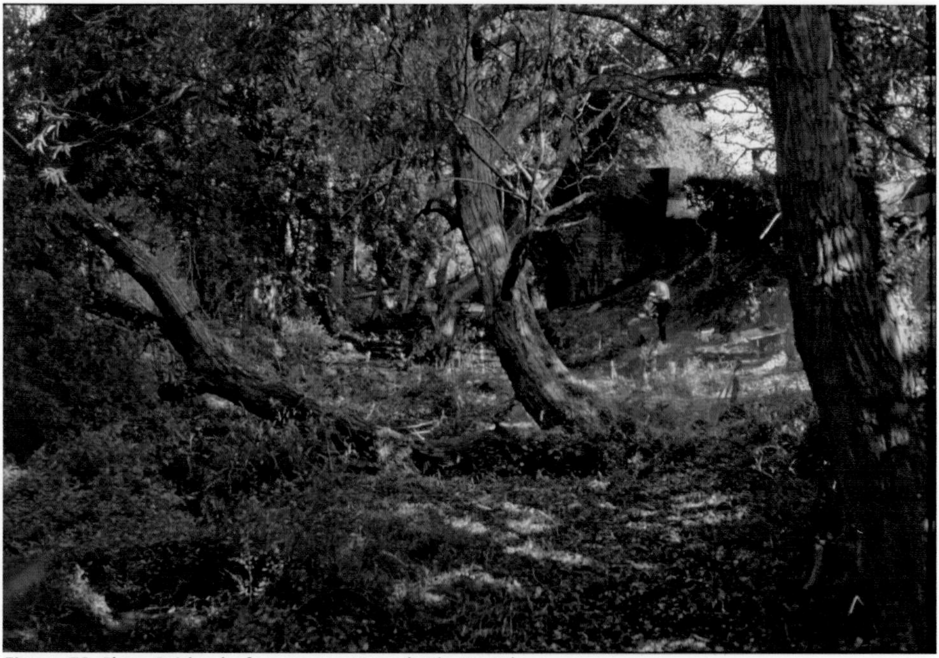

Figure 78: Skew Bridge before restoration. *(Mike Potts)*

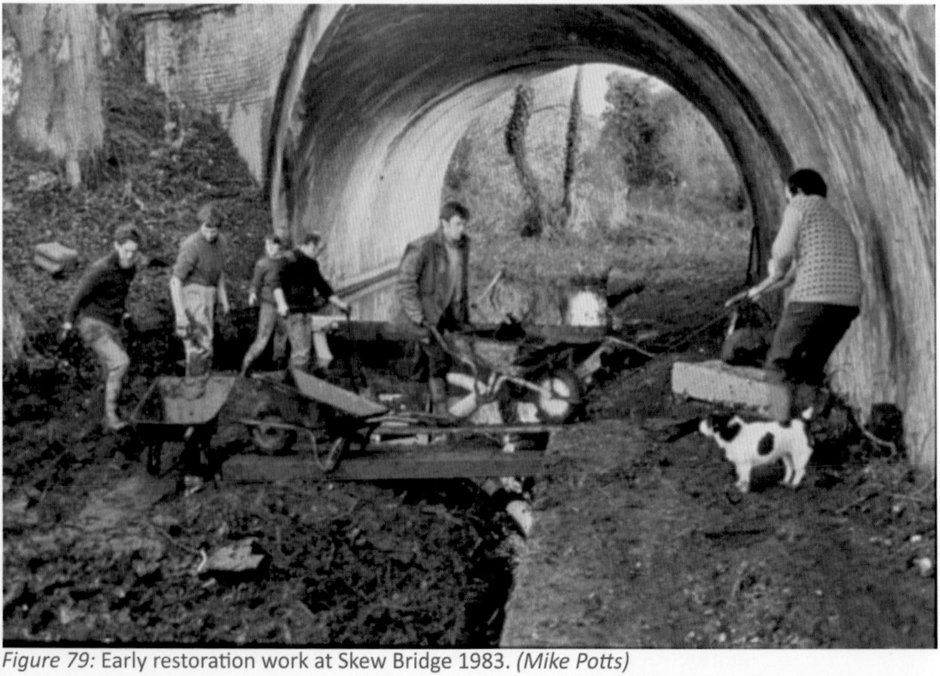

Figure 79: Early restoration work at Skew Bridge 1983. *(Mike Potts)*

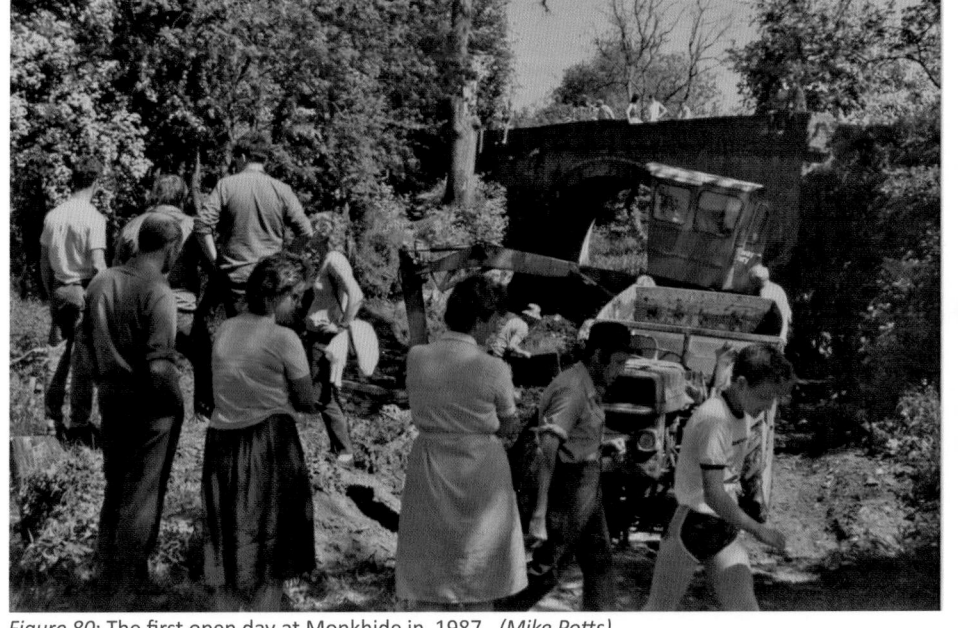

Figure 80: The first open day at Monkhide in 1987. *(Mike Potts)*

Beneath Skew Bridge the towpath had deteriorated considerably and a quantity of hard core was required to strengthen it. Fortunately the Society managed to source a free supply which was duly delivered to the site. As it was being broken up fragments of paper were found in it, enough to indicate that the source of the rubble was none other than the demolished Hereford Canal Office which the Society had been unable to save a few months before!

By this time enough progress had been made to justify opening the site to the general public and the official opening of this short length of restored canal. The open day was a great success and, much encouraged, the Society began to extend the canal further. Its achievements and ambitions were recognised by a grant of £2,000 from the IWA.

There was, at this stage, no public admission that the Society harboured any aspirations to restore the whole canal to full navigation, though some of its members were privately beginning to develop such a vision and the Society's Committee began to debate whether a change of policy should be made.

This was at least partly at the suggestion of both the Hereford and Worcester and the Gloucestershire County Councils. David Bick, a member of the Committee sought advice from Charles Hadfield, one of

the country's leading authorities on canals, a co-founder of the Inland Waterways Association and vice-president of three canal restoration societies. Hadfield's advice was unequivocal and not encouraging.

In a letter to Bick dated January 12th 1988 Hadfield lists a whole host of reasons why restoration of the Hereford and Gloucester was a completely ridiculous idea. He listed issues of huge cost, both of restoration and maintenance, the time it would take and the fact that so little of the original canal remained. What about landowners, water supply and access from the Severn now that Maisemore lock had been sold? And who would want to cruise it anyway, well away from the main cruising areas and a dead end?

He concludes his advice to David Bick thus:

> 66 These are a few of the obvious objections. All round the country lie the wrecks of good intentions – The Thames & Severn, the Portsmouth and Arundel, the Wey and Arun, the Grantham (in spite of being a BWB canal) etc. etc. They finish up as a hobby of a few dozen enthusiasts who potter about in welllies in a lock here and there, and pretend to themselves that they are doing good, when all they are doing – to be blunt – is to inflate their egos.
>
> My suggestion is that you have nothing to do with it. Resign from the Society, and form an amenity group to work with the local authorities on (a) preserving important structures as they are; (b) putting up informative historical notices; (c) issuing a trail guide for school and tourist use and a series of trail walks led by experts; and so on. In other words, keep the memory of the canal alive but do no restoration. The Americans are very good at this ... 99
>
> *Hadfield, Charles: Letter to David Bick 12th January 1988*

Hadfield undoubtedly raised some very important issues, which might well have convinced the Society that restoration was, indeed, out of the question. But for the second time in the canal's history, optimism triumphed over pragmatism and privately, at least, the Society changed its aims. Although David Bick shared Hadfield's view that full restoration was impossible, he remained a member of the Society and Trust to the end of his life.

The few dozen has now grown to many hundreds spending millions of pounds and making great strides in restoring these derelict waterways. Charles Hadfield would have been delighted.

In spite of Hadfield's reservations, public promotional meetings and exhaustive negotiations with the local authorities on restoration of the canal continued. In 1990 South Herefordshire Council agreed to protect the route of the canal from development, noting that the Society's

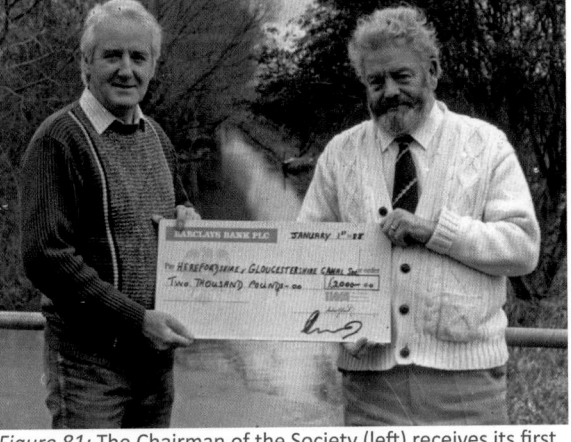

Figure 81: The Chairman of the Society (left) receives its first grant cheque presented by Ken Goodwin, IWA Chairman, in 1988. *(Mike Potts)*

proposals were "formidable" and that it "had a realistic approach to restoration over a long period." Hereford & Worcester County Council was also supportive, recognising the canal and its towpath as a major asset in its Recreation Strategy.

By 1990 the Society was openly speaking of full restoration and attended the Inland Waterways Festival at Gloucester with a large stand and display which won many new members to the Society, including the author.

The canal was forced further into public notice in the following year when proposals were published for a Hereford bypass to be built on the eastern side of the city. This would have cut through the Lugg Meadows, the largest and most important Lammas Meadows in England and a Site of Special Scientific Interest. For the Canal Society, more to the point, it would run across the line of the canal preventing it from ever reaching Hereford. The argument for including provision for the canal was valid only if full restoration between Hereford and Gloucester was a realistic possibility.

The original proposals had rejected a canal crossing on the basis of cost. At the Public Inquiry the Society's Chairman, a chartered civil engineer by profession, prepared and presented formal Proof of Evidence running to 39 pages plus appendices and argued that the Department of Transport's costs for a navigable culvert were double what they should have been and that a number of other false assumptions had been made. After two lengthy adjournments requested by the DoT so it could consult its experts and refine its arguments the Inspector recommended in 1992 that provision for the canal should be made and fully funded by the DoT, a decision accepted by the Secretaries of State for Transport and for the Environment. Michael Handford, Chairman of the IWA Restoration Committee, wrote: "I must congratulate you on your superb appendices and evidence. It was without doubt the best and most comprehensive ever presented by any Canal Society at any Inquiry I ever attended. Your whole presentation was most professional. It was great fun too to see you tie in knots both the DoT Barrister and the Chief Witness."

Over 20 years later Hereford is still waiting for its bypass, but the argument had been won and an important stake had been driven into the ground: a precedent was established which would prove its value in many subsequent planning decisions. Of almost equal importance, the cat was now completely out of the bag. The Society intended to restore the entire canal to full navigation.

In the same year, 1991, Robin Stiles, the owner of House Lock at Oxenhall near Newent allowed members of the Society to begin clearance of the lock site. This was important, as hitherto all restoration work had been carried out in Herefordshire and the Committee was concerned to have a restoration site in both counties.

While House Lock was the only one on the canal where there was anything at all to see, it was in a very sorry state indeed. Much of the stonework had crumbled away and there was a prolific growth of trees rising from the base of the chamber. It was a sad and daunting prospect.

In 1992, following 18 months of complex negotiations with the Charity Commission including advice from specialist parliamentary lawyers and with funding support from IWA, the Society took an important step forward when it became registered as a Charitable Trust, now with the clearly stated aim of restoring the canal from its junction with the River Severn at Over to the centre of the City of Hereford.

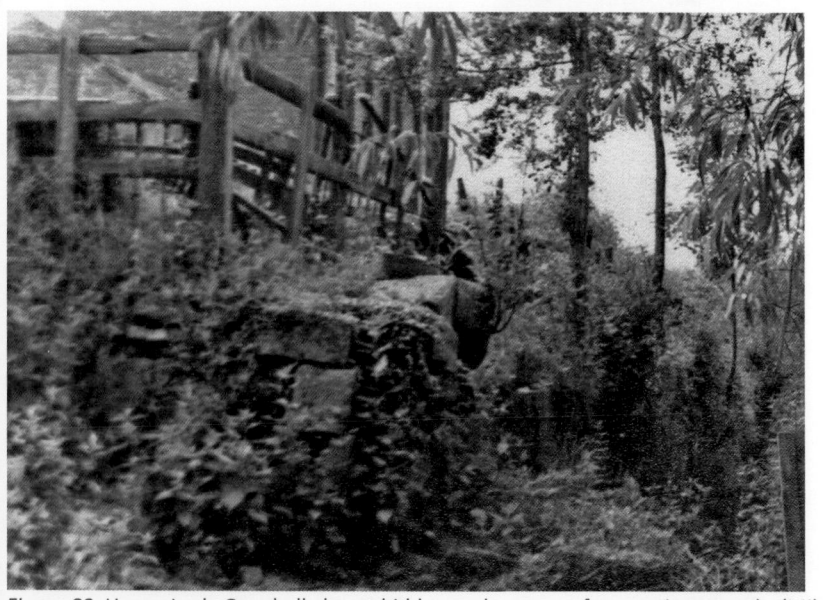

Figure 82: House Lock, Oxenhall almost hidden under years of vegetation growth. *(Mike Potts)*

CHAPTER 9

The Herefordshire & Gloucestershire Canal Trust

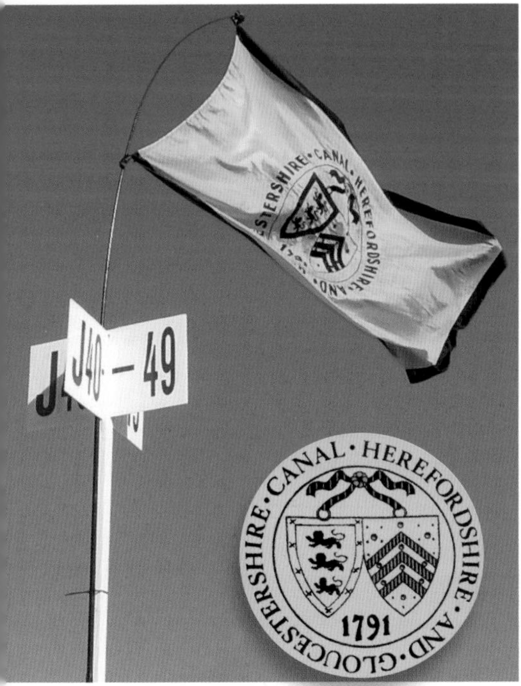

While the transition from Society to Charitable Trust in 1992 made little outward appearance it gave significant advantages, opening up new ways of securing grant aid for restoration and equipment and putting things on a more secure legal footing. The establishment of Hereford and Gloucester Canal Sales, a Not for Profit Trading Company associated with the Trust, also opened up new possibilities.

It was essential in these early days to establish the identity and ethos of the Trust, building on what had already been developed by the Canal Society. The Company Seal made an ideal logo, reproduced in black on yellow.

Trust members working on display stands at external events became easily recognisable by their yellow and black sweatshirts and a large yellow flag bearing the Company crest flew over their stand at outdoor events.

Figure 83: The Trust flag flying at the Crick Boat Show. *(Janet Moult)*

Figure 84: The Company Seal *(H&GCT)*

With a steadily growing sense of self-confidence it was essential to build on the established professionalism of the Trust as demonstrated at the Hereford Bypass Inquiry. There was a determination that, whatever the Trust attempted to do, it must do it well. This extended far beyond work on the canal itself – it was to apply across the board, from rigorous financial management, high quality publicity material and excellence in the Trust's quarterly magazine, The Wharfinger. Health and Safety was established as being of paramount importance, not only for restoration work but covering all the activities of the Trust and the Trading Company. Comprehensive protocols were developed, regularly reviewed and followed as a matter of course.

The threats to the canal experienced in Herefordshire indicated that the first priority for the Trust must be to maintain and extend the commitments of the Local Authorities, through periodic reviews and against numerous challenges, to protect the line of the canal from any developments which could compromise restoration, however far in the future that might be. Local government is subject to reorganisation from time to time and it was vital to ensure that the protection afforded to the canal corridor was carried through from one body to another. The short-lived county of Hereford and Worcester was abolished in 1998 and Herefordshire re-established as a unitary authority. The campaigning carried out by the Society to protect the canal under Hereford and Worcester had to be reiterated for the new authority, with the resulting following robust planning policy:

RST 9 Herefordshire and Gloucestershire Canal

The historic route of the Herefordshire and Gloucestershire Canal together with its associated infrastructure, buildings, towpath and features will be safeguarded. Where the original alignment cannot be re-established, a corridor allowing for deviations is safeguarded. New developments within the safeguarded corridor, or on adjacent sites, will be required to incorporate land for the Canal restoration. Development not connected with the Canal that would prevent or prejudice the restoration of a continuous route will not be permitted.

Herefordshire Council: Herefordshire Unitary Development Plan ☐ March 2007

In Gloucestershire both the County Council and Tewkesbury Borough Council have supportive and protective policies in place. Most of the canal in Gloucestershire lies within the Forest of Dean District Council. When the Local Plan was reviewed in 1993-4 the Trust's representations were supported by 450 individual letters and a far stronger policy on protecting the canal was secured. This has been maintained in a subsequent review and is supported by the following narrative:

Part of the former Herefordshire and Gloucestershire canal lies within the District. It is the long term aim of the Herefordshire and Gloucestershire Canal Trust to restore the entire length of the canal between the River Severn and Hereford, a distance of 34 miles. Considerable effort has already resulted in the

restoration of several sections of the canal and it is important that the ultimate reinstatement is not compromised by development. The Plan will therefore safeguard the historic line of the Canal where it is not already obstructed by permanent structures. Where so obstructed, the Council will safeguard any agreed diversion routes. The Plan will therefore safeguard the route of the canal and shall seek to ensure its restoration as part of any adjacent development. Where appropriate, the District Council may view favourably development that enables a significant contribution to the restoration of the canal. Where the canal has been restored, it offers considerable recreational opportunities and, when the restoration of this important water feature is complete, tourism, economic, and recreation benefits will accrue to the area. The Council will seek to ensure that the canal restoration does not have an adverse impact on water resources through the production of a management structure, if required, or on existing features of wildlife interest, and will encourage habitat enhancement wherever possible to provide nature conservation benefits. The Council supports the Herefordshire and Gloucestershire Canal Trust in their endeavours to restore the Canal to a fully navigable waterway.

The Forest of Dean District Local Plan Review, 2005

Subsequent revisions to planning policies have maintained or strengthened these safeguards.

While fighting to secure the protection of the canal it was easy to see property development as the enemy and planning objections where restoration was threatened, an automatic response. A number of such developments were successfully opposed, with amendments to secure the line of the canal achieved. However, with increasing recognition that the Trust would be vigorous and effective in presenting its case, many developers realised that working with the Trust rather than against it was a much more effective way forward. In particular, agreements under Section 106 of the Town and Country Planning Act (1990) by which developments could be permitted subject to making the associated canal land available or even providing the funding for restoration along it, were found to be invaluable. Over only the first few years of the Trust's existence a number of spectacularly successful agreements were reached securing millions of pounds worth of investment in the canal, while adverse developments

were turned down. In a planning appeal decision letter in 1997, rejecting a proposed industrial development on the line of the canal in Hereford, the Government Planning Inspector wrote: "The Canal Trust's credibility is apparent from the role it has played in successfully influencing the planning policy framework both within Hereford City and along the entire length of the Canal. As such, I am in no doubt as to the standing and substance of its considered position prior to and at the hearing and in post-hearing correspondence."

But undoubtedly the greatest difficulty facing the new Trust in restoring the entire canal was that it owned none of it. Following the closure of the canal in 1881 the Proprietors attempted to get what they could for the parts of the canal line not used by the railway. In some cases they could scarcely give it away, but retrieving it from the present owners was never going to be easy. However it was important that there was visible progress towards eventual restoration and therefore, like other similar projects elsewhere, this would take the form of the restoration of short, isolated lengths of canal, the property of sympathetic land-owners, as opportunities arose.

Volunteer teams were set up at each site as it became available. A designated Site Leader managed the work programme within an agreed budget. While often the Site Leader and some of the volunteers were initially associated with an existing site, in each case a new site brought new volunteers, usually local people attracted by the challenge of worthwhile voluntary work and the opportunity to join a team of like-minded people. Rapidly the teams developed their own identity and, with training always being provided, their own skills.

The Trust also recognised from the start that simply restoring the canal was not enough to secure its future. It had to be able to generate sufficient income to support the continuing maintenance costs of operating the canal. Sustainability became a key element in the Trust's thinking and working, constantly exploring ways in which income could be maximised, expenditure minimised and a positive approach to environmental issues exploited.

Experience of other waterways, including those owned by British Waterways was that income from the paying users of the canal, principally boating licenses, mooring fees, and rental from canal based businesses, would never be adequate. It is known that most people visiting canals do so on foot and therefore more imaginative ways have to be found to

generate sufficient revenue. Over time this meant that the Trust had to spend some of its hard-won resources on securing income for the future rather than on restoring the canal itself. For some members this appeared to be a distraction from the stated aims of the Trust; to others, these were investments that simply had to be made to ensure a long term future for the canal.

Consideration of the wider economic aspects was also important. The benefits of a fully restored canal to the local communities through which it passes are numerous and varied, but the impact on the local economy is a vital factor in securing support from local authorities, grant giving bodies, potential sponsors and the public. British Waterways carried out a study of the canal in 1995, using comparative data from similar existing waterways, and estimated an additional local spend resulting from the canal of some £6million per year. A further study in 2009 updated this figure to £20million, the increase related to both inflation and the increased tourism engagement with canals, and added an estimate of extra jobs created at some 500 full time equivalent. It is anticipated that the continued growth of the Trust's ambitions, looking at the broader corridor of the canal rather than just the canal itself, will see an increase in these estimates.

Other principles were also established from the start. The membership of the Trust had to be built up and maintained, for this is a measure of public support for the restoration, a key determinant for funding bodies. In those early days the very existence of the old canal was still unknown to a great many people, even to those living close to its original line.

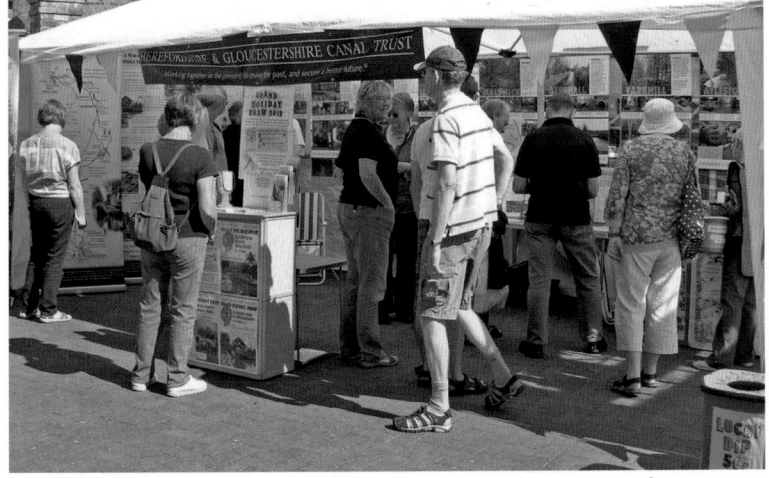

Figure 85: The Trust's stand at the Lock 200 event at Gloucester Docks.
(Maggie Jones)

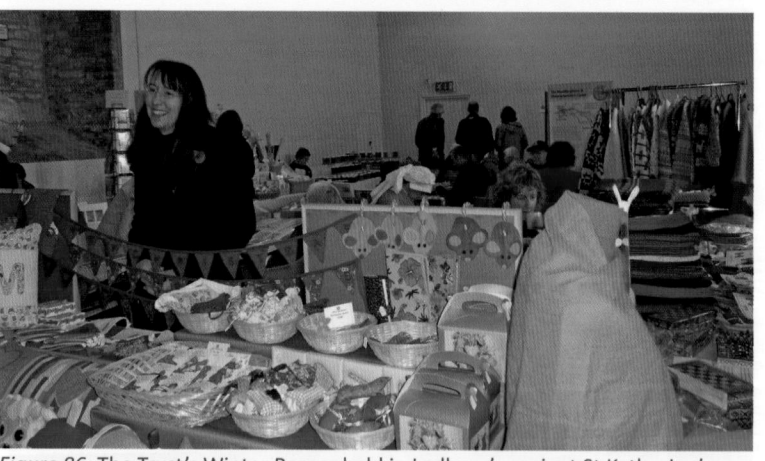

Figure 86: The Trust's Winter Bazaar held in Ledbury's ancient St Katherine's Hall in 2013. *(Author)*

The Trading Company took stands at all major waterway and many local events and continues to have a busy programme during the summer months – sometimes having to split its resources over more than one event on the same day. A programme of monthly Social Evenings, generally with an invited speaker, was established and is well supported to this day.

Members of the Trust gave talks to groups both in the two counties and further afield and still do so, though now the interest is more in progress towards restoration than discovering the canal itself. Tours of the canal are also arranged from time to time visiting restoration sites and other points of interest.

The Society's magazine, "The Wharfinger", which began as a simple duplicated news sheet evolved into an attractive high quality magazine running to some 40 full colour pages. It was not until Edition 115 in Spring 2013 that the words "Rebuilding 34 miles of canal between Gloucester and Hereford" appeared on the front cover, leaving the reader in no doubt of the objectives of the Trust. "The Wharfinger" is now widely regarded as one of the best journals produced by any canal Trust or Society.

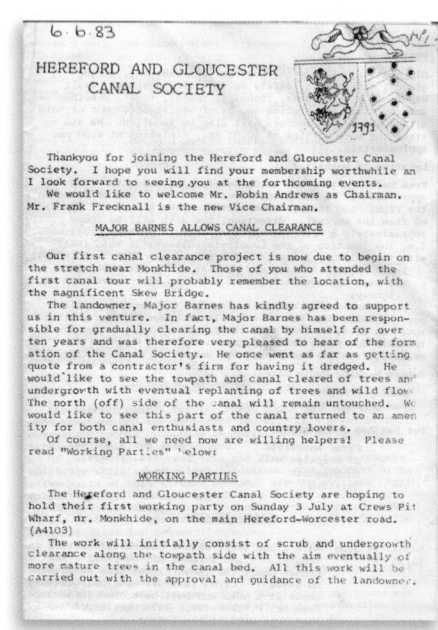

Figure 87: The first newletter from the Canal Society – June 1983.

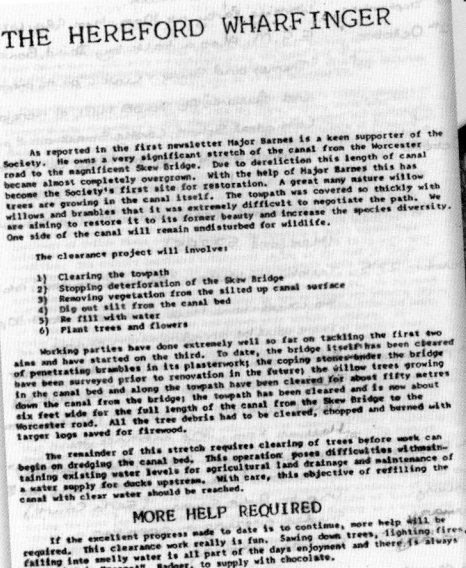

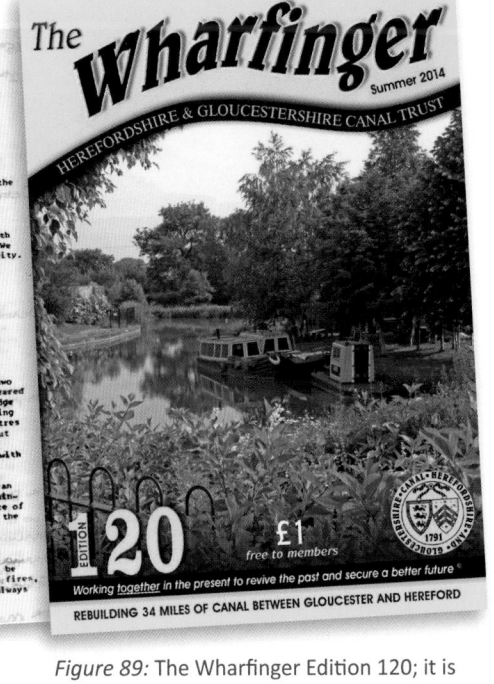

Figure 88: The second newsletter – the first edition to be called "The Wharfinger".

Figure 89: The Wharfinger Edition 120; it is now a 40-page full colour magazine with over 2,000 copies printed each quarter.

The Trust also accepted from an early stage that it could not restore 34 miles of canal on its own. This would have to be done in close partnership with other bodies and organisations which shared the vision of the restored canal. In particular, working with local authorities and with developers would prove essential. It looked for, and found, support from the Inland Waterways Association and the Waterway Recovery Group (WRG) the huge contribution of which will be told in the following pages.

An essential partnership in all canal restorations is with the Environment Agency. Water supply for any canal is essential, and this is a significant issue for a canal with many locks and a summit level, as all boat movements result in the removal to the lower level of a lock-full of water – close to 200 tons in the case of the Hereford & Gloucester Canal's locks. An independent study on water supply and management for the Canal was commissioned jointly by the Trust and the EA and carried out by Birmingham University's School of Civil Engineering between 1996 and 2001, drawing on data from British Waterways, the EA and other sources, as well as considerations of the rivers, catchment areas and countryside through which the Canal will pass. This concluded that the foreseeable demands of the fully restored Canal would be met adequately from a combination of some historic sources, specific identified new sources and water conservation measures including back pumping.

These conclusions now form the basis of the Trust's overall plan for water supply for the restored canal.

As the Trust matured these basic principles were developed and enhanced. Lessons would be learnt, sometimes painfully, but the foundations have proved to be sound.

A recent introduction which now seems to have become established firmly as an annual event is the Over Canal Festival held over the last weekend in August. Over Basin is thronged with people enjoying the waterside and a whole range of activities including cruises on *Mr. Maysey*, the Trust's trip boat, a procession of the Trust's heritage boats, a horse-drawn boat, classic cars and the handiwork of the members of the Gloucester Model Boat Club. There are craft and produce stalls, great food and beer, cider and perry.

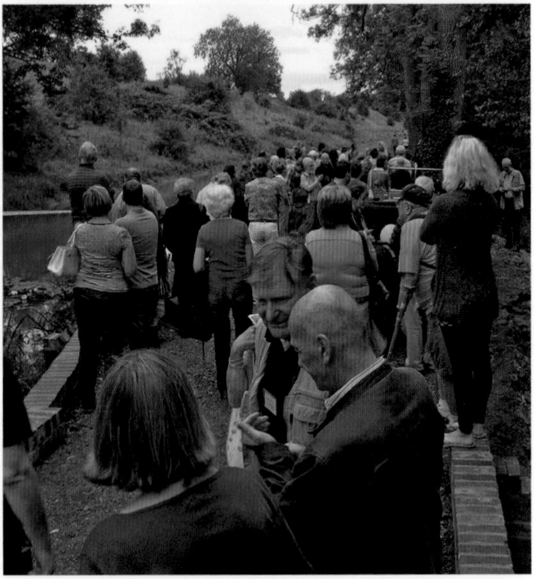

Figure 90: Crowds of people at the Over Canal Festival 2012. *(Ted Beagles)*

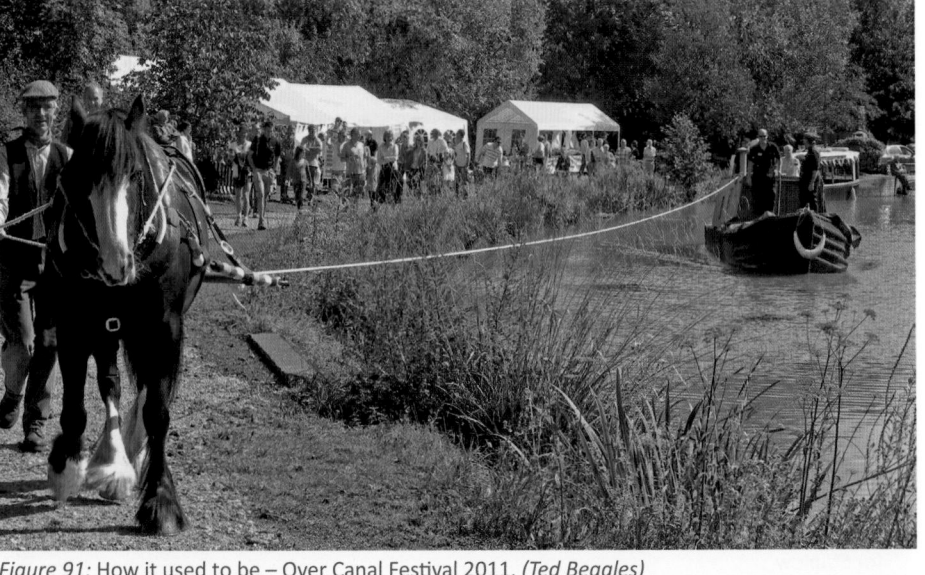

Figure 91: How it used to be – Over Canal Festival 2011. *(Ted Beagles)*

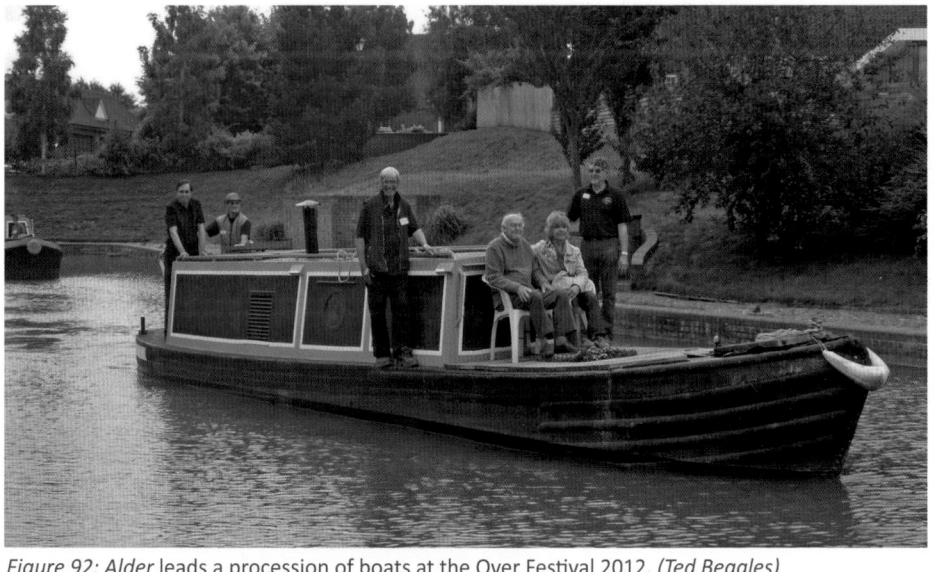

Figure 92: Alder leads a procession of boats at the Over Festival 2012. *(Ted Beagles)*

Although almost the whole of the canal lies in private land and many parts of it are not easily accessible the Trust has produced a series of attractive leaflets describing walks along footpaths and such lengths of the towpath where this is possible.

Each leaflet describes the route of the walk and the places of interest along the canal.

By 2014 five leaflets were available covering areas around Staplow, Withington, Dymock, Llanthony Lock and Oxenhall.

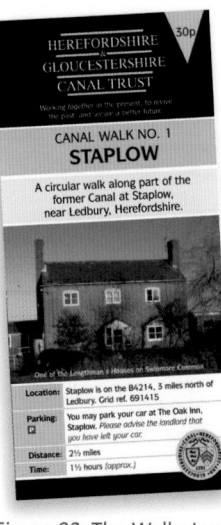

Figure 93: The Walks Leaflet for Staplow

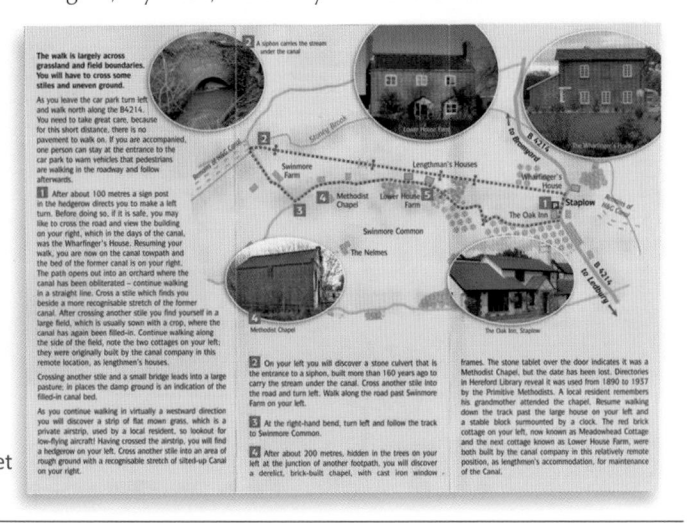

Restoration in Herefordshire

Returning to our story of the Canal itself, following the formation of the Trust, the Society's work on the canal at Monkhide continued apace and in 1992 another open day was held – this time an Open Weekend, attracting large numbers of people with a variety of attractions alongside the canal. Trip boats, including one of the very first fibre-glass cruisers ever to use the canal, gave the public a taste of being afloat on their own local waterway.

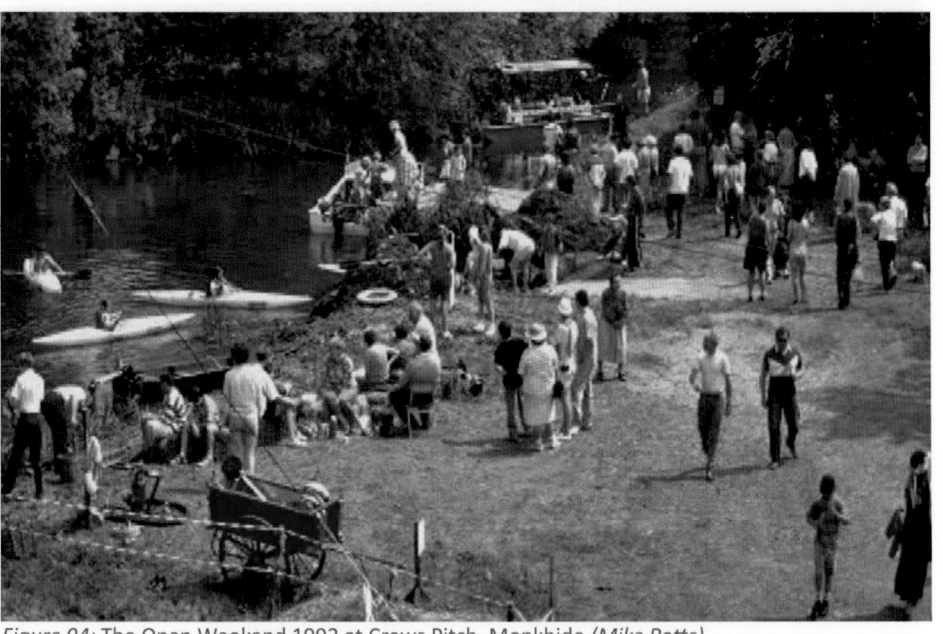

Figure 94: The Open Weekend 1992 at Crews Pitch, Monkhide *(Mike Potts)*

The Society had been given *"Mallard"* a trip boat by the late Sir John Knill. It had been refurbished and provided with an outboard motor. Major Barnes' own trip boat, *"Brindley"* was also in service, these boats mingling with canoes, a coracle and a steam launch.

A brass band, Morris dancers, demonstrations of country crafts, plenty of food and displays promoting the restoration of the canal kept visitors busy for the whole weekend.

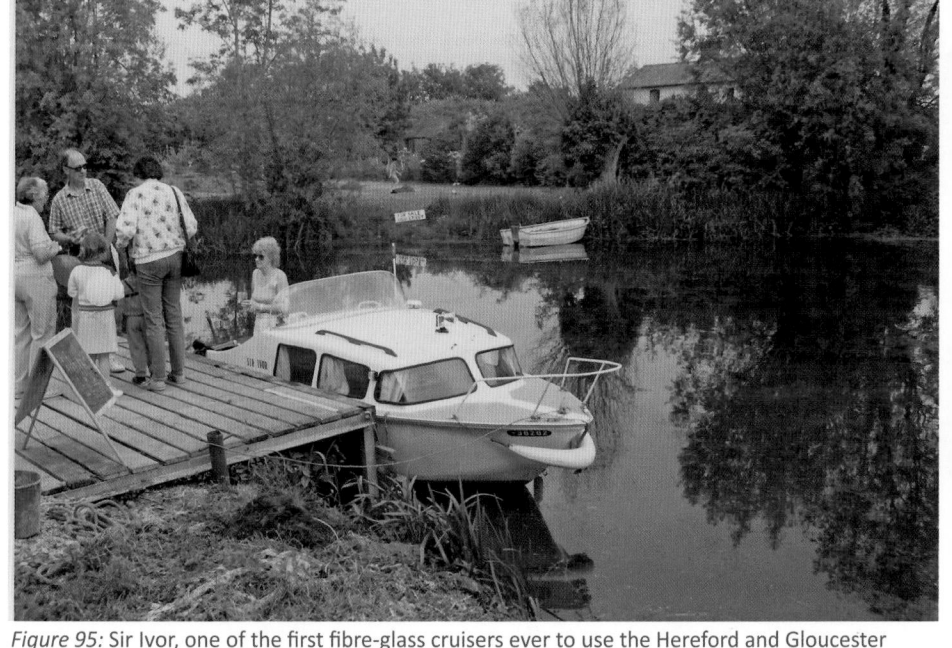

Figure 95: Sir Ivor, one of the first fibre-glass cruisers ever to use the Hereford and Gloucester
Canal, serves as a trip boat at the Open Weekend 1992. *(Mike Potts)*

Despite the publicity the canal was now receiving and the Inspector's
decision in the bypass Inquiry, when the Hereford and Worcester County
Council carried out its Roman Road improvements in 1995 it planned to
lower the road at the canal crossing, thus once again threatening to prevent
the canal ever reaching the centre of Hereford, though tantalisingly within
arm's reach.

The Trust successfully challenged this decision and the County Council
funded the £100,000 cost of the approach ramps and the navigable culvert
which will allow boats to reach Hereford in the future. The concrete
culvert has little of the charm of the old canal bridge, but another vital
battle had been won.

Another Open Weekend was held in 1995 and once again this was a great
success with many visitors, both local and from further afield. To celebrate
the opening of a further length of the canal Major Barnes had his narrow
boat Maria Ballard, named after Stephen Ballard's wife, transported from
its home mooring at Worcester and for the first time cruised Ballard's
canal. There was a display of vintage cars and other attractions and the
Society's Trading Company had displays about the canal and sold various
items in order to raise money towards further restoration.

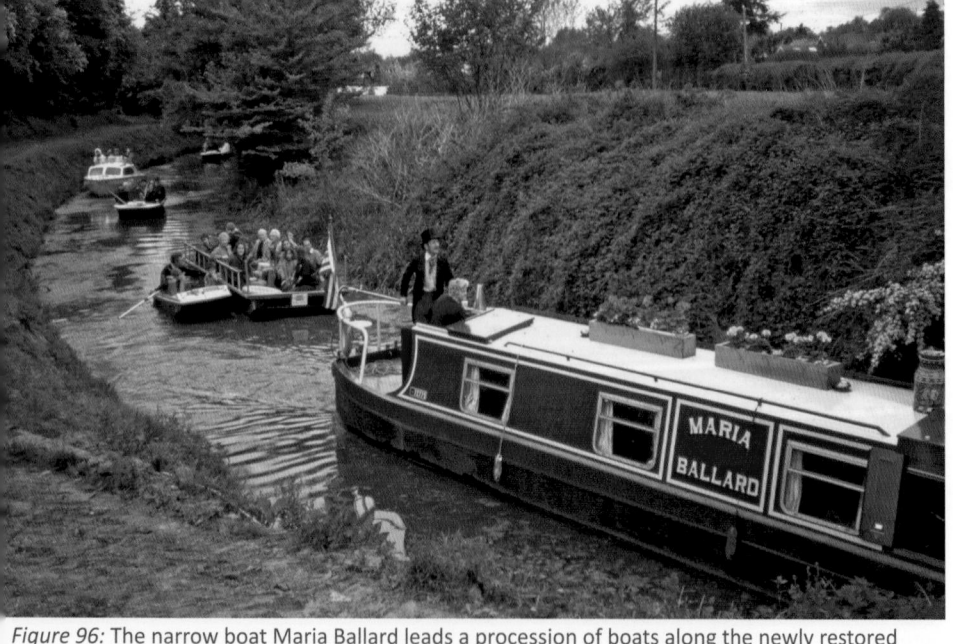

Figure 96: The narrow boat Maria Ballard leads a procession of boats along the newly restored length of canal at the Monkhide Canal Open Weekend 1995. *(Mike Potts)*

While restoration at Monkhide had been carried out in association with the landowner there was no legal agreement between the two parties, and in particular, any arrangement by which the public could be guaranteed unrestricted free access to the restored canal. A similar situation existed in Gloucestershire on the lengths approaching Oxenhall Tunnel. As the restoration had been carried out mainly by volunteers and funded by public donations, this was a situation unacceptable to the Trust. It led directly to the adoption of a fundamental principle that the Trust would only allow restoration work to commence on sites that it owned, or were the subject of a legal agreement which guaranteed access for restoration and maintenance and by the general public, though this would be subject to health and safety restrictions while work is in progress.

In consequence, although major preliminary restoration works were completed on these sites there has not been any further restoration or maintenance undertaken by the Trust at any site which the Trust does not own or where appropriate legal agreements are not in place.

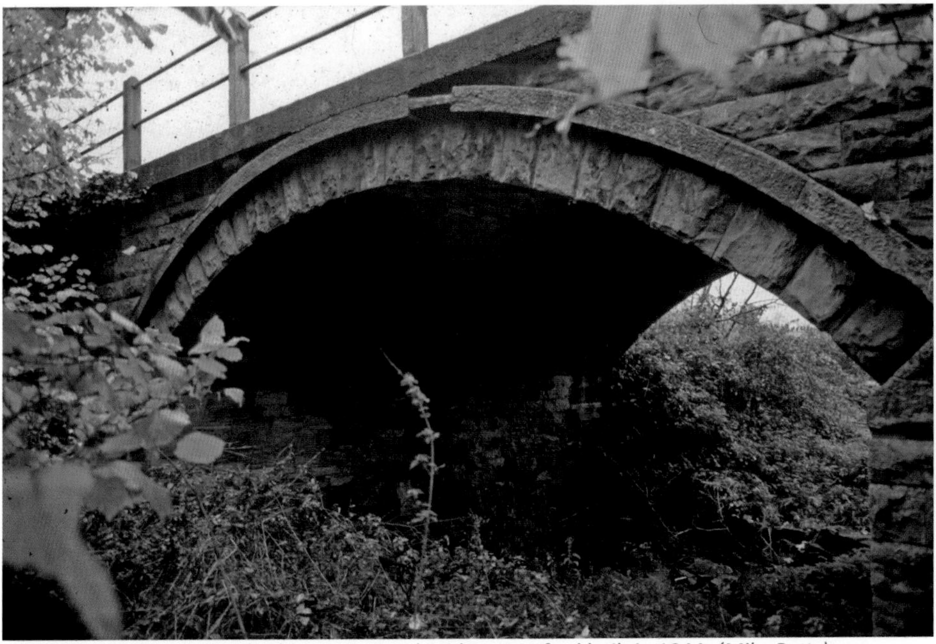

Figure 97: Stephen Ballard's old Roman Road Bridge, Hereford built in 1844. *(Mike Potts)*

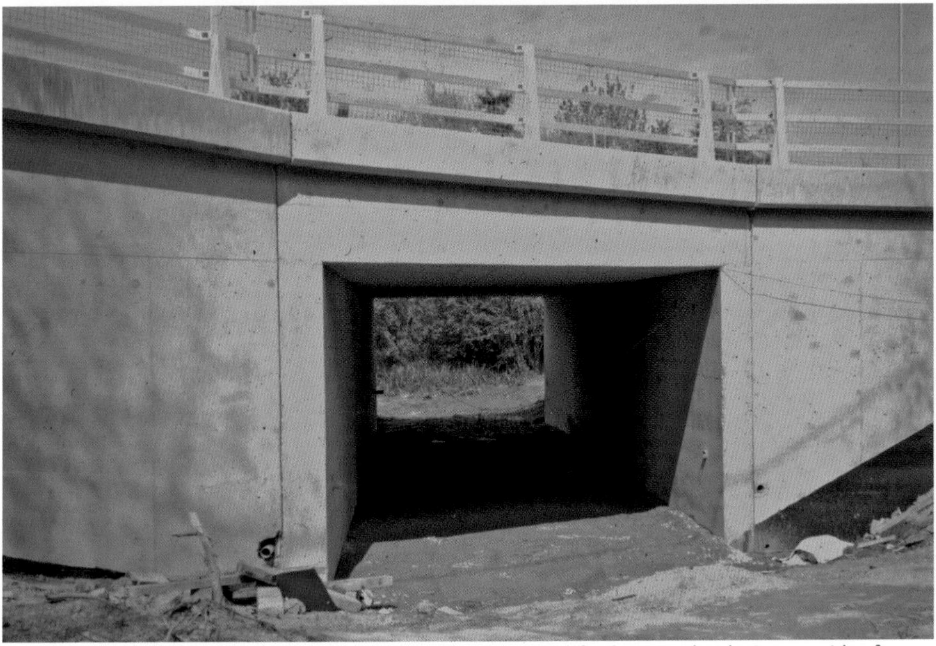

Figure 98: The navigable culvert under the Roman Road, Hereford 1995. The design provides for a facing of stone or brick when the canal is restored which will greatly improve its appearance. The towpath will be at about the present ground level. *(Cliff Penny)*

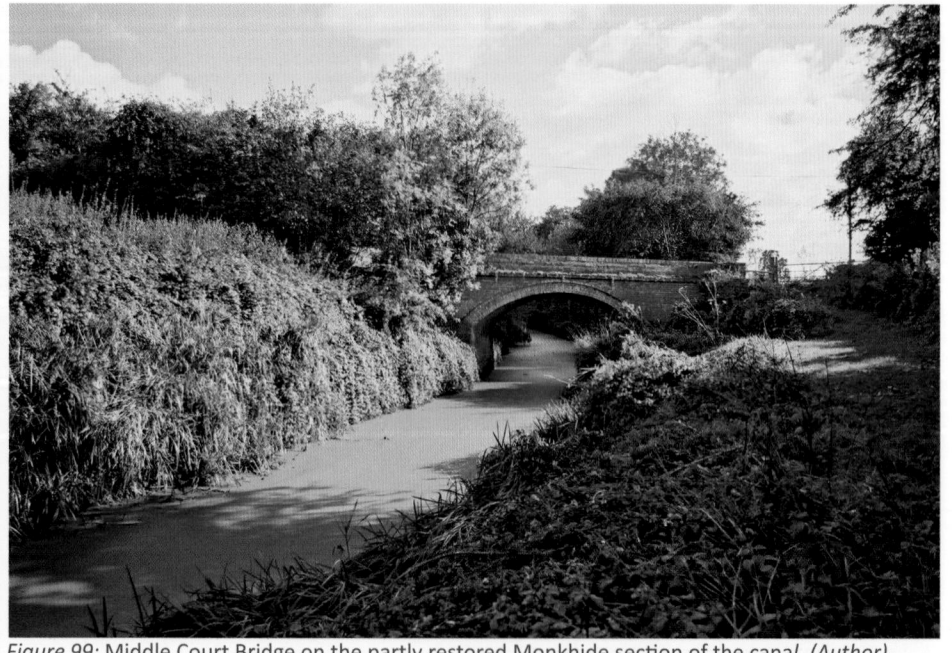

Figure 99: Middle Court Bridge on the partly restored Monkhide section of the canal. *(Author)*

In November 1994 a legal agreement was reached between the Trust and Mrs Patricia Oram of Whitwick Manor in relation to a stretch of canal some 1000 yards long on the northern side of the A4103 at Yarkhill, close to the Monkhide stretch partly restored previously. This led to, but did not include, the site of Barr's Lock the first of the three locks which lowered the canal towards Hereford.

A major clearance of the site began immediately and excavation of the canal and grading of the towpath was carried out in the autumn by an energetic work camp. Though plagued by extremely wet weather, great progress was made and after further work the following year the canal filled with water from natural drainage of adjoining streams. Although not part of the site, with the neighbour's agreement a trial excavation was carried out to determine the exact position of the lock. Nothing was found – either the excavation was not deep enough or no stone or brickwork remained.

While this length of the canal includes no bridges or other structures requiring restoration, the canal bed and banks have been badly damaged by the growth of large trees which had to be removed. Consequently, while the stretch held water well in winter, in summer, with evaporation and little feed from land drainage it could dry up completely.

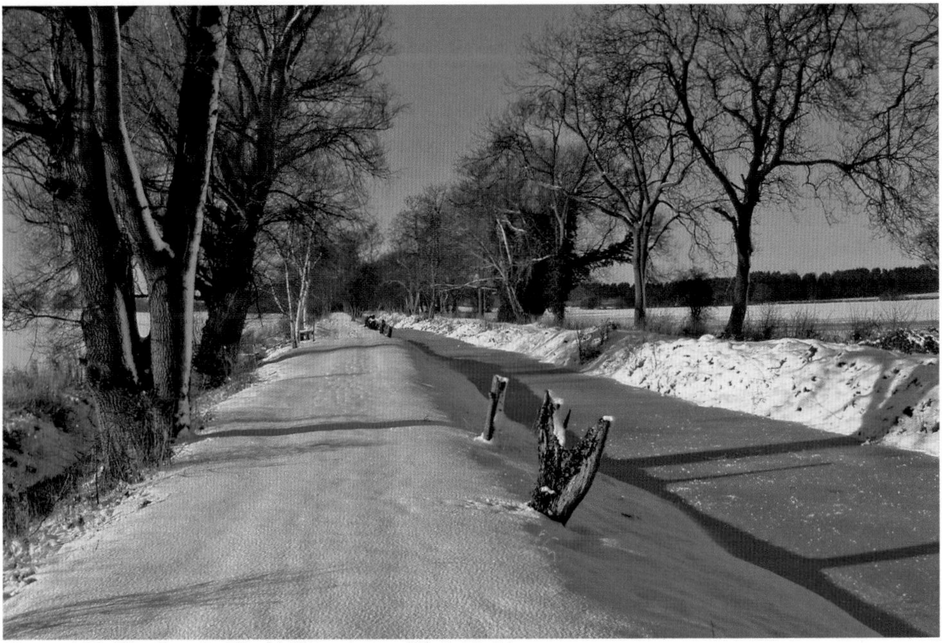

Figure 100: The Canal at Yarkhill in winter. *(Chris High)*

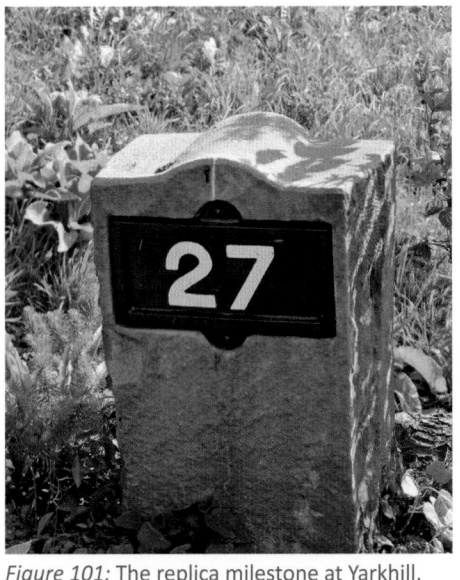

Figure 101: The replica milestone at Yarkhill, 27 miles from the River Severn. This was carved by Trust volunteers demonstrating their versatility in the art of masonry. *(Author)*

In 2005 a new restoration team was formed and, with some help from the Waterway Recovery Group, has done much to bring the site up to a high standard. Encouraged by the Site Leader, the towpath, despite the remote location, is now used and much appreciated by local people. A great number of tree stumps have been removed and considerable work still needs to be done to restore the original profile. Some leaks have been sealed including the excavation of the canal bed at the Barr's Lock end to repair a hole in the culvert that passes under the canal but more work is necessary to make it watertight. This is a difficult and time-consuming task.

In 2008 a replica of milestone 27 was erected by the canal, the first of the new set of milestones which will be required to replace all those lost. Open days have been

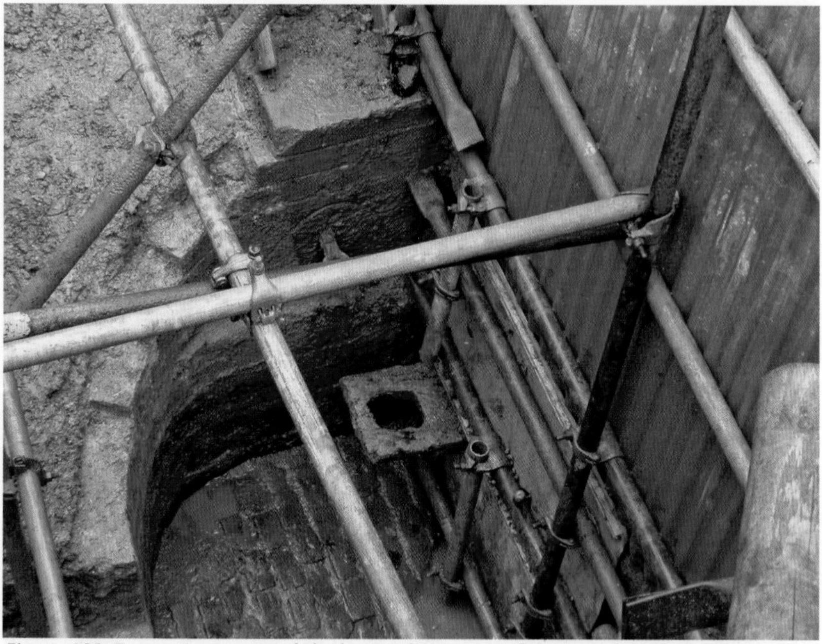

Figure 102: Excavations at Barr's lock revealing some of the remaining masonry and brickwork. (Chris High)

held when large numbers of people walked the towpath, but the remote location, the want of a slipway and lack of water during the summer has not made it practical to hold major public events here.

With the permission of the owner, Mr. Peter Clews, further excavation work has also been carried out at the site of Barr's Lock on a slightly different alignment, this time with considerable success. While little evidence of the stone or brickwork of the lock walls has been found, masonry at the bottom of the lock has been discovered and brickwork forming the bottom offside corner and lock invert uncovered.

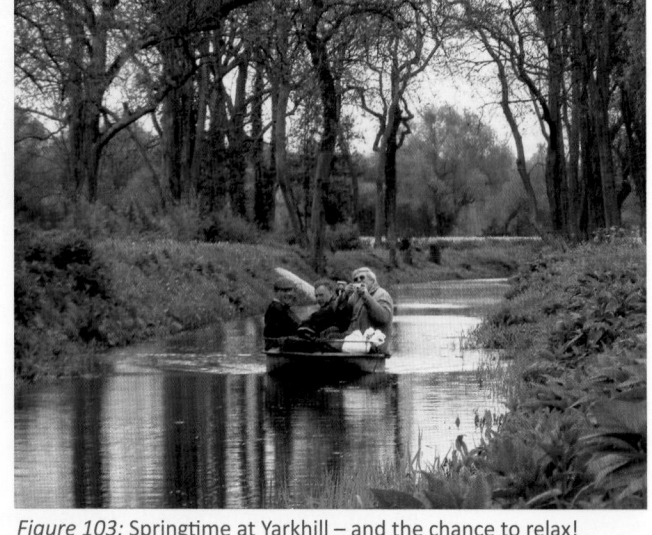

Figure 103: Springtime at Yarkhill – and the chance to relax! (Chris High)

Some five miles towards Hereford, on the outskirts of the City itself, another length of canal became available for restoration in 2002 following the compulsory purchase by the Herefordshire Council of a considerable area of land adjoining Aylestone Hill for development into a public park. The line of the canal ran along the northern edge of the site and, following a request from the Trust, this was included in the compulsory purchase.

One of the first tasks was to build the secure compound to house the paraphernalia required to carry out work on the site in association with the Waterway Recovery Group in the most appalling, freezing cold wind. Such is the devotion of the restorers of canals!

Work on scrub clearance and tree felling followed in preparation for the excavation of a quarter of a mile of canal.

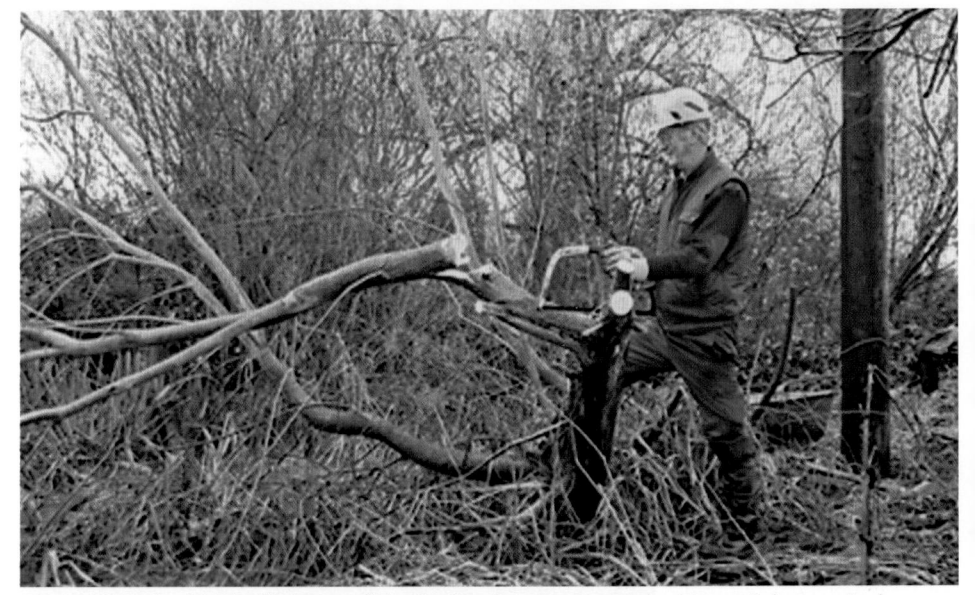

Figure 104: Brian Moult, Chairman of the Trading Company, scrub-bashing at Aylestone Park. Sadly, Brian died the following morning. *(Keith Kitson)*

The canal itself had not been infilled but had accumulated a large quantity of silt almost to the level of the surrounding ground. There had been some factories bordering the canal, including a tile works and many years ago it had been the custom to dispose of unwanted paints and other materials into the canal. Indeed, after the present author had given a talk about the canal in Hereford and spoken of this, an elderly gentleman introduced himself and, much embarrassed, confessed that, as a boy of about 15, this had been his job at the end of his working day!

Preliminary tests had shown the silt to be uncontaminated and a Waterway Recovery Group work-camp was planned for Easter 2004. However, further tests carried out shortly before the camp indicated significant levels of contamination by heavy metals. The camp was cancelled and the Trust faced the challenge of how to excavate and dispose of many tons of contaminated silt. The transportation and disposal of this material is extremely expensive – far beyond the budget of the Trust at the time. The solution was found within the park itself, where a number of roadways and parking areas were to be constructed. In return for the Trust's undertaking agreed work in the park, Herefordshire Council let a contract to Celtic Technologies in 2007 to excavate 1800 cubic metres of silt from the canal which was processed on site to create a solid, inert compound from which the contaminants cannot leach, and this formed the foundations of these hard areas.

Over the next few years Trust volunteers, again with assistance from the Waterway Recovery Group, completed the preliminary restoration of the canal, constructed fencing around the park and over a mile and a half of footpaths within it.

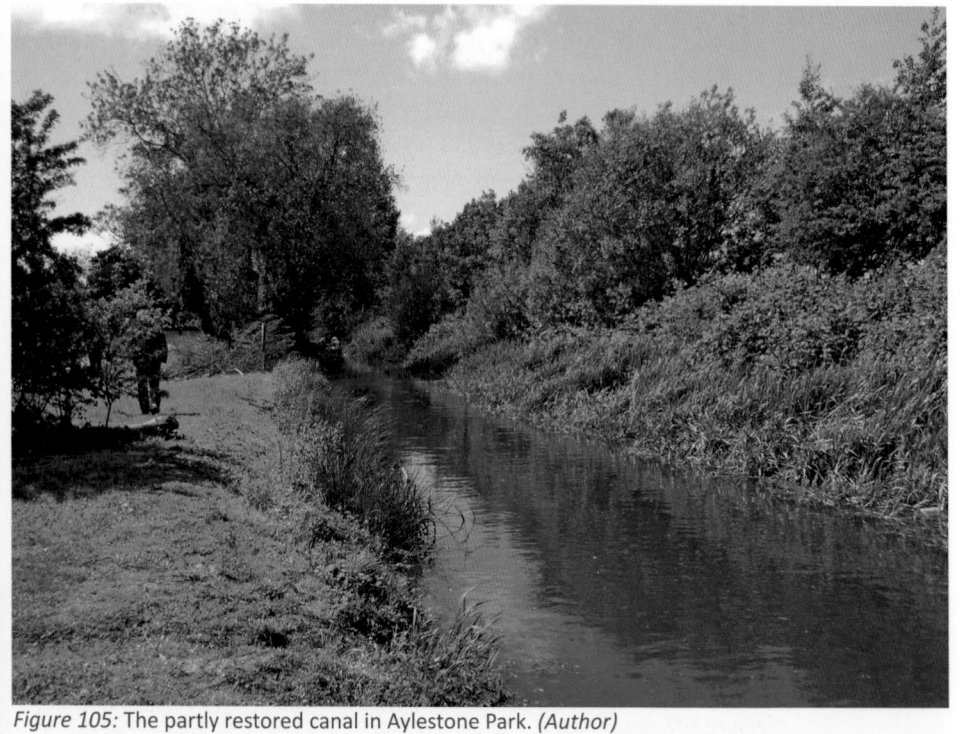

Figure 105: The partly restored canal in Aylestone Park. *(Author)*

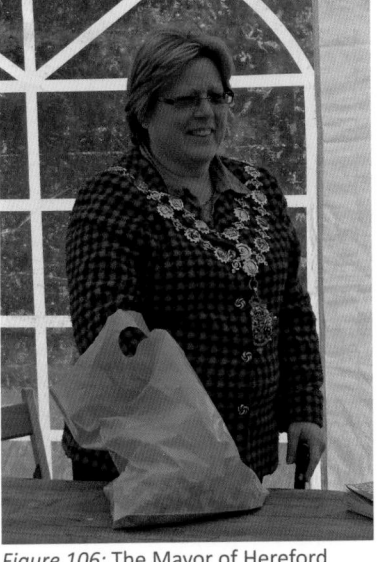

In May 2011 the first Boat Gathering was held following the completion of a slipway. This was another of the landmark events in the history of the canal's restoration when an estimated 2000+ people came to Aylestone Park. All day there were queues for the trip boats travelling the canal. The steam vehicles and vintage cars were much admired and the sales stand did a roaring trade in goods and raffle tickets – such that it was difficult to keep up with the paper-work!

The Mayor of Hereford, the late Councillor Julie Woodward, attended on the Sunday morning and "opened" the new stretch of canal cutting a ribbon across the slipway. She had to leave for another engagement at lunchtime – only to return in the afternoon!

Figure 106: The Mayor of Hereford draws the winning raffle tickets at Aylestone Park. *(Author)*

Four Wilderness Boats were moored in the park for the weekend, stopping off on the way to the IWA National Trail-boat Rally on the Neath Canal the following weekend. Other boats, including a steam boat were launched from the new slipway. It was a remarkable day, the first canal event in the City's history. Despite the Canal Society and Trust promoting the canal for nearly 30 years there were still people who said they never knew there was a canal in Hereford and many more who knew that there once was a canal but had never expected to see boats on it again.

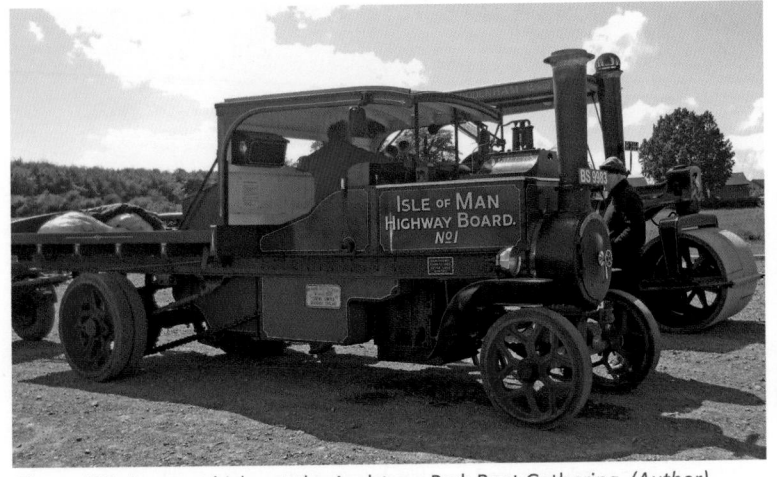

Figure 107: Steam vehicles at the Ayelstone Park Boat Gathering. *(Author)*

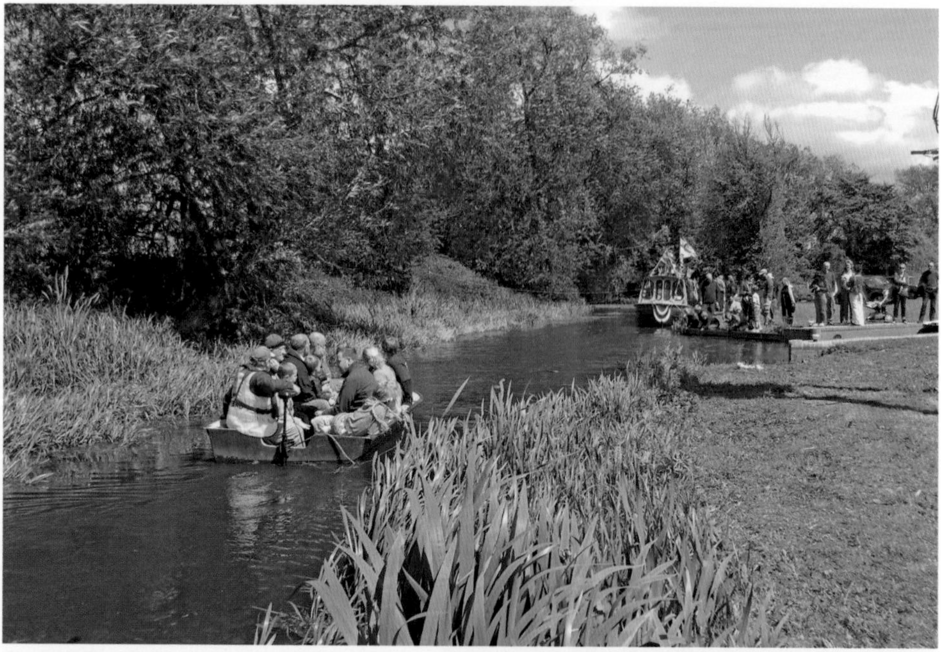

Figure 108: Trip boats in operation on the canal in Aylestone Park. *(Author)*

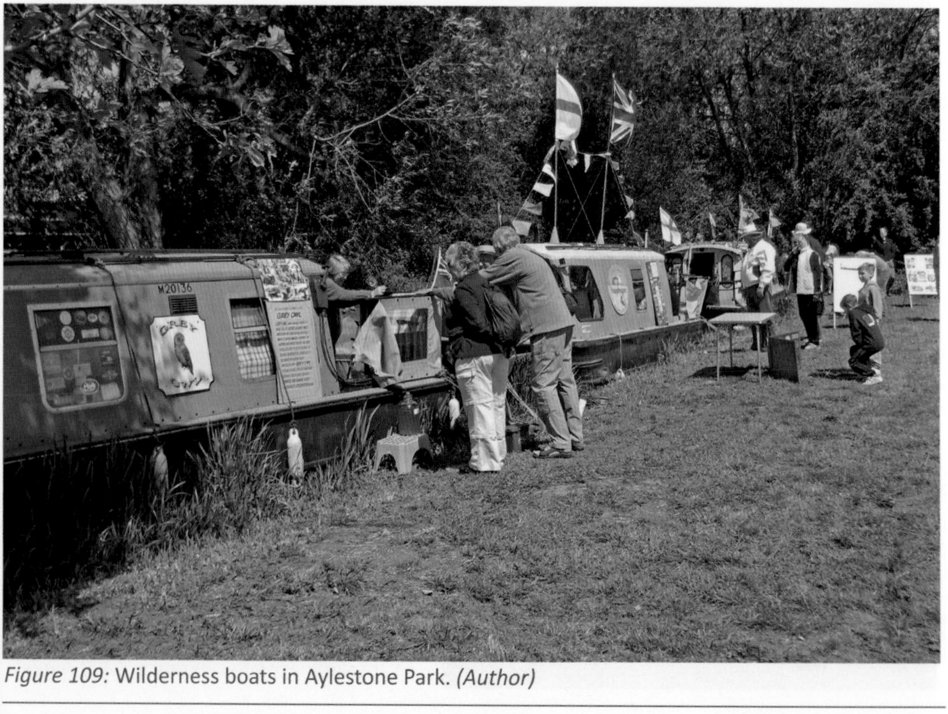

Figure 109: Wilderness boats in Aylestone Park. *(Author)*

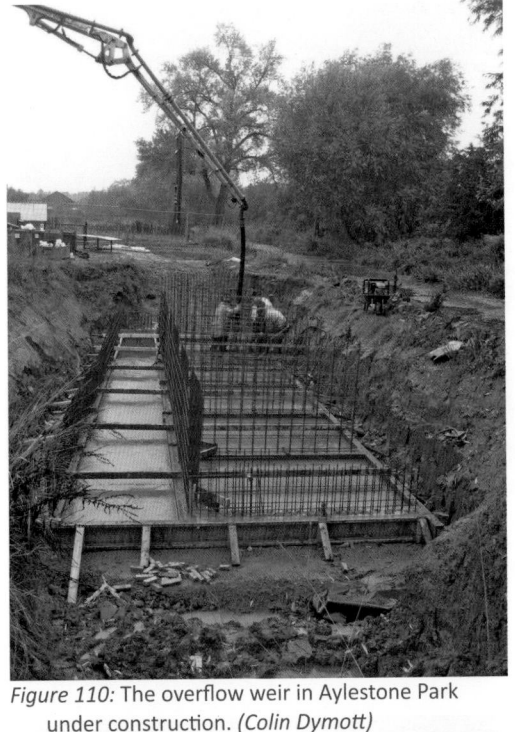

Figure 110: The overflow weir in Aylestone Park under construction. *(Colin Dymott)*

In 2013 the Trust let a contract to build a large overflow weir in the park which will not only manage the water level in the Hereford pound but is crucial to the management of surface water in parts of the City, some of which will drain into the restored canal.

In 2012 agreement was reached with Peter Clews, owner of the land between Barr's Lock and Kymin to restore 1000 yards of canal. This is adjacent to the Yarkhill stretch already under restoration and has the advantage of road access at Kymin. Being a heavily wooded stretch, the restoration is designed to retain as many trees as possible such that from the surrounding countryside the landscape will appear little changed. Work began in November with the Waterway Recovery Group National Reunion Weekend when over 100 "WRGies" descended on the site and began to clear the line to be restored. About 800 yards were cleared, the remaining 200 being dealt with in two weekends by Trust volunteers early in 2013. Although much scrub and some trees on the line of the canal and towpath had to be removed, over 150 trees have been planted as part of the restoration. During the summer of the same year final site clearance was undertaken, tree stumps removed and a drainage channel dug to drain water away from the canal itself to allow the excavation work to be completed. Restoration of this site has not been carried out by a restoration

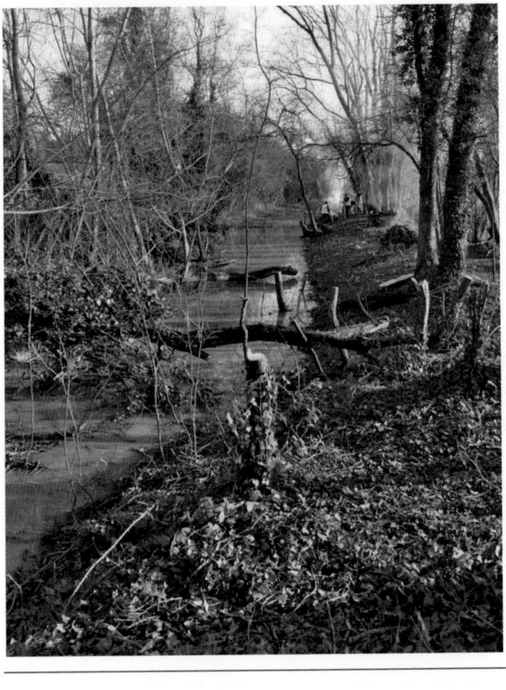

Figure 111: The Canal at Kymin after preliminary site clearance. *(Wilf Jones)*

group specifically devoted to the site, but by relatively short periods of intensive work by specialist members of the Trust's other groups.

The Trust owns a short stretch of the canal corridor in Hereford, the Burcott Road Site. This was acquired under a Section 106 Agreement associated with a small housing development alongside the canal line together with two adjoining small parcels of land owned by the Herefordshire Council. Apart from general tidying of the site, restoration has not begun as it is possible that much of the engineering works to restore the canal into the City and construct the terminal basin will be carried out by contractors as part of the major redevelopment of Hereford City which is currently taking place.

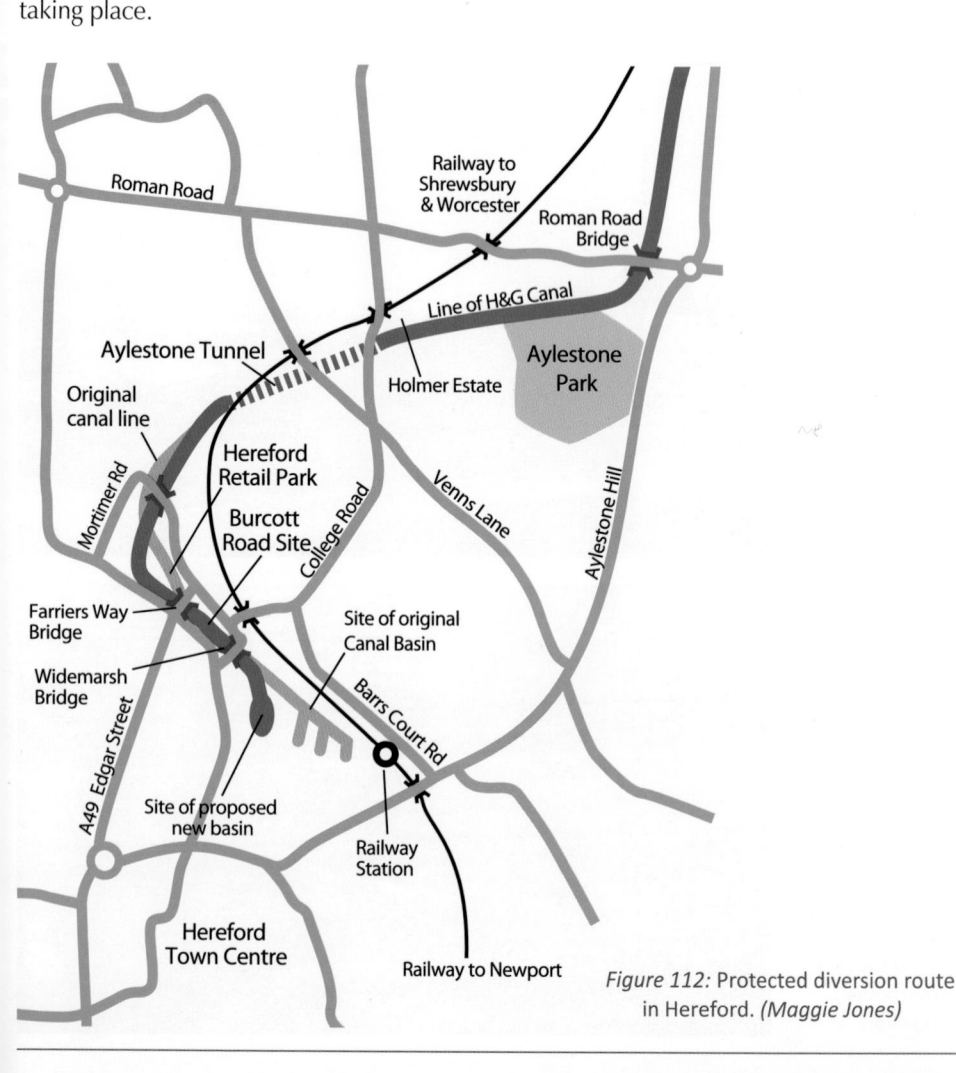

Figure 112: Protected diversion route in Hereford. *(Maggie Jones)*

Adjacent to this length, as part of the development of the retail park on the site of the former Farriery College, a road bridge and a substantial footbridge over the route of the canal have already been built under another Section 106 Planning Agreement. This followed extended negotiations between the Trust and the developer, who agreed to forego some 10% of the potential retail space as well as to bear the cost of constructing two bridges over the canal. When the developer failed to get permission to divert Widemarsh Brook, thus jeopardising the economic viability of the whole development, the Trust negotiated a solution with the Environment Agency. The agreement has more significance than first appears as the crossings have been provided, not over the original line on which properties were built in the last century, but on an approved diversion. This creates an important precedent for the Trust, establishing the same protection for diversions as for the original line.

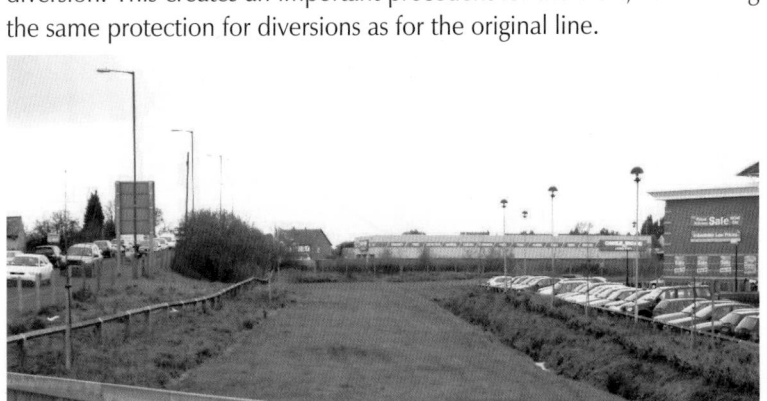

Figure 113:
The protected canal corridor beside Hereford Retail Park, from the new footbridge.
(Cliff Penny)

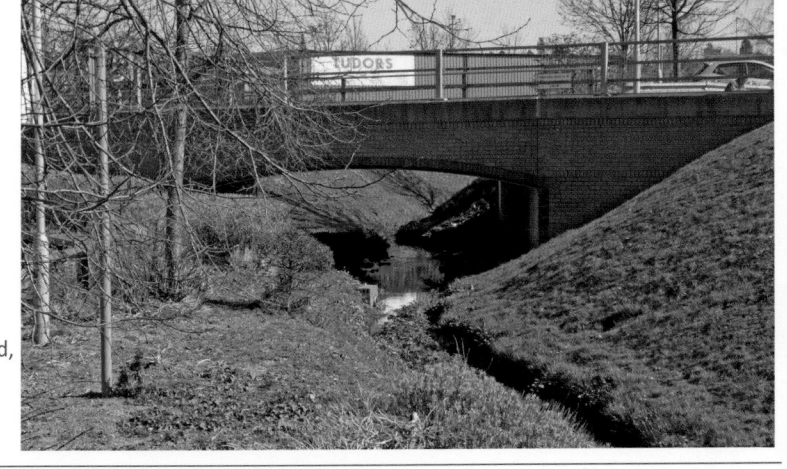

Figure 114:
Farriers Way Bridge, Hereford, from the new footbridge.
(Author)

Restoration in Gloucestershire

The work begun at Oxenhall by the Canal Society continued under the Trust. After the area around House Lock had been cleared, attention turned to the stretch of the canal towards Oxenhall Tunnel. The towpath under Cold Harbour Bridge was reinstated and some minor work carried out to restore the bridge itself. This is one of the only two remaining canal bridges surviving between Gloucester and Ledbury, the others having been replaced by railway bridges after 1881.

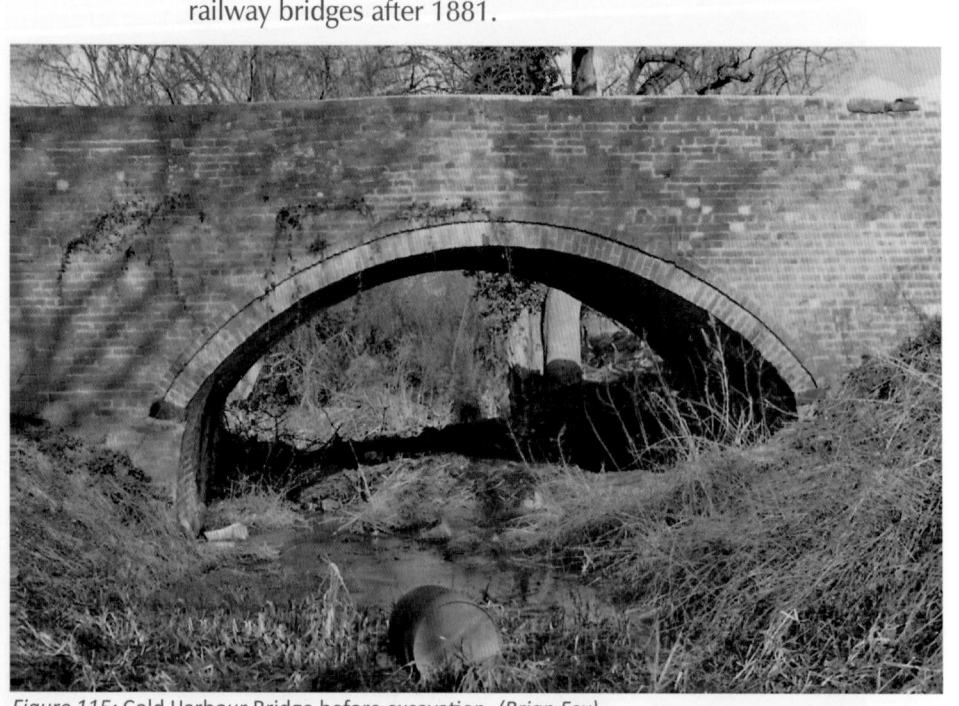

Figure 115: Cold Harbour Bridge before excavation. *(Brian Fox)*

The canal was then cleared and dredged up to the Tunnel Mouth with many tons of silt being removed. Only after this had been done was the true nature of the cutting revealed, hewn out of solid rock. The Southern Portal of the tunnel was also restored. On the side of the towpath a brick structure was unearthed, the true nature of which may never be fully established. Known by the work parties as the "leggers rest" it may have been a refuge used by the professional leggers while waiting for boats to

work through the tunnel. There were clear signs of an "upper floor" which gave rise to suggestions that this might have been a stable with a hayloft above. Certainly it is an unusual structure, the like of which I have never seen on the British canal system.

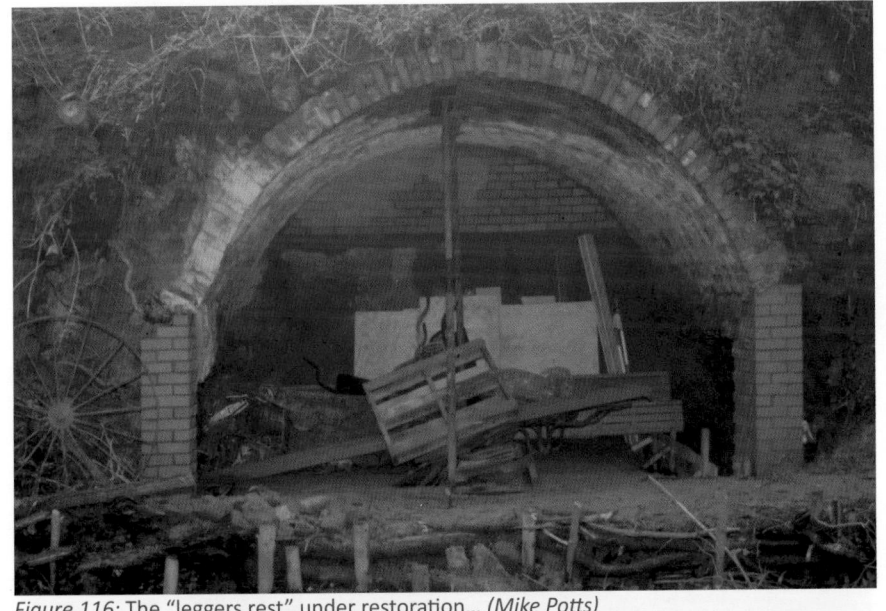

Figure 116: The "leggers rest" under restoration... *(Mike Potts)*

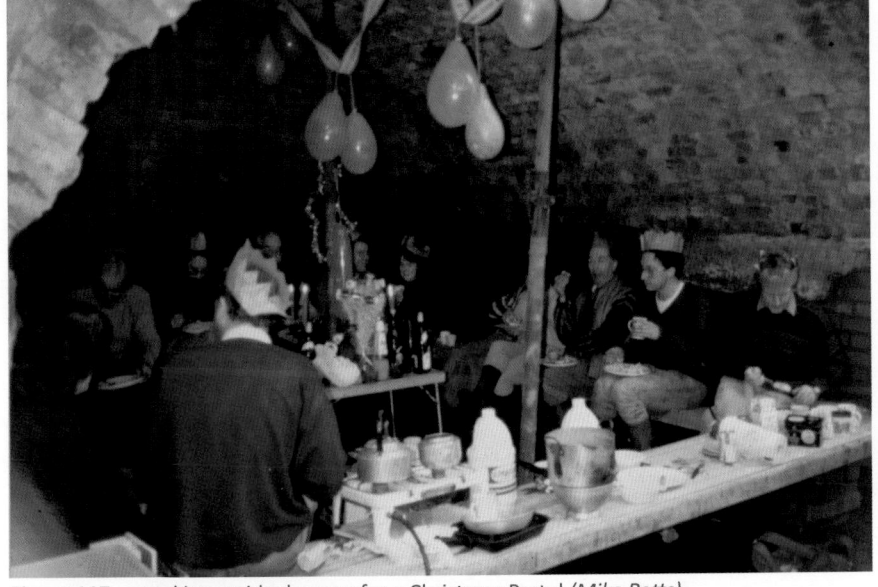

Figure 117: ... making an ideal venue for a Christmas Party! *(Mike Potts)*

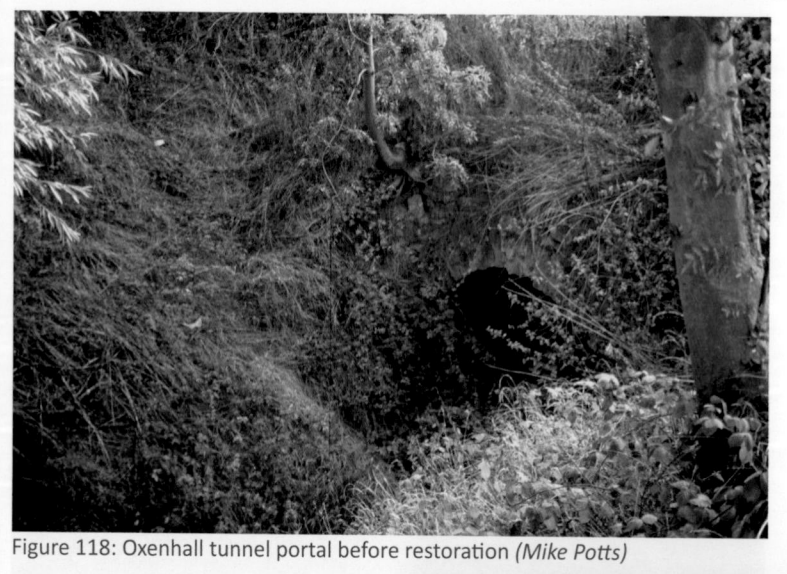

Figure 118: Oxenhall tunnel portal before restoration *(Mike Potts)*

The excavation of the cutting in 1996 proved extremely difficult. Water was constantly flowing out of the tunnel and from streams in the side of the cutting. Dumpers and the excavator were working in semi-liquid mud and on more than one occasion drivers had to be rescued from their equipment after it had become hopelessly stuck.

Eventually the whole length between Cold Harbour Bridge and the tunnel was cleared but it proved impossible at the time to prevent the channel rapidly silting up again.

At present there is no agreement with landowners to enable further work to be carried out, which will involve the building of silt traps on land adjoining the canal to prevent further silting.

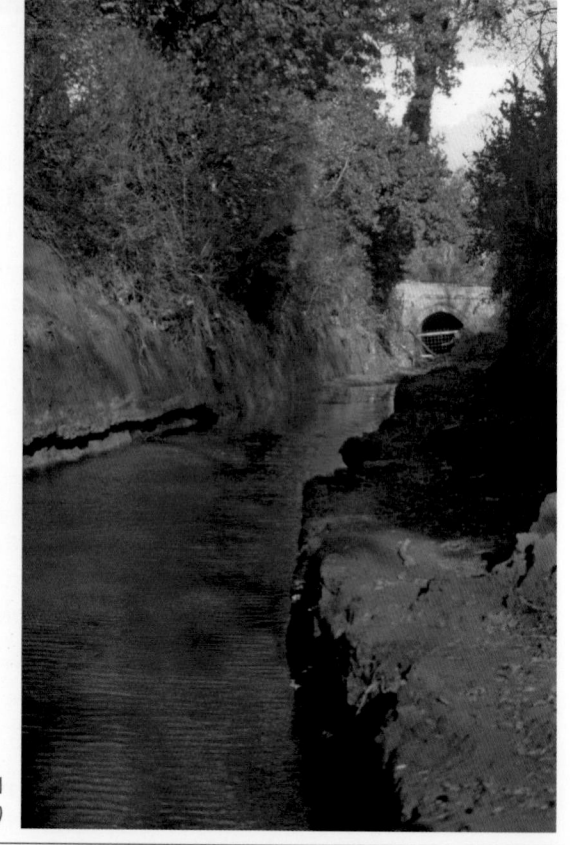

Figure 119: The approach to Oxenhall Tunnel *(Mike Potts)*

Work was also carried out dredging the canal between Cold Harbour Bridge and Winter's Lane at the site of Top Lock. Lack of boat movement along this stretch has resulted in much weed growth but the towpath provides a pleasant walk.

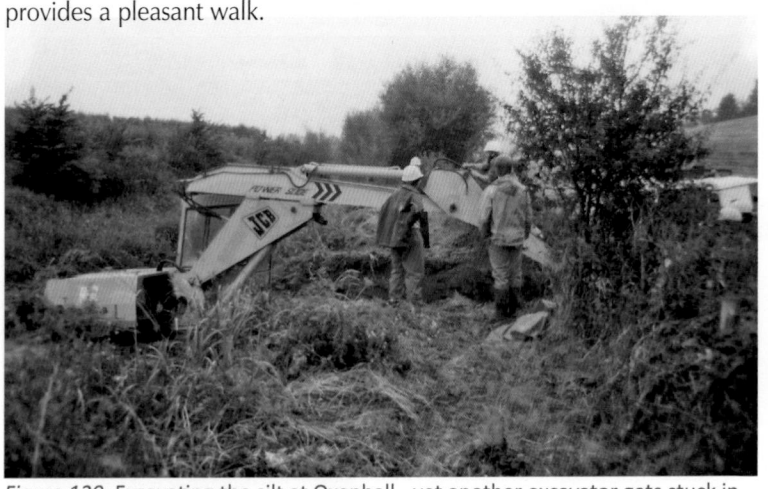

Figure 120: Excavating the silt at Oxenhall - yet another excavator gets stuck in the mud. *(Brian Fox)*

Meanwhile, House Lock and the adjacent lock cottage were in a poor and deteriorating condition, with the unoccupied cottage suffering from repeated vandalism. Both were listed structures, so the Forest of Dean District Council issued several repair notices in the 1990s but the owner, Robin Stiles, was facing a constant battle with vandals and was unable to

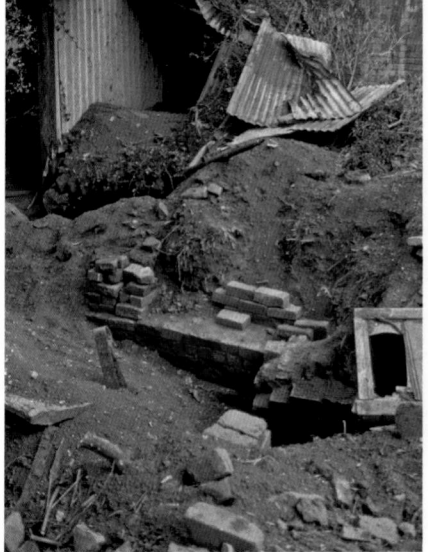

meet the requirements. It was judged the value of the site, consisting of the cottage, House Lock and the line of the canal to beyond Ell Brook Aqueduct, was less than the commercial cost of repairs. The Council threatened Compulsory Purchase but to avert this a deal was struck such that the entire site was transferred to the Trust, with the proviso that when the cottage was sold, 10% of the value would go to Robin Stiles. Thanks to his generosity, this therefore became the first piece of land owned by the Trust.

The removal of a garage adjacent to the lock cottage revealed the remains of a circular spill-weir, the outflow being culverted underneath

Figure 121: The scant remains of the spill-weir at House Lock after removal of the garage. *(Mike Potts)*

the cottage to emerge below the lock. The spill-weir was painstakingly restored and used to divert water round the lock itself on which restoration was to begin. Being a listed structure it was necessary to restore the lock, as far as possible, to its condition at the time the canal was closed.

A small team of volunteers, working one day a week, began cutting and dressing stone, removing the existing unstable masonry and learning the craft of the mason as they did so.

While there was plenty of masonry remaining, much of it was in poor condition and could not be reused. Most conveniently, what remained of a nearby bridge from the Ledbury-Gloucester Railway was bought from British Railways for a nominal sum. When some of the stone blocks from this bridge were dressed for reuse they were found to be curiously recessed on their reverse side. These were quickly recognised as quoin-stones, presumably from one of the locks in the Oxenhall flight which had been demolished at the time of the building of the railway. They have now been returned to the lock! The restoration involved the first substantial use of lime mortar by the Trust's volunteers, who also designed and installed special stainless steel ties to secure the new stonework to the sound original inner structure of the lock.

The cottage was sold to a new owner who under-took to repair it in accordance with the listed building requirements once the head of the lock and the spill-weir had been completed. As a canalside property,

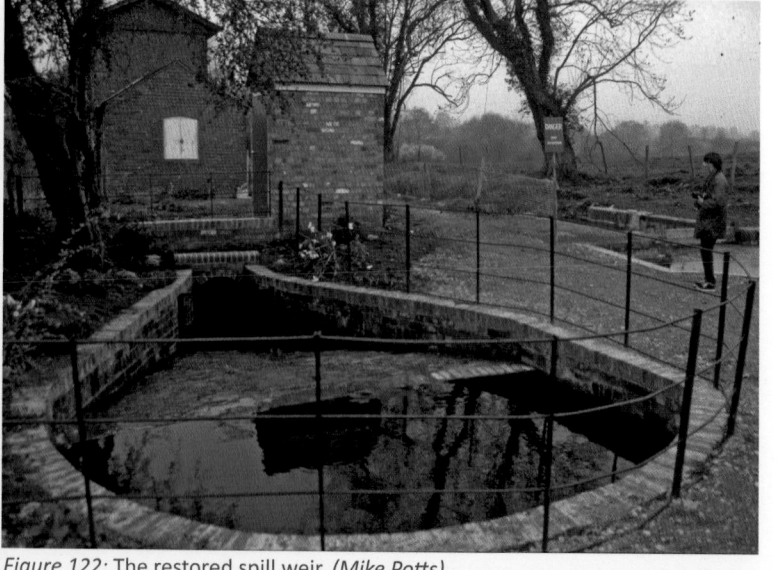

Figure 122: The restored spill weir. *(Mike Potts)*

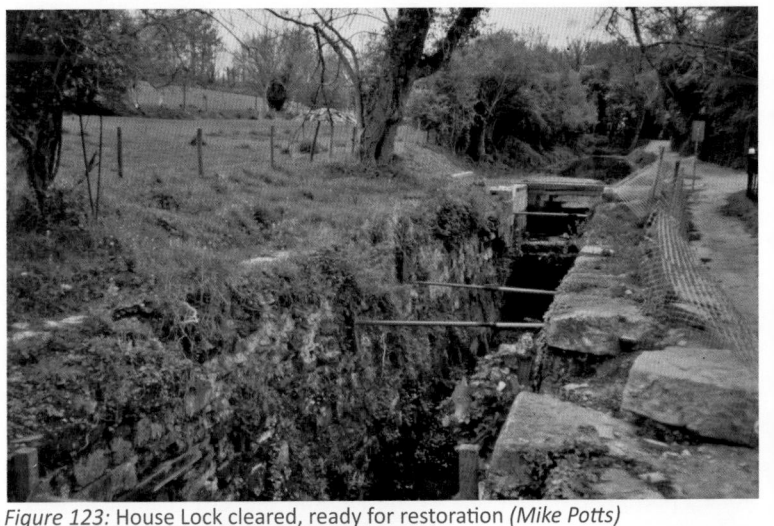

Figure 123: House Lock cleared, ready for restoration *(Mike Potts)*

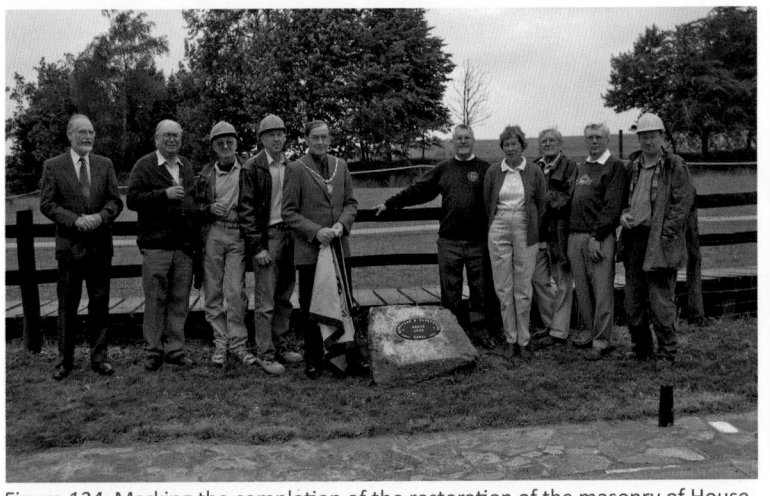

Figure 124: Marking the completion of the restoration of the masonry of House
Lock. *(Sallie Hopper)*

the sale included a provision for an annual index linked payment to the
Trust, setting a precedent which has been followed with all subsequent
canalside developments. The sale proceeds provided funding to complete
restoration of the lock itself.

More stone was needed. Fortunately a redundant railway bridge in
Herefordshire was being demolished as part of the improvements to
Roman Road, and several lorry loads of stone were donated to the Trust and
delivered to the site. By June 2004 the stonework had been completed and
a formal ceremony was held at the lock-side to mark the achievement.

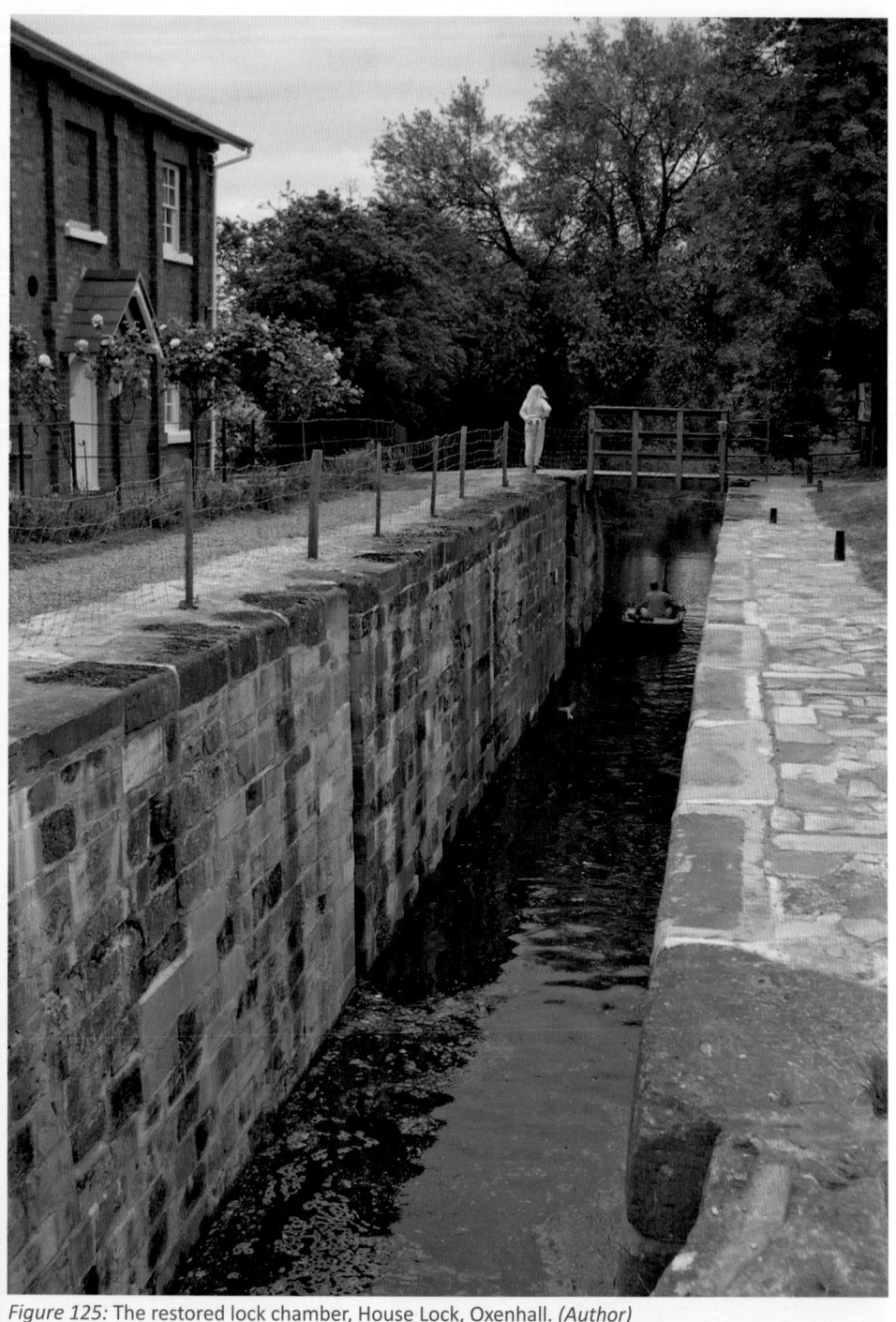

Figure 125: The restored lock chamber, House Lock, Oxenhall. *(Author)*

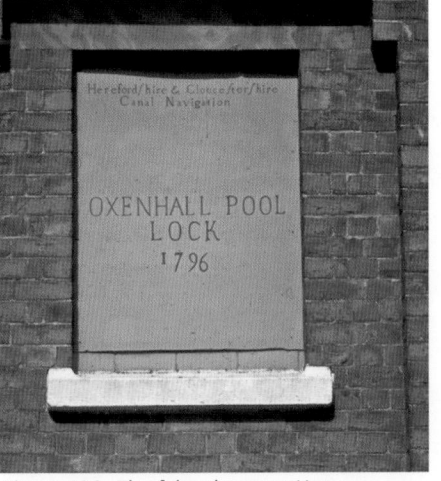

Figure 126 : The fake plaque at House Lock. *(Mike Potts)*

As the actual use of the lock was inevitably some years off, gates and paddle gear were not installed. A footbridge, was however, erected over the tail of the lock. This was constructed of timbers from the Over Isolation Hospital which was being demolished at the time and which will feature again later in our story.

Around this time a fake plaque mysteriously appeared above the door of the lock cottage. The date and name are entirely wrong. It looked impressive but upon closer inspection was discovered to be made of cardboard. No one knows how it got there. The cottage, more properly, now bears one of the Trust's aluminium cast plaques.

Once the masonry of the lock was completed the Oxenhall team turned its attentions to the single-arched aqueduct which carried the canal over the Ell Brook, some 350 yards from the lock.

This is the largest surviving aqueduct on the canal and is of a rather strange design, being unusually wide. It appears that the canal may even have crossed it at an angle. It had fallen into a serious state of disrepair and threatened to collapse entirely into the brook below. While the Oxenhall group had acquired considerable skill in preparing and laying masonry in rebuilding the lock, the construction of a stone aqueduct was quite a different matter and very much less straightforward.

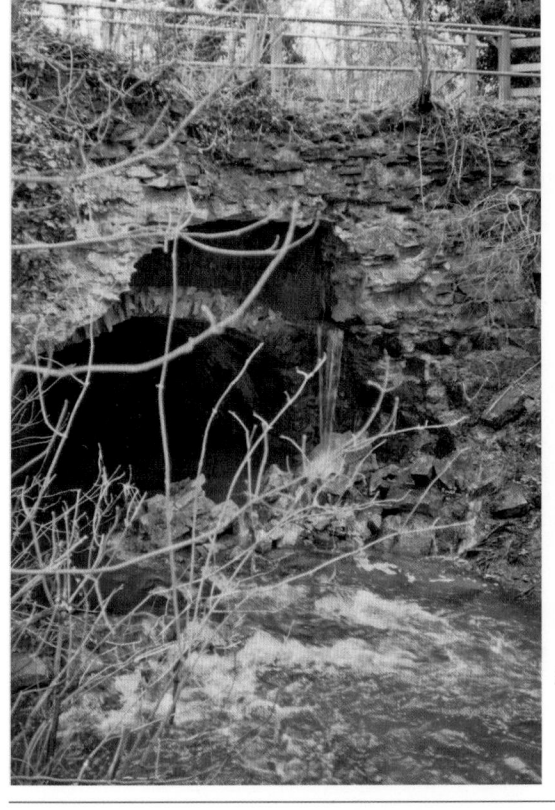

Figure 127: The Ell Brook Aqueduct before restoration. The facing stone had collapsed and the whole structure was at risk. *(Cliff Penny)*

The first task was to stabilise the arch itself and fortunately within the group there were skills to design and construct a steel support to prevent further movement and allow the work to proceed safely. This also acted as a former to enable the new masonry to be laid on the correct alignment. The spandrel walls were then reconstructed using stone from a variety of sources, most of the original stone being unusable.

During the summer months the Ell Brook is a placid stream, with perhaps six inches depth of water, but after heavy rain the level can rise dramatically to within inches of the top of the arch. Work on more than one occasion had to be suspended because of these conditions as the site was inundated with rocks and silt being carried downstream.

The rebuilding of the aqueduct took the small Oxenhall group four years to complete. The canal was not reinstated over the aqueduct because changes to the canal level are required elsewhere and it is proposed that the canal will eventually pass over the aqueduct on an embankment. It was fortunate indeed that the original structure was of sufficient dimensions to allow for this.

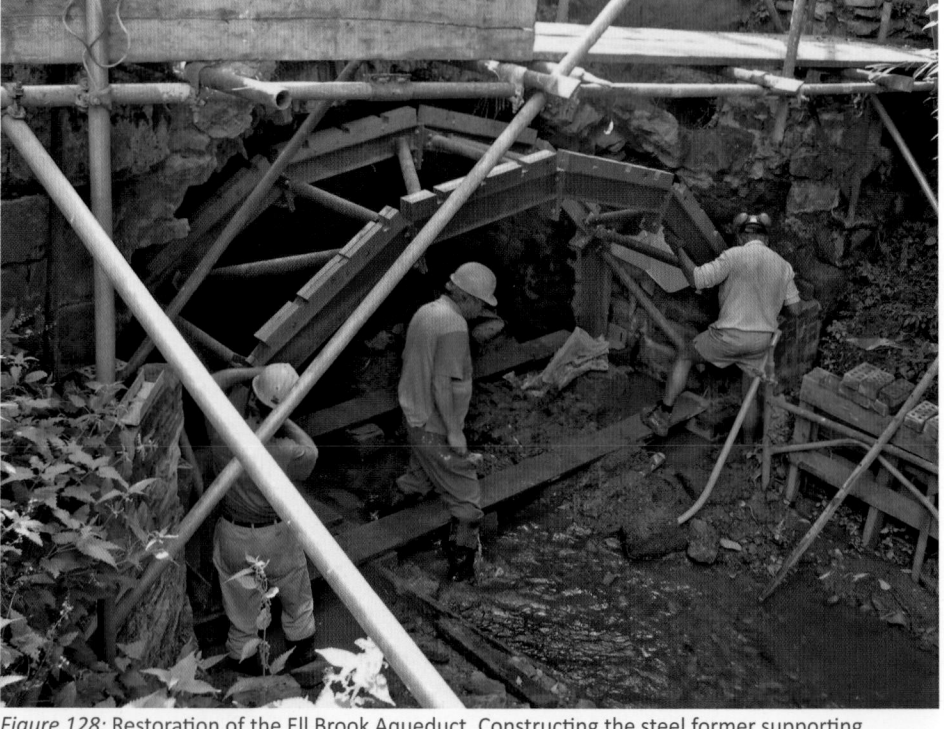

Figure 128: Restoration of the Ell Brook Aqueduct. Constructing the steel former supporting the arch. *(Geoff Hopper)*

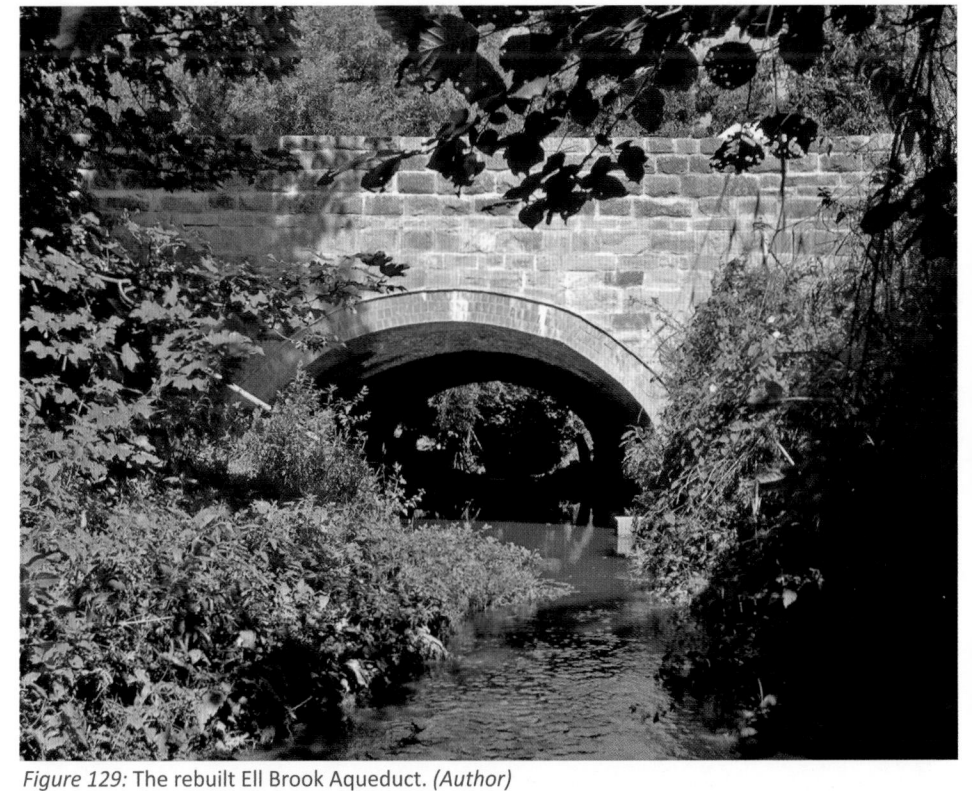

Figure 129: The rebuilt Ell Brook Aqueduct. *(Author)*

Adjacent to the site of the Ell Brook aqueduct is a large area of land through which the canal originally ran before passing under the B4215, Newent to Dymock Road. Previously occupied by the Willows Nursery, this had been compulsorily purchased by the Highways Agency to enable improvements to the A40 to be made but these plans were subsequently scrapped and the land was no longer required. In 2000 the Agency announced that the land was to be auctioned as a whole – far beyond what the Trust could realistically bid. The Trust had been unable to persuade the Agency to split the site and to sell the land formerly occupied by the canal to the Trust for a nominal sum, as had been the case with British Rail at another small site adjacent to Ell Brook restoration site.

The auction was announced for July 7th just ten days after the Deputy Prime Minister, John Prescott, launched "Waterways for Tomorrow" which required both local and national government departments to recognise the value of our waterways and to support restoration projects by, among other means, not allowing developments to take place which could impede future schemes.

Armed with an obscure government circular identified by the Trust covering the interpretation of "best value" in sales of land, the MP for the Forest of Dean, Diana Organ, swung into immediate action and demanded that the sale be postponed. At 3.30pm John Prescott cancelled the auction just three hours before it was due to take place, no doubt much to the astonishment and disappointment of a number of potential bidders. Smith's, the auctioneers, were equally surprised. John Parrott, of Smiths, said he has never come across a situation like this before.

> **66** It was a real shock, **99** he said.
>
> **66** We had an inclination *(sic)* that there was a bit of bother over it but then, at 3.30pm, the Highways Agency cancelled it.
>
> It was pretty tough because there were a lot of people geared up to buy it. **99**
>
> *Worcester News, July 7th 2000. Copyright and courtesy of the Worcester News.*

While the immediate danger from the auction was averted, the matter was far from resolved as the Highways Agency still took the view that it was obliged to obtain the best value it could for the land it held.

From the outset the Trust had argued that, under the Local Government Act 1972 General Disposal Consents (1998), "best value" was not limited to financial return but could include the value of benefits to the local community and the environment. Important though the Newent site was to the Trust, there were implications for restoration schemes across the country. It was vital that the argument was resolved in the Trust's favour.

Diana Organ continued her battle in Parliament and Whitehall and in May 2002 succeeded in arranging a meeting of two of the Trust Directors, supported by the Chief Executive of the Waterways Trust, with the then Transport Minister, David Jamieson MP. The Trust went to the Palace of Westminster well prepared. The case that the long term benefits which the restored canal would bring to the area must far outweigh the short term financial gain to the Agency was strongly argued. A letter was produced from the Forest of Dean District Council confirming that it would be prepared to use its powers of compulsory purchase, if necessary, to enable restoration to take place– so why sell to a third party only to have it compulsorily purchased later? The Minister expressed surprise that land could be so acquired for canal restoration – and was even more astonished to learn that the Waterways Trust had facilitated the compulsory purchase of part of a Sainsbury's store for the Huddersfield Narrow Canal!

The meeting, however, was a positive one and it was clear that the Minister was sympathetic and would do what he could to help. A formal, lengthy, submission was made by the Trust. This resulted in the land being offered to the Trust, but as another party had already offered some £20,000 for the land, that was the sum demanded. The Trust rejected this and went back to the Minister to argue for a further change to Government policy such that not only would any land in public ownership on the line of the canal have to be made available for restoration but it would also have to be offered at nominal value – a most crucial rider. This was accepted and in September 2003 the Highways Agency offered all of the land to the Trust for an agreed nominal sum of £1,000, or some £600 per acre.

It had been a long battle, but a vital victory had been won to the benefit not only of the Trust but of all other canal restorations.

Restoration of the canal through The Willows site has still to be commenced. The original line of the canal passed below what is now the B4215 but that road was lowered to allow the railway to pass above it. Any crossing would require significant changes to the level of the canal and it is now planned that an embankment will carry the canal over the Ell Brook Aqueduct, across the Willows site and to a new aqueduct over the B4215, using the old railway abutments. The parcel of land acquired from the Highways Agency was specified such that it would be large enough to enable this.

In the meantime, nine miles away in Gloucester, the Trust had for several years also been addressing quite different concerns. The canal's connection with the River Severn by means of Over Lock was situated on land owned by the West Midlands Regional Health Authority, having been the site of Over Isolation Hospital which had closed in 1992. The following year the Authority began the process of disposing of the buildings and the large site they occupied. At the first meeting of the Secretary of State's advisers with Tewkesbury Borough Council, the Council made it clear that proposals would not be considered unless provision for the canal restoration was included; the Council had agreed to protection for the line of the canal only the previous year. Various proposals were made, including an offenders' rehabilitation centre and a supermarket, but both were overtaken by changes in policy before being considered by the Council.

Eventually a plan for a residential development of 44 houses was proposed, but this was then amended to 33 houses before submission to the Council. The Trust lodged a technical objection to these proposals to ensure it had a place at the Inquiry where it could negotiate the gain for the canal.

The Trust saw this as an opportunity not to be missed and worked closely with both developer and Council to prepare a scheme which brought mutual benefit. Under the leadership of one of the Trust's Directors, revised plans were drawn up around the concept of a development which made a feature of the canal and its junction basin on which the proposed housing would be focused.

At the Inquiry in December 1997 the Trust obtained an adjournment in order to draw up a Section 106 agreement which had long been promised by the Department of Health, but had not materialised. A tight deadline for early January 1998 imposed by the planning inspector, otherwise he was "minded to grant planning permission without it", meant frantic preparation over Christmas and New Year of the Trust's proposals, including gaining approval from both Tewkesbury Borough Council and the Secretary of State for Health.

The case was made and the Inquiry then found in favour of the Trust. In essence this required the developer, whoever that might be, to transfer to the Trust the ownership of the land occupied by the canal, the basin and lock, together with the lock cottage which had first to be made safe and weather-tight. The developer was also required to accept the soil excavated from the canal and contribute a significant sum of money to fund the Trust's work which would be carried out by volunteers.

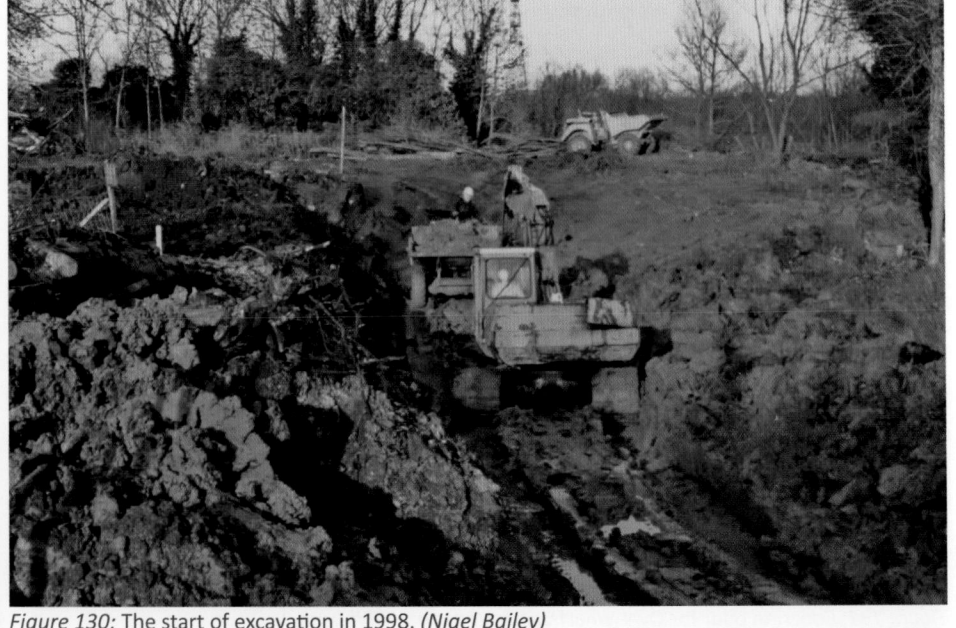

Figure 130: The start of excavation in 1998. *(Nigel Bailey)*

For its part, the Trust was required to excavate the line of the canal and the basin, build a new wharf wall 75 metres long, and make arrangements for water to be abstracted from the River Leadon to maintain the water level of the basin. It also had to provide a surfaced towpath. But there was a sting in the tail of this agreement – the Trust's work had to be completed by September 2000 when it was expected the first houses would be for sale.

Early in 1998 – before the start of the nesting season, all of the trees which had become established on the line of the canal and surrounding areas were removed. In the summer the site was cleared of scrub in preparation for the excavation of the canal and basin.

In the space of nine days a small team of volunteers using a large hired excavator and dumpers carrying 25 tons of soil at a time made an impressive start to the excavation. Some of the spoil was used to infill the site of the old mill pond, the rest for landscaping and to build noise bunds to reduce the sound of the traffic on the adjacent A40 trunk road. In the Spring of 1999 a Waterway Recovery Group work camp completed that part of the task and the task of building the wharf wall could begin. Three of the required twelve pours of concrete for the foundations of the wall were completed by the start of the summer.

The project plan had assumed that the bricks for the wharf wall would be recycled from the parts of the hospital which were to be demolished,

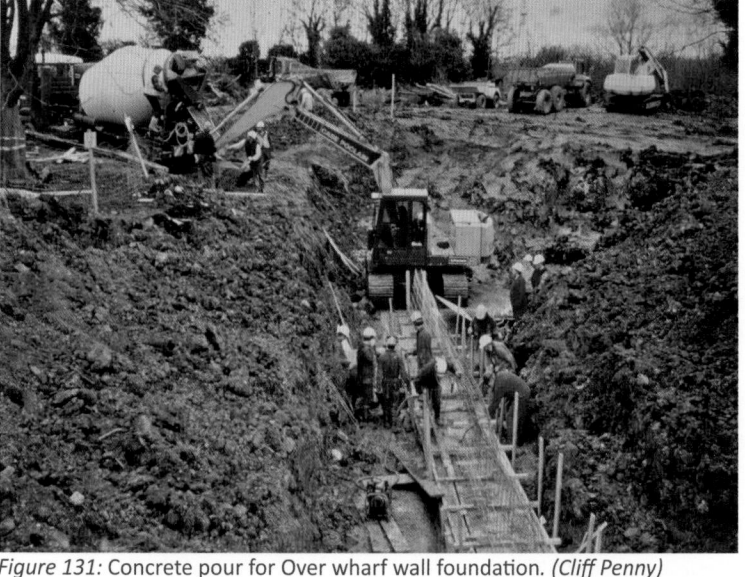

but by May 1999 demolition had not begun. A WRG training weekend had been arranged and it been expected that bricks would be available for this and a start made on the brickwork of the wharf wall. The Trust said it would take a building down itself if the bricks

Figure 131: Concrete pour for Over wharf wall foundation. *(Cliff Penny)*

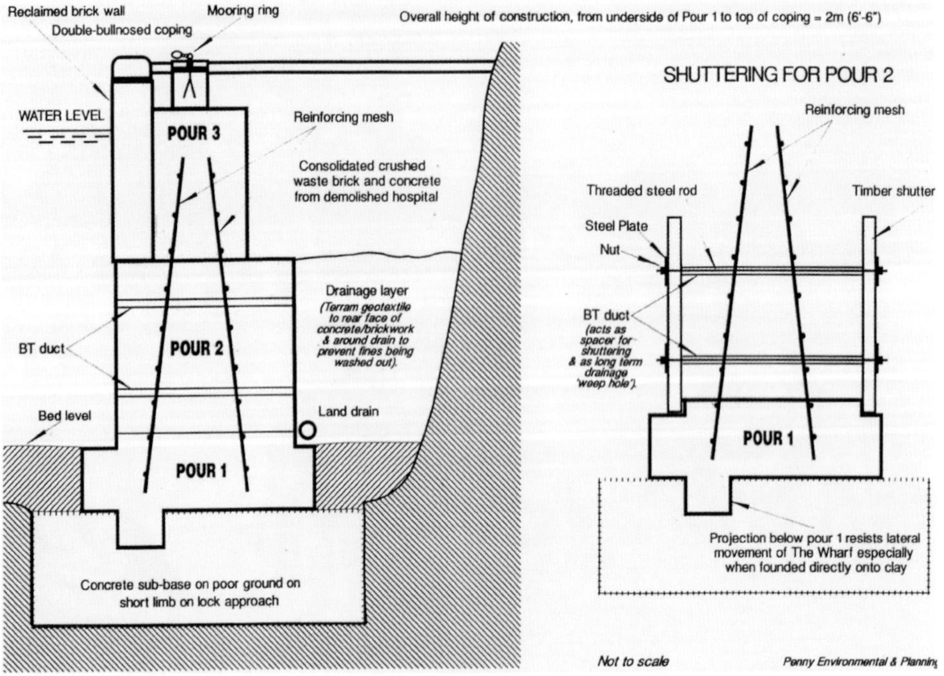

Reclaimed brick wall   Mooring ring   Overall height of construction, from underside of Pour 1 to top of coping = 2m (6'-6")
Double-bullnosed coping

WATER LEVEL

POUR 3

Reinforcing mesh

Consolidated crushed
waste brick and concrete
from demolished hospital

Drainage layer
*(Terram geotextile
to rear face of
concrete/brickwork
& around drain to
prevent fines being
washed out).*

BT duct

POUR 2

Bed level

Land drain

POUR 1

Concrete sub-base on poor ground on
short limb on lock approach

SHUTTERING FOR POUR 2

Reinforcing mesh

Threaded steel rod   Timber shutter

Steel Plate
Nut

BT duct
*(acts as
spacer for
shuttering
& as long term
drainage
'weep hole').*

POUR 1

Projection below pour 1 resists lateral
movement of The Wharf especially
when founded directly onto clay

Not to scale   *Penny Environmental & Planning*

*Figure 132: Cross section of the Over wharf wall; like an iceberg, most is now out of sight.
(Penny Environmental & Planning)*

did not arrive in time, a comment the developer did not take seriously until the Trust did precisely that. A single storey part of one of the wards was carefully demolished to provide a supply of bricks to be sorted and cleaned ready for the weekend.

As the demolition contractors' work got under way a ready supply of bricks became available for cleaning for reuse. Anything else of possible value was also salvaged – doors, skirtings, architraves and nearly 8000 wood floor blocks. All the materials were cleaned and carefully stored, a major and often tedious task.

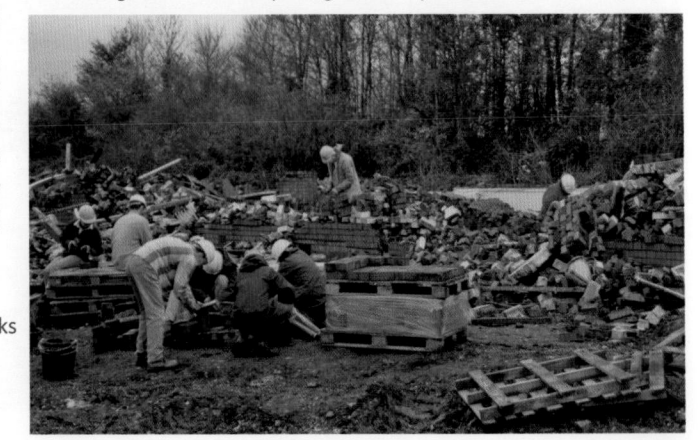

Figure 133: Recycling bricks
from the 1903 block
of the Over Hospital.
(Nigel Bailey)

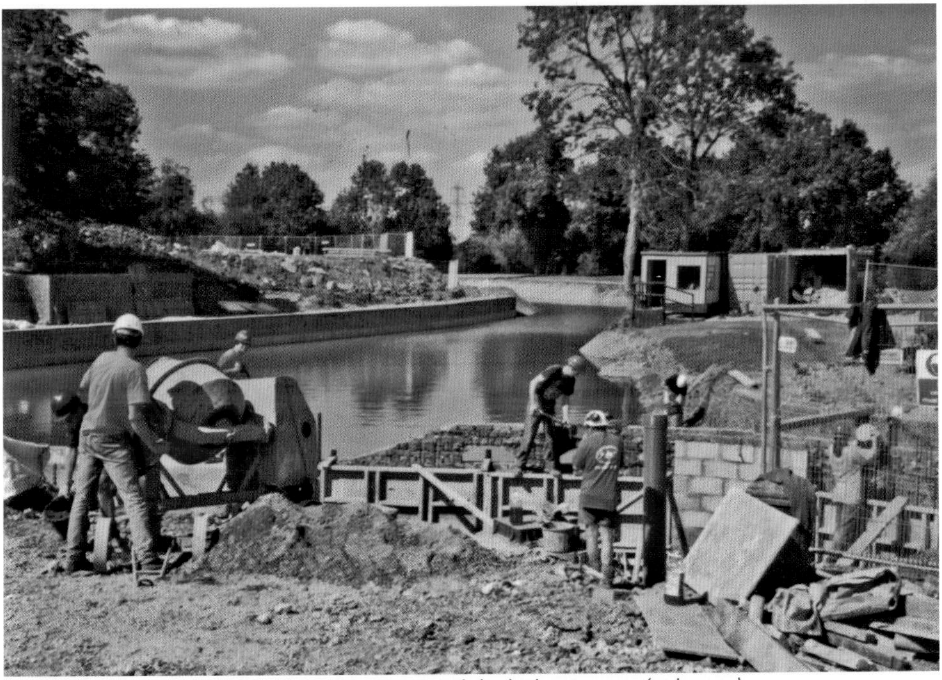

Figure 134: The construction of Over Basin around the lock entrance. *(unknown)*

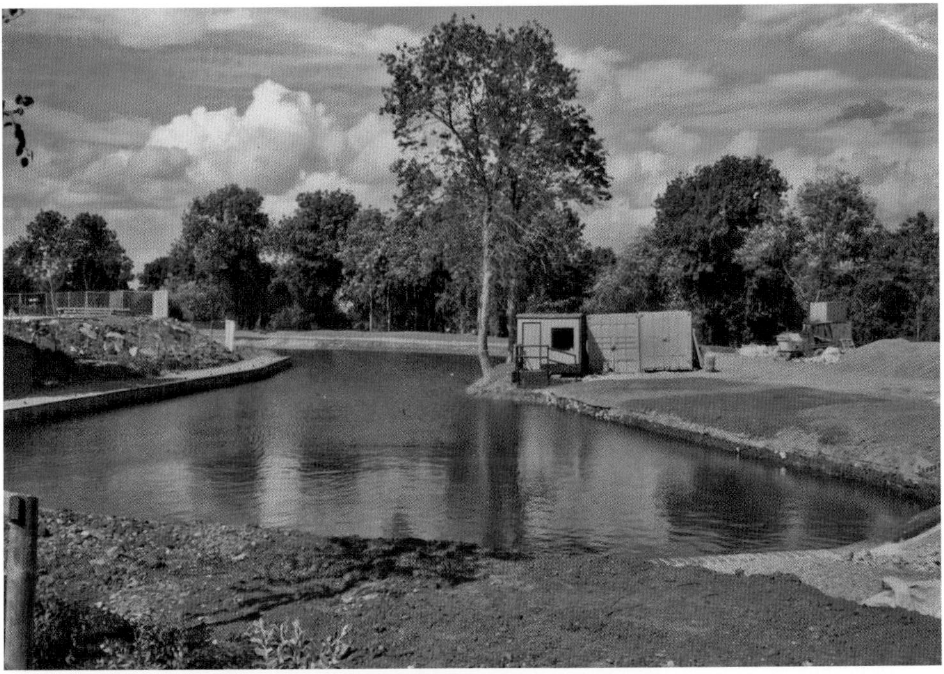

Figure 135: The newly filled basin. *(Nigel Bailey)*

During the rest of 1999 local volunteers and a number of WRG camps saw the construction of the two brick wharf walls and the slipway. At the WRG Reunion Weekend about 140 volunteers were divided into teams working on different parts of the site. Work continued unabated with further WRG camps and long hours of local volunteer labour.

In early August 2000, as the deadline for completion approached, the last of the bricks of the wharf walls were laid and on Thursday August 10th the pump lent to the Trust by Sterling Fluid Systems began to lift water from the River Leadon to feed the basin and canal. By the following Wednesday both were full.

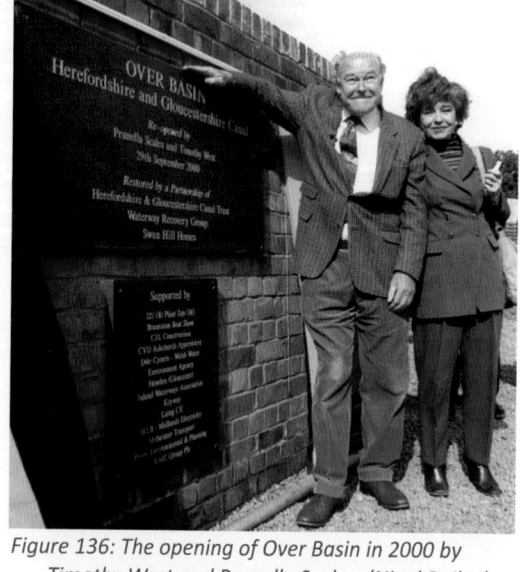

For two years this had been the largest all-volunteer waterway restoration project in the country. Following years of frustrating negotiations, a large area of scrubby, untidy land had been transformed into an attractive landscaped canal basin entirely by volunteers and at a tenth of the cost which would have been incurred had contractors been used.

Figure 136: The opening of Over Basin in 2000 by Timothy West and Prunella Scales. (Nigel Bailey)

On September 29th 2000 Timothy West and Prunella Scales performed the opening ceremony, unveiling plaques on the feature wall beside the basin. This wall, built, like almost everything else, of recycled bricks, has the letters "H & G" and "WRG" picked out in blue bricks, a permanent reminder of the partnership which delivered the restored basin on time and on budget. Notwithstanding the huge efforts of the Trust's volunteers, it was the support from the Waterway Recovery Group which made the task possible in the time allowed.

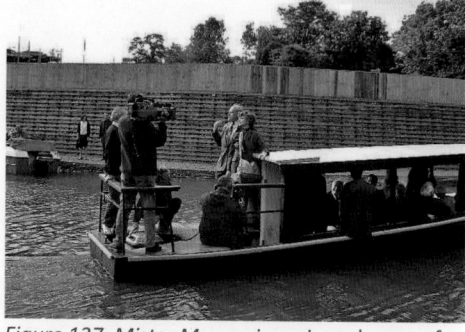

Part of the opening ceremony was filmed by Central TV as part of their Water World series. The Trust's small trip boat, *Mister Maysey*, began the event by carrying the VIPs across the basin.

Figure 137: Mister Maysey in serious danger of sinking while recording an episode of Water World at the opening of Over Basin. (Source Unknown)

The cabin was filled with local dignitaries, much weighed down with mayoral chains of office. The skipper, your author, watched in horror as the boat dropped lower and lower in the water. The petrol tank, which normally sat at the stern well above water level now bobbed alarmingly around. Mr. West and Miss Scales then boarded and stood on the stern deck ready to be interviewed as we cruised across the basin, so we were joined by the film crew – cameraman, sound recordist and director together with all the accoutrements required for modern TV recording.

* The distance between the water and the lowest point of the hull above which water may enter a boat.

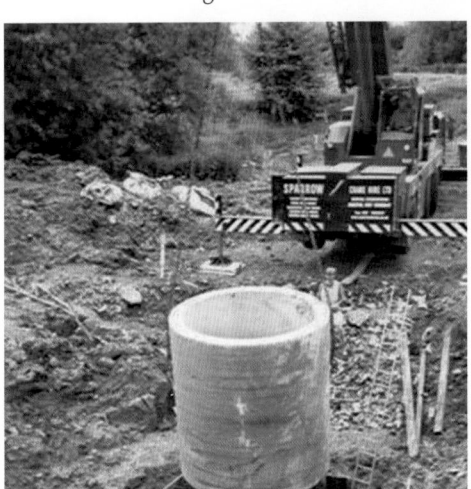

Figure 138: One of three 2.5 metre diameter concrete rings being lowered to form the 9 metre deep pump shaft. (David Penny)

With almost zero freeboard* the boat set out across the basin – a journey of only fifty yards or so. To the skipper, watching for the first signs of the boat actually sinking, the trip seemed interminable, everyone else on board quite oblivious of the very real danger of the whole party having to swim for the shore. While this would have made sensational television, it was with great relief that the wharf was reached, the boat secured to the mooring rings and the passengers discharged on to dry land.

In 2001 work started on another major but largely invisible project, the building of the pump shaft, silt trap and abstraction and feeder channels to allow for the canal to be permanently filled. Three 2.5 metre diameter pipes, surplus to a long sea outfall project in Cardiff, were set on end to form the 9 metre deep pump shaft. Underground ducting was installed to carry services to the wharf, where the outlets are housed in "dog kennels" and to the pump house. The car park for the basin and The Wharf House was also built, carefully landscaped to intrude as little as possible into the site.

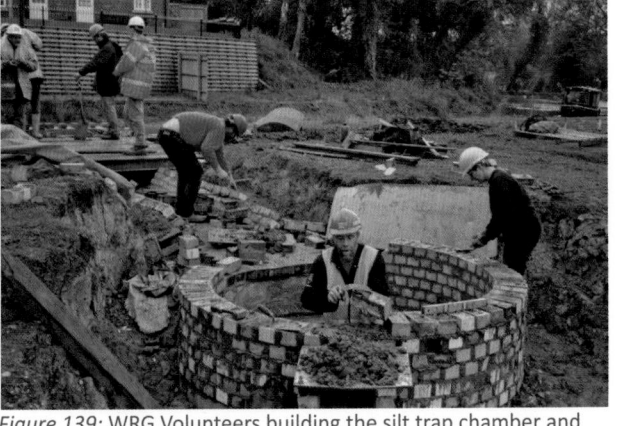

Figure 139: WRG Volunteers building the silt trap chamber and feeder channel at Over Basin. This is one of the new water sources for the Canal. (Nigel Bailey)

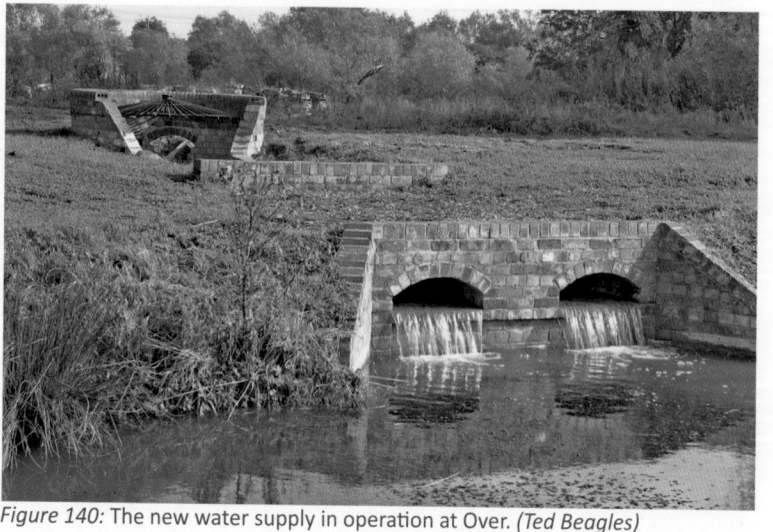

Figure 140: The new water supply in operation at Over. *(Ted Beagles)*

Seen from Over Basin, the canal shortly disappears round a left hand bend, but walking the towpath quickly brought one to the end of the restored canal – still a very long way from Hereford! The next length of the canal passed through a piece of land bought in 2004 by a consortium of 28 residents of Staunton's Hill, the development occupying the rest of the Over Hospital site. In 2011 negotiations with the owners resulted in the sale of the line of the canal to the Trust, potentially allowing the length of the canal at Over to be more than doubled. A condition of the sale was that restoration work had to be completed within 12 months, by September 2012.

On September 3rd 2011 two longstanding volunteers at Over ceremoniously cut through the wire fence separating the new site from the old and work on site clearance began.

With a new project came new volunteers. During the first few weeks, 26 different people turned up to help, ten of whom had not worked at Over before.

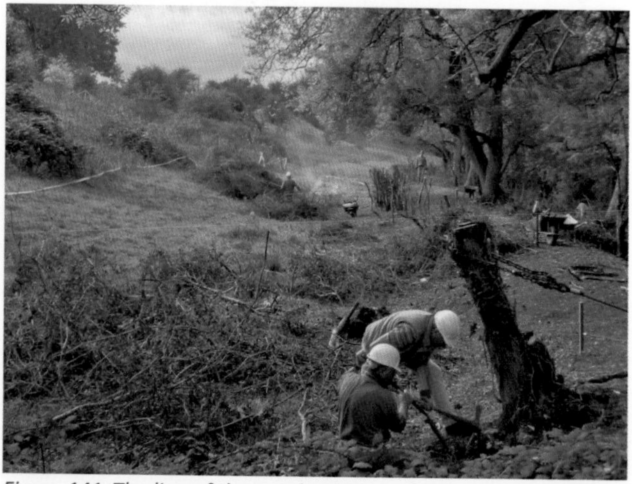

Figure 141: The line of the canal at Vineyard Hill at the start of site clearance in 2011. *(Ted Beagles)*

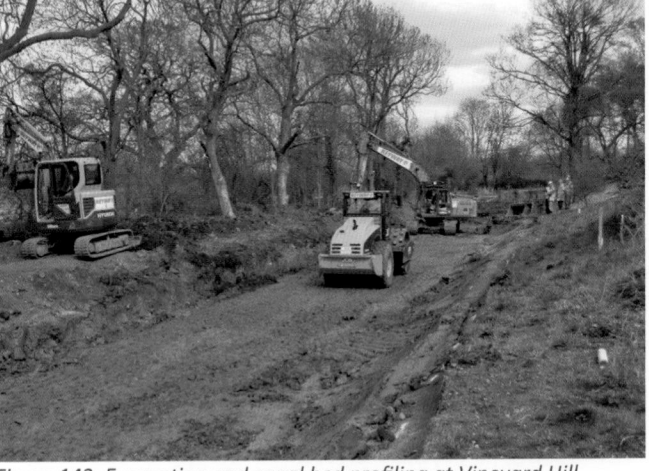

Figure 142: Excavation and canal bed profiling at Vineyard Hill. (Ted Beagles)

All the scrub and trees which had to be removed had gone long before the nesting season began and the top soil had been stripped from the canal line. At one point a major failure of an excavator engine brought work to a temporary halt. Despite being stuck in the middle of the site 150 yards from the end of the towpath, the engine was winched out, the accessory parts transferred to a new engine before this was winched in and installed into the machine. Only four working days were lost.

During the first two weeks of April 2012 members of the Waterway Recovery Group assisted in carrying out the actual excavation of the canal. On April 15th the dam between the existing canal and the newly excavated stretch was lowered slightly, the pump lifting water from the River Leadon was started and water flowed from the old to the new length. Three hours later the first pair of ducks arrived on the new stretch of canal.

Although five months ahead of schedule, there was still much to be done finishing the towpath and landscaping the rest of the site. Progress towards this was interrupted by an unexpected rise in the water level caused by persistent rainfall in the spring and early summer. The canal bank was raised to prevent damage by water overflowing on to the towpath. The first boat, albeit of the rowing variety, navigated the canal from the slipway to the winding hole at the far end of the new length and back on May 2nd.

By July the dam between the two lengths was removed and the Trust's ex-British Waterways pusher tug *Alder* navigated from the basin to new winding hole. After further tidying the site was ready for its official opening as part of the Over Canal Festival on September 1st and 2nd. The ribbon across the canal was cut by Jason Pullen, Managing Director at Gloucester Quays *(see title page)*. Prunella Scales and Timothy West returned to Over to unveil a plaque to mark the occasion. Once again a restored length of canal had been completed on time entirely by volunteers.

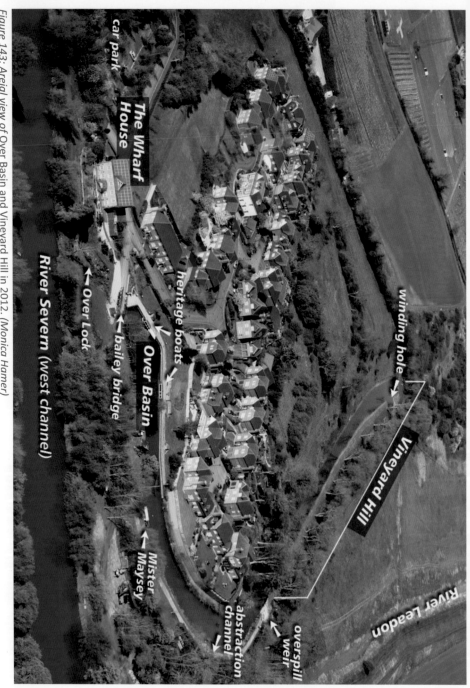

Figure 143: Areial view of Over Basin and Vineyard Hill in 2012. (Monica Hamer)

The Wharf House

car park

River Severn (west channel)

Over Lock

bailey bridge

heritage boats

Over Basin

Mister Maysey

abstraction channel

overspill weir

River Leadon

Vineyard Hill

winding hole

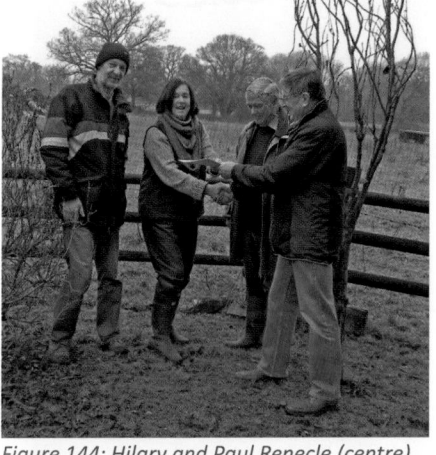

Figure 144: Hilary and Paul Renecle (centre) handing the signed documents to Trust representatives. (Ted Beagles)

In 2012 the Trust reached agreement with the Mr. and Mrs. Paul Renecle, owners of Moat Farm at Malswick some five and a half miles from Gloucester. Although this part of the canal was largely obliterated by the railway, the latter took a more direct route at this point leaving a stretch of canal very much overgrown by trees and scrub but normally retaining a reasonable depth of water. Steady progress has been made in clearing the site ready for future excavation when the water has been drained.

The site extends to some 600 yards with about 100 yards at each end over which the railway line passed. Some of the railway embankment at the Gloucester end of the site has been removed and the canal bed and towpath reinstated. At the other end of this length is the site of the bottom lock of the staircase which caused so much trouble for Howard Williams and his friends in 1875.

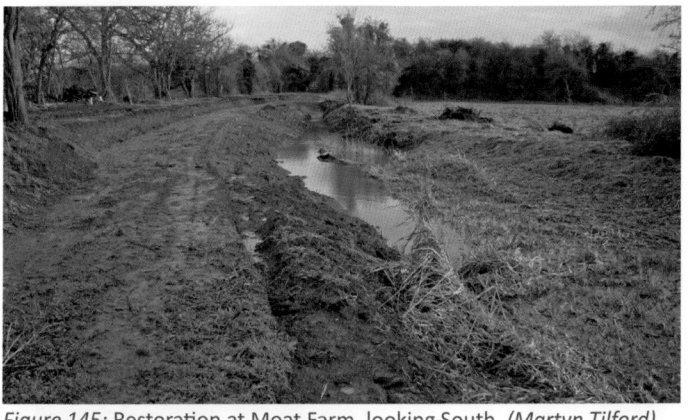

Figure 145: Restoration at Moat Farm, looking South. (Martyn Tilford)

A bridge over the railway line, which was constructed here on top of the abandoned canal, provided a very useful temporary 'amenity' and storage area for the site until a modular site hut could be erected.

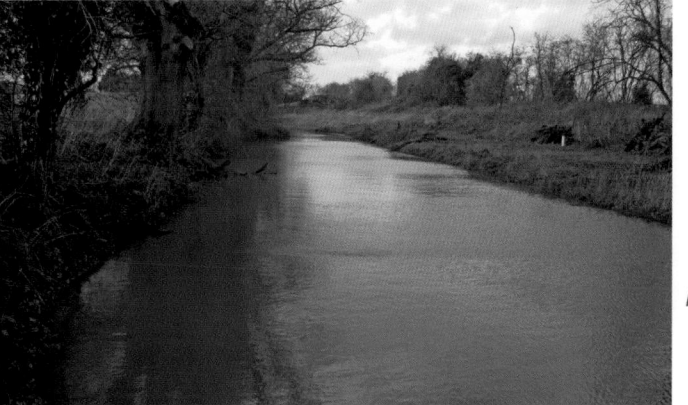

Figure 146: The partially restored canal at Moat farm looking North. *(Martyn Tilford)*

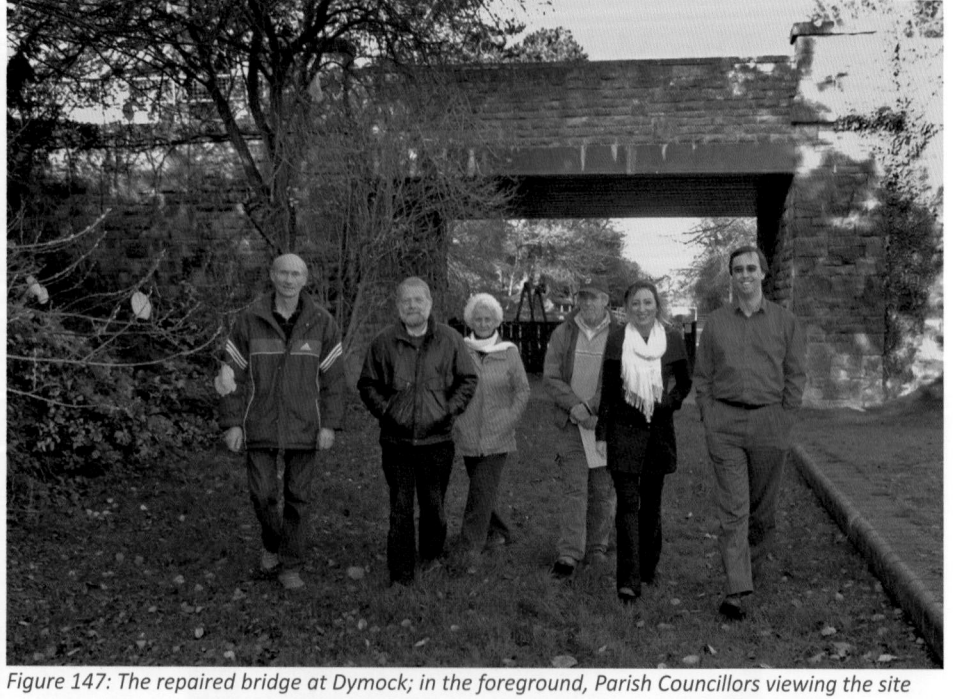

Figure 147: The repaired bridge at Dymock; in the foreground, Parish Councillors viewing the site with members of the Trust's Legal and Project Development Team. (Martin Perry/The Forester)

Another bridge, carrying a road out of Dymock over the old railway line and course of the canal, was judged to be unsafe. The cheaper and simpler option, planned initially, would have been to fill the opening below the road. However, as it crossed the protected route of the canal, the Trust made representations to Gloucestershire County Council. The Council then agreed to carry out substantial repairs to the bridge, including replacement of the bridge deck, which were completed in 2004. This demonstrated a commitment to facilitate restoration even though the Trust had no plans to restore this section for many years. The repaired bridge over the canal route became a focal point in discussions of more recent developments in Dymock, including a canal basin, as described in chapter 16.

The Wharf House

CHAPTER 12

The agreement with the developers of the Over Hospital site included an undertaking to stabilise and make weatherproof the former Lock Cottage in order for it to be the converted by the Trust, perhaps to provide a Visitor Centre, shop and small tea-room. This cottage had been built by Stephen Ballard in 1831 to house the Over lock keeper. It originally had three rooms upstairs and two down with a back kitchen. It was later extended and named "The Lodge" and used by the hospital to house the Hospital Engineer. It was occupied until 1971, after which time the structure of the building deteriorated rapidly.

Bailey, Nigel: Over and Over Again Red Osier Publishing, 2000 p.37

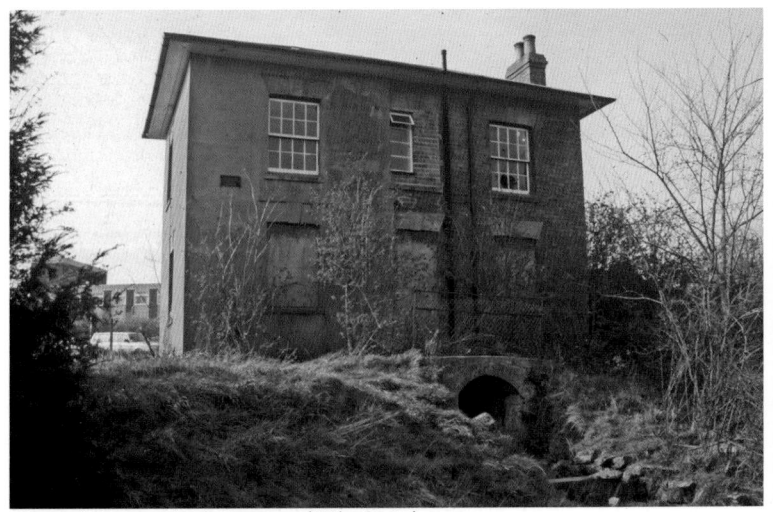

Figure 148: Over Lock Cottage. (Mike Potts)

When daylight appeared between the original part of the house and the extension it became apparent that it was impractical to make the building safe at reasonable cost and the agreement was changed such that the cottage was demolished and a new building erected on the site.

While the loss of any building associated with the canal was to be regretted, it was not an object of great beauty and even if a sympathetic restoration had been possible, the much altered building would have been a dubious asset of limited practical value to the Trust.

The new agreement provided for a building five times the size of the original cottage, on three floors, designed to complement the houses being built nearby while expressing the style of traditional canal architecture. The developer was required to deliver just the shell of the building, the only internal walls being those around the central staircase. The building, to be called The Wharf House, was handed over from Swan Hill Homes to the Trust in November 2002.

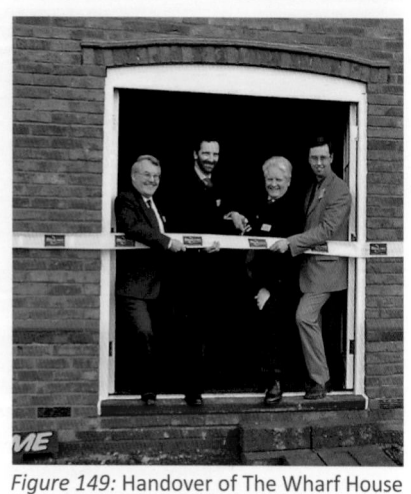

Figure 149: Handover of The Wharf House – November 2002 *(Mike Hunt)*

The volunteers who had been working outdoors on the Over site now swung into action building walls, laying floors and fitting doors, skirtings, and ceilings. Plumbing and electrical systems were installed and gradually the rough shell of the building began to be transformed. As many as possible of the materials used were recycled from the old hospital which had been built to a high standard. Thousands of wooden floor blocks were cleaned and relaid, skirtings, doors and architraves were stripped of paint and reused.

In 2003 the Wharf House Company was established to oversee the fit-out and plan for the commercial use of the building. The ground floor was divided into a restaurant area and a spacious Visitor Centre and shop.

Some professional help was necessary to deal with specialised work including the provision of a commercial kitchen. After thousands of hours of volunteer effort supported by five-figure grants from the Heritage Lottery Fund, DEFRA, and the Gloucester Environmental Trust as well as generous donations from local businesses and supporters of the Trust, the ground floor was opened in 2005.

It had been a mammoth task – and now work could be concentrated on the two upper floors. Here there were to be six luxury bedrooms together with staff and storage facilities. There followed

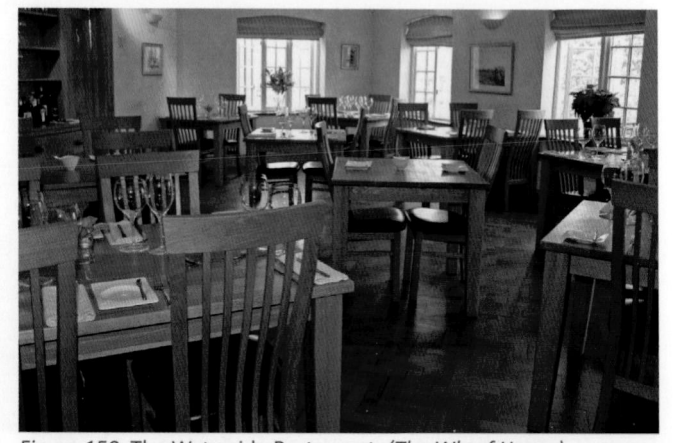

Figure 150: The Waterside Restaurant. *(The Wharf House)*

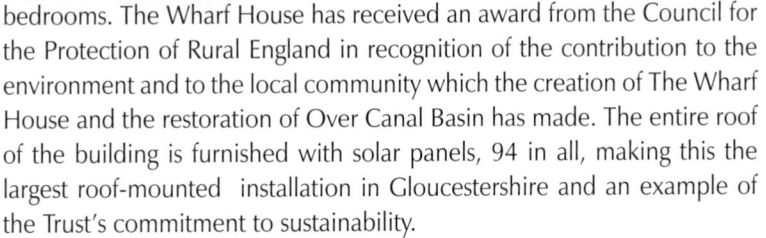

Figure 151: One of the seven beautifully appointed
bedrooms in the Wharf House. *(The Wharf House)*

five years of intense work, almost all of it by volunteers until, in 2010, there was an informal "private opening" for Trust members to celebrate the completion of this part of the task.

In 2012, a seventh bedroom was opened; this, being on the ground floor, is ideally suited for less-abled guests and for those with canine companions.

The restaurant has received the AA's Red Rosette for the excellence of the cuisine and four Gold Stars for the seven bedrooms. The Wharf House has received an award from the Council for the Protection of Rural England in recognition of the contribution to the environment and to the local community which the creation of The Wharf House and the restoration of Over Canal Basin has made. The entire roof of the building is furnished with solar panels, 94 in all, making this the largest roof-mounted installation in Gloucestershire and an example of the Trust's commitment to sustainability.

The location of the Wharf House adjacent to the basin and, above the River Severn creates a splendid setting, and when a Severn Bore is due, a very dramatic one. The Waterside Restaurant has become recognised as one of the highest quality restaurants in Gloucestershire and on summer evenings Tapas on the Terrace has proved very popular.

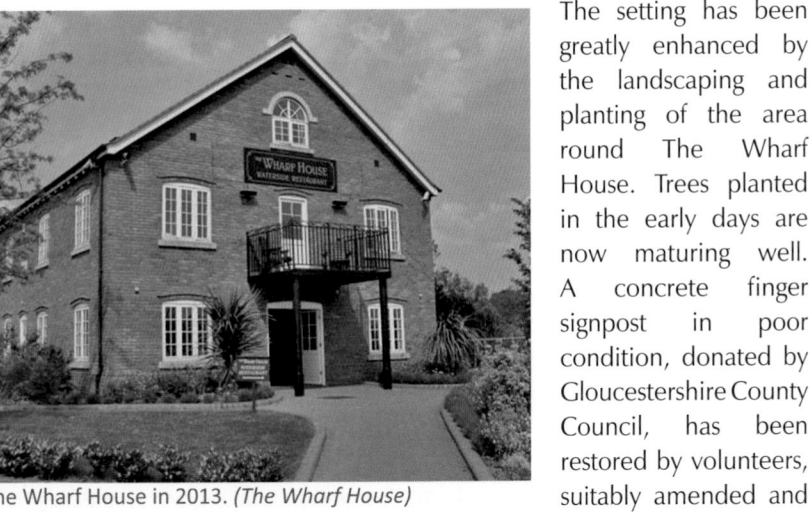

The setting has been greatly enhanced by the landscaping and planting of the area round The Wharf House. Trees planted in the early days are now maturing well. A concrete finger signpost in poor condition, donated by Gloucestershire County Council, has been restored by volunteers, suitably amended and

Figure 152: The Wharf House in 2013. *(The Wharf House)*

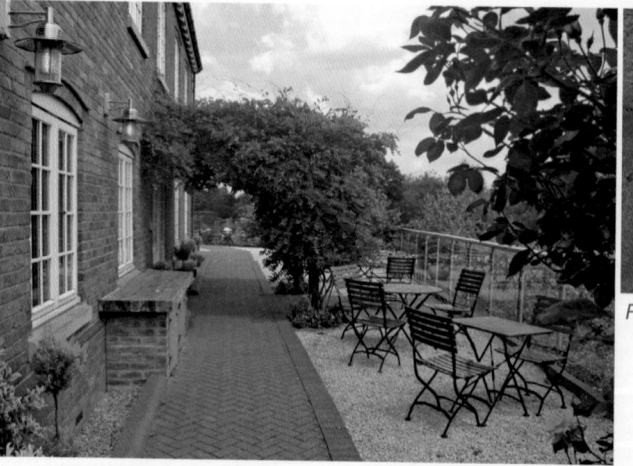

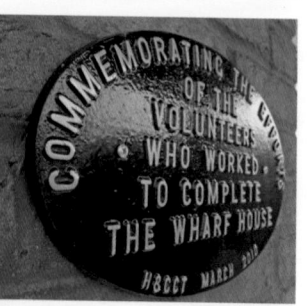

Figure 154: The commemorative plaque. (The Wharf House)

Figure 153: The Terrace. (The Wharf House)

erected. As a reminder of the canal's most famous bridge, the grounds were soon christened "Skew Gardens" by the volunteers. A sense of humour has always been a necessary virtue among the Over team.

In addition to its core business as a restaurant with rooms, The Wharf House also hosts the Trust's Visitor Centre and provides accommodation for the Trust's Legal & Project Development Team. It is seen as the headquarters of the Trust and provides a prestigious and welcoming venue for important meetings with external bodies. The site for which it is responsible includes the line of the canal as far as Rudford, plus the Trust's fleet of heritage boats which are held at Over. All profits from the operation of The Wharf House are used for the promotion and restoration of the canal.

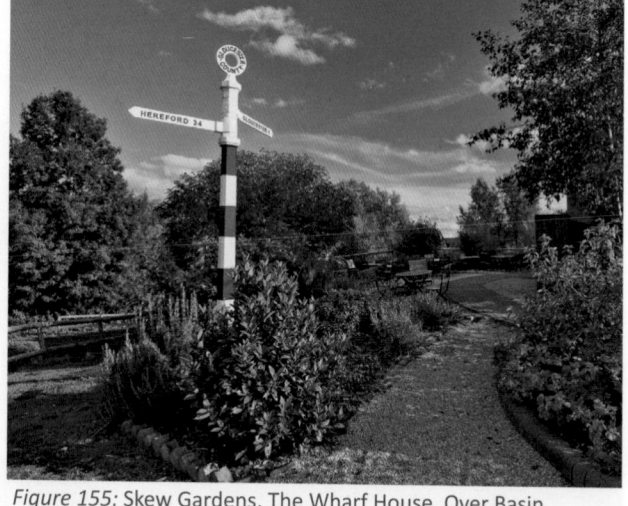

In September 2013 The Wharf House acquired the freehold of The Traveller's Rest at Malswick, situated on the main Gloucester to Newent road. This was achieved in a remarkably short time as the auction was held only a week after

Figure 155: Skew Gardens, The Wharf House, Over Basin. (© Jonathon Wakins, Photoglow photography)

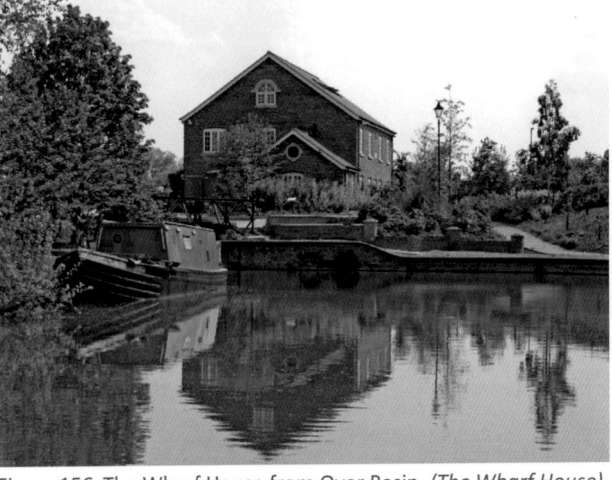

the proposed sale of the pub came to the notice of the Trust, the previous tenant having ceased trading less than a month before. Paperwork supporting a bid, including a financial analysis, was prepared and the Trust's Council of Management discussed this in a 1½ hour telephone conference involving all members, reaching a unanimous agreement to go ahead.

Figure 156: The Wharf House from Over Basin. *(The Wharf House)*

The principal reason why the Trust, through The Wharf House Company, was anxious to secure the freehold of the property is that it is the only remaining pub alongside the route of the Hereford and Gloucester Canal in Gloucestershire, the line of the canal adjoining its rear garden. After initial renovation by Canal Trust volunteers The Travellers Rest is now open for business, run by a tenant on a lease which includes payment of a proportion of turnover.

As restoration proceeds The Travellers Rest will provide a focus for this section of the canal with displays and other material promoting the waterway. Once it is restored, the canal will vastly increase the attraction of the pub in its unique location and continue to provide an enhanced and permanent income stream for the Trust.

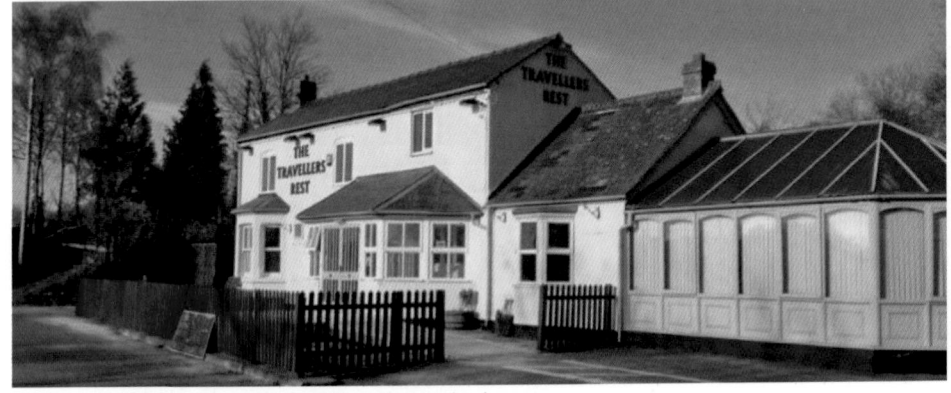

Figure 157: The Travellers Rest, Malswick. *(Author)*

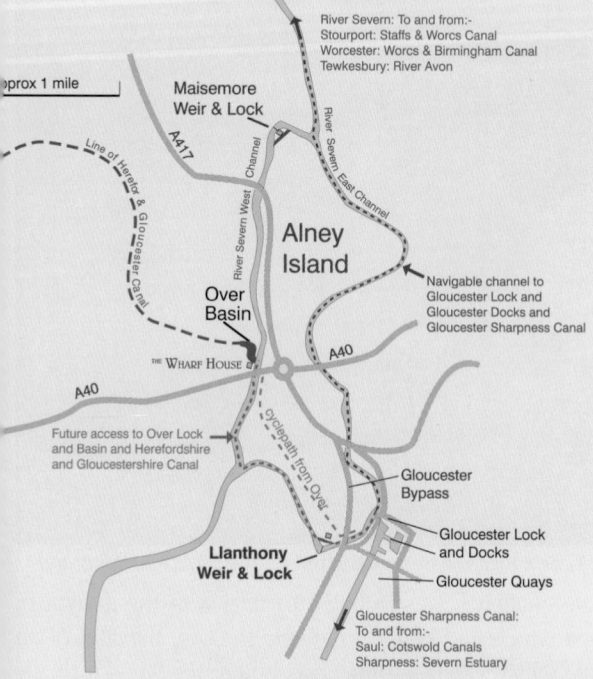

Llanthony Lock

The canal's connection to the river Severn at Over and thence to the rest of the waterway network has been something of a challenge since its very earliest days. Entry into the deep lock at Over from the tidal river required some very tricky manoeuvring on the part of the boatmen and while help was given, there were a number of serious accidents and sinking of boats.

Figure 158: The River Severn in Gloucester. *(Maggie Jones)*

Navigation on the river may have become a little easier for the last 10 years of the canal's working life when Maisemore and Llanthony locks were built on the river. Maisemore Lock and its cottage were sold by British Waterways in the 1980s before restoration of the canal it served was thought a serious possibility, but Llanthony Lock, though partly infilled, remained in the possession of British Waterways until 2008

Although not, of course, part of the Hereford and Gloucester Canal, after lengthy negotiations it was bought by the Canal Trust for £150,000, together with the pair of lock cottages, a considerable area of surrounding land and a stretch of the river Severn including both banks and Llanthony Weir. Very significantly, the agreement also gave the Trust control of both Maisemore and Llanthony weirs but no liability for them. The purchase was made possible through a legacy from Miss Beth Gadesden.

Restoration of Llanthony lock secures access to the Severn below Over Lock giving a much easier upstream approach than would have been

made downstream from Maisemore. This would have involved a turn just before the railway bridge, the central piers of which would constitute a significant navigational hazard.

A project team was set up to carry out a programme of work to prevent further deterioration of the site and the cottages and the first steps towards restoration of the lock. The team would have a wide range of work to do, from major site clearance and continuing maintenance to general repairs to the cottages.

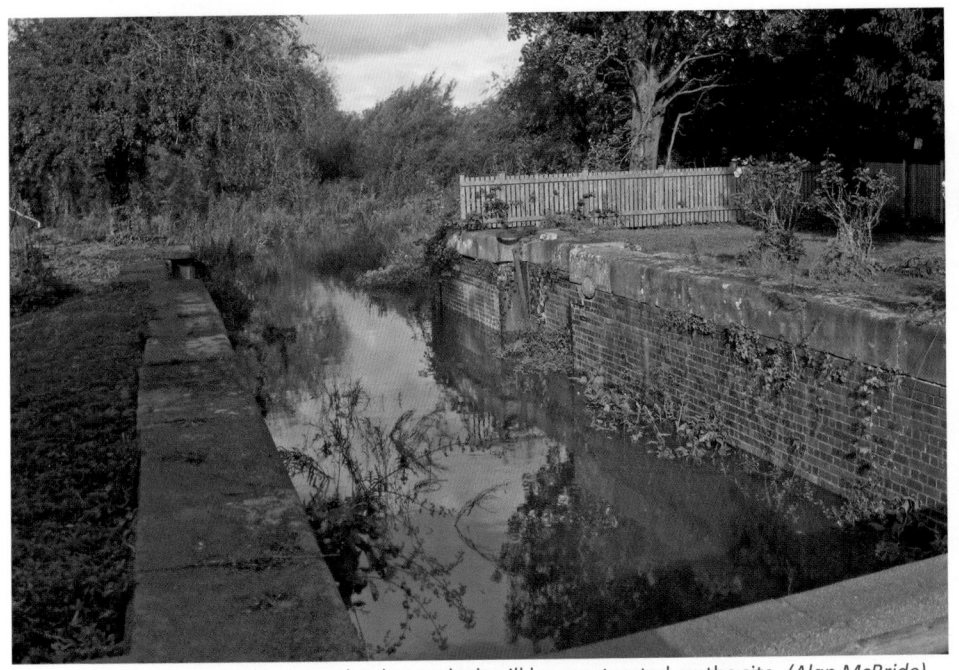

Figure 159: Llanthony Lock. A completely new lock will be constructed on the site. *(Alan McBride)*

The first immediate challenge was to begin to deal with the growth of Japanese Knotweed which had begun to invade the site, the start of an a determined battle which will last some years before the weed is finally eradicated.

During the summer of 2009 a large site hut was erected on the site – no small feat as all the sections had to be carried on to the site over the footbridge. Unfortunately the roof sections were too large to fit under the cross-braces of the bridge and had to be carried a far longer way around. The next job was to provide a car park and toilet facilities.

Having provided the basic infrastructure for work to be carried out on the site, attention was turned to the cottages where guttering was replaced

and new fencing erected. Scrub clearance around the site continued, as did the long battle against the knotweed. The lock cut approach to the top of the lock was cleared.

In 2010 a team from the Waterway Recovery Group helped the local volunteers with several necessary tasks including the removal of an old footbridge over the lock and stump clearance in the downstream lock cut. Later in the year further fencing was erected, power and water supplies brought to the site hut from the cottages and new windows installed in the cottages themselves.

The following year further work improving the cottages was carried out including renovation of the lock-keeper's office – ready for the first boats to arrive! The painstaking and tedious task of stripping years of old paint from the very decorative Victorian railings in front of the cottages prior to repainting was begun – and yet more fencing was erected! A new floor was provided for cottage No. 1 and further restoration carried out on both cottages. The pipe-box enclosing the water supply as it is carried over the Severn on the river footbridge was replaced without any volunteers having an unexpected swim, and other important landscaping work was carried out across the site.

The cottages are now let, providing a reliable income stream for the Trust. The main access to the cottages is via the footbridge over the river which

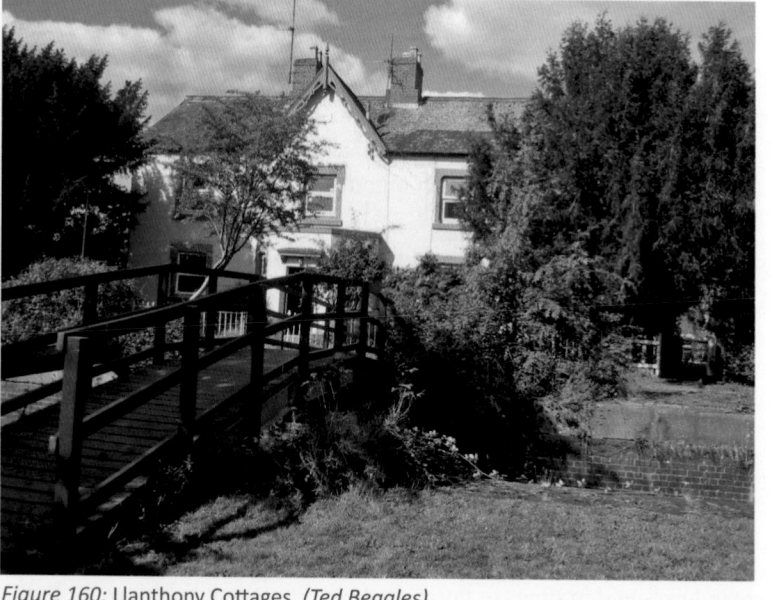

Figure 160: Llanthony Cottages. *(Ted Beagles)*

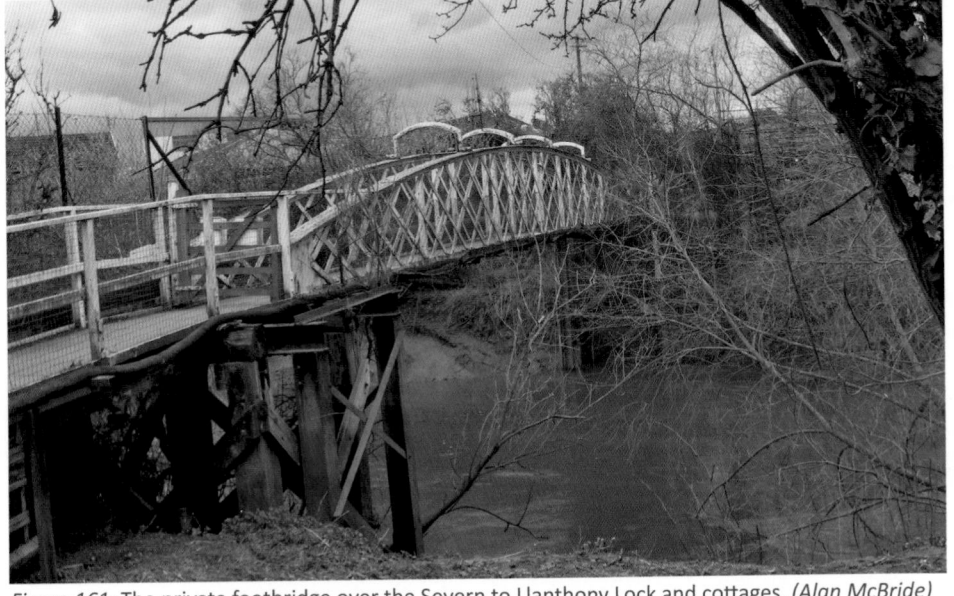

Figure 161: The private footbridge over the Severn to Llanthony Lock and cottages. *(Alan McBride)*

the Trust acquired as part of the agreement with British Waterways. In addition to foot traffic and services to the cottages, the bridge also carries an important pipe forming part of the Government Pipeline and Storage System. Negotiation by the Trust's Legal and Project Development Team with the Government Pipeline Agency in 2012 led to a transfer of liability for maintenance of the footbridge, at no cost, from the Trust to the Agency.

While it was clear why the Trust had wanted to purchase Llanthony Lock, less obvious was why it should also want so much land around the lock, control of the weirs and a stretch of the Severn itself. In 2012 the 'hidden agenda' for the site was revealed.

The restoration of the lock was only part of the Trust's vision for the site. In December, Richard Benyon MP, the Environment Minister, chaired a meeting attended by senior officers from British Waterways (soon to become the Canal and River Trust), Gloucestershire and Herefordshire Councils, the Environment Agency and other interested parties. At this meeting the Trust's Commercial and Development Director launched Llanthony Hydro, a Hydro-Electric, Flood Relief and Lock scheme.

Under the proposals outlined, inflatable weirs at Llanthony and Maisemore would significantly increase control of the river Severn, both at normal river levels and in times of flood, and would prevent tidal flows with the

accompanying debris above the weirs. This will greatly help navigation through the East Channel and the access to Gloucester Docks. It will also very significantly reduce the silting of the river, the docks and the Gloucester and Sharpness Canal as currently water carrying fine estuarine silt is pumped into the docks from just above the weir. A new lock to replace the old Llanthony Lock would be fitted with radial gates which would enable the lock and lock cut to function as a flood relief channel. A major component of the scheme would include hydro-electricity generation to meet the long-term energy requirements of operating the canal – another example of the Trust's commitment to sustainability.

There are obvious advantages in this scheme far beyond those to the Trust. There is equally clearly an immense amount of planning to be done to develop the scheme to the point where contractors can begin the work. Because of the number of beneficiaries of the scheme, funding is potentially available from a variety of sources, but it will be some years before very much becomes visible at the site.

The design, construction and operation of a modern tidal river lock is a very significant and expensive undertaking and one which the Trust could hardly dream of undertaking on its own. A partnership with players far bigger and stronger than itself, and with a wide range of additional benefits, makes the project not only achievable but a potential source of lasting income for the Trust rather than a drain on resources.

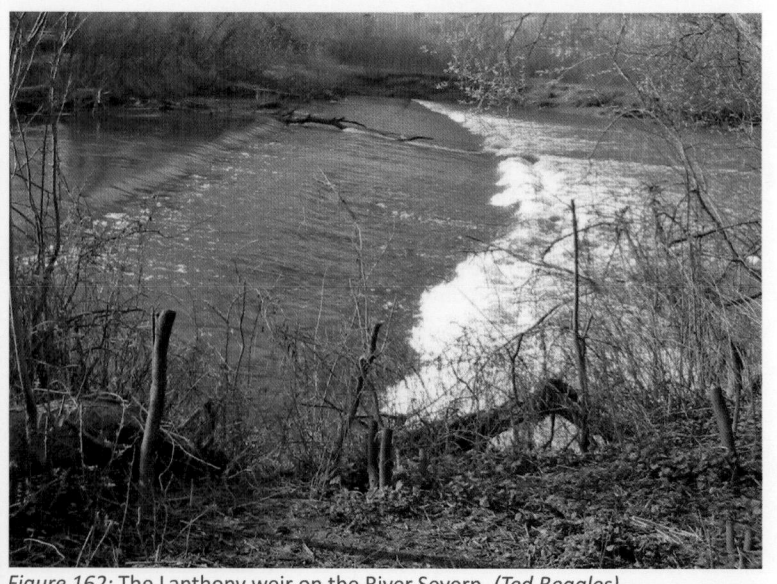

Figure 162: The Lanthony weir on the River Severn. *(Ted Beagles)*

CHAPTER 14

The Canal Trust's fleet

The Trust has four boats currently moored in Over Basin, a trip boat and three 'heritage boats' which were acquired from British Waterways initially on a lease basis, but with the prospect of Trust ownership.

* Named after William Maysey, who had worked for the Canal Company for the 35 years, from the time construction commenced. He fullfilled various roles including assistant engineer, manager and general dogsbody. He had a reputation for getting things done.

The trip boat *Mister Maysey** was purchased by the Trust from the IWA West Country Branch in 1999 having served as the trip boat *RUBY II* on the Bridgwater and Taunton Canal. She was brought to Oxenhall where initial restoration work was carried out. She was then moved to Over Basin in time for the opening of the basin in 2000. Since then her superstructure has been almost entirely replaced, the interior refurbished and repairs to the hull undertaken. Painted in the Trust's yellow and black colours and with an eye-catching name scroll she now carries visitors along the newly restored length of the canal on Over Open Days.

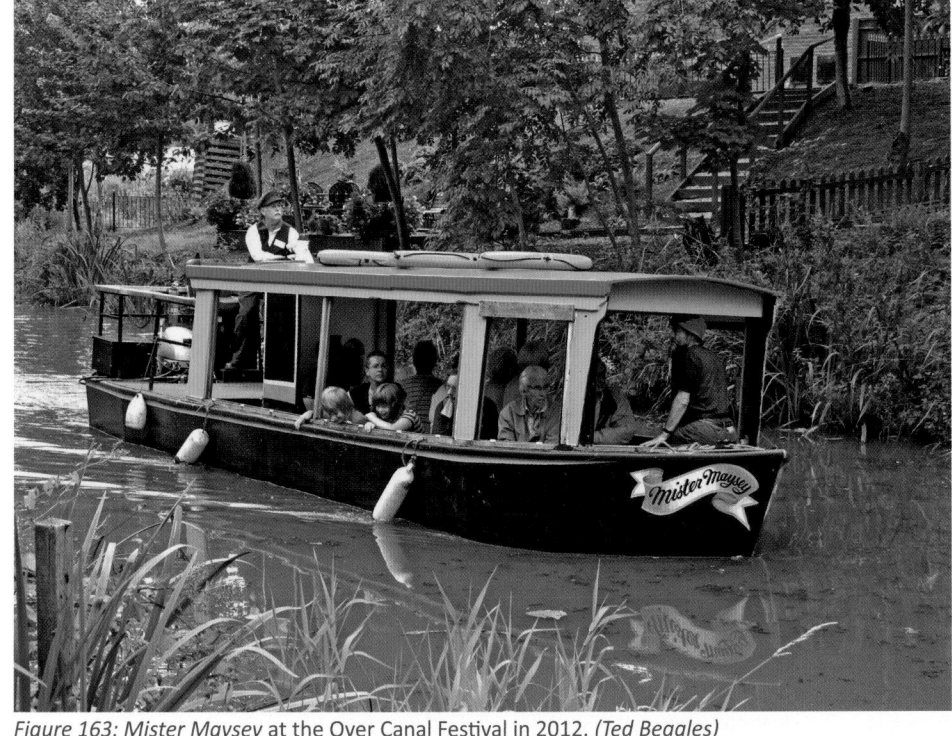

Figure 163: Mister Maysey at the Over Canal Festival in 2012. (Ted Beagles)

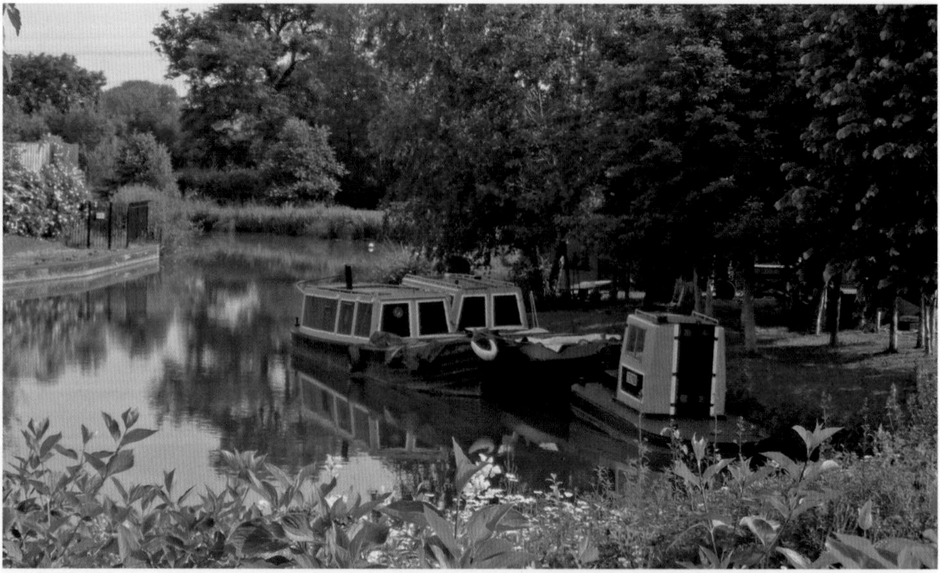

Figure 164 : The Trust's heritage boats at Over Basin in 2013. *(Ted Beagles)*

The Trust's three other boats are all from the British Waterways Heritage Fleet. Following a decision in 2005 to modernise its fleet of workboats, British Waterways auctioned many of its old fleet, but a number were leased to voluntary organisations who were required to restore them to a satisfactory standard, and if that was achieved by the end of the lease, the boat would become theirs.

In 2007 the Trust acquired *Alder* on this basis. *Alder* has an interesting history. Originally built by Yarwoods in 1931, as a Bolinder-powered motor, she became Fellows, Morton and Clayton No. 301. In 1965 she was converted by British Waterways at the Bradley yard into two workboats. *Alder* is the stern of the original FMC narrow boat fitted with a new bow and a Lister HR2 engine. Becoming only 37' long, she worked as a push tug on the Kennet and Avon Canal.

She arrived at Over from Devizes on October 15th on a low-loader and was craned into the

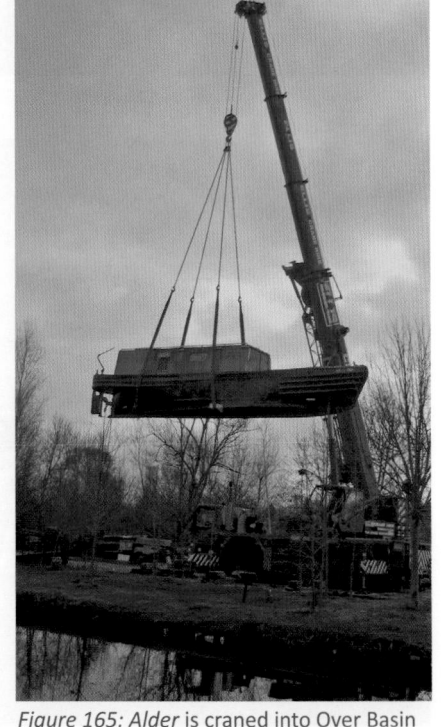

Figure 165: Alder is craned into Over Basin in October 2007. *(Ted Beagles)*

basin after maintenance and repairs to the hull and the fitting of a new propeller. Much work has been done to bring her to her present excellent condition in H & G livery and *Alder* is now in the Trust's ownership.

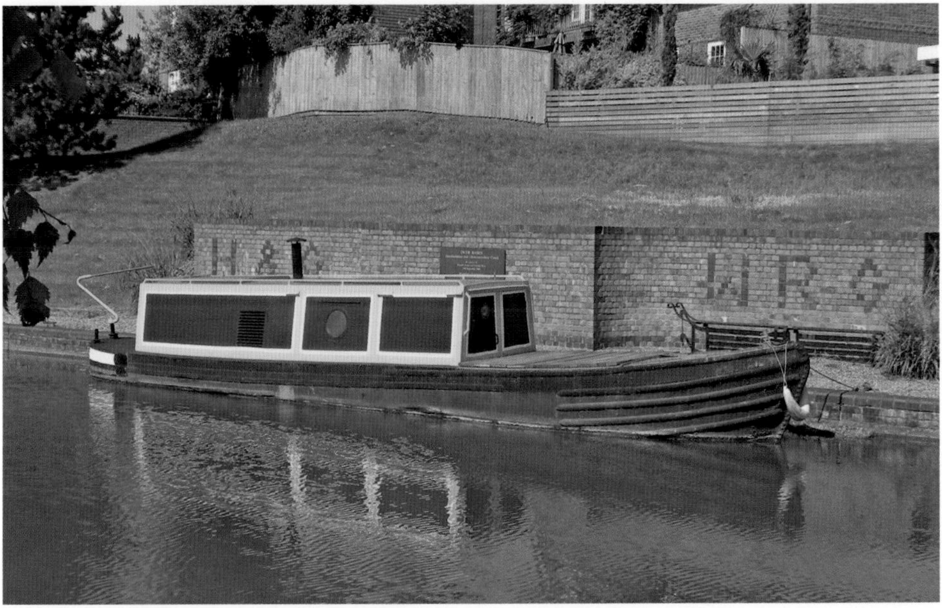

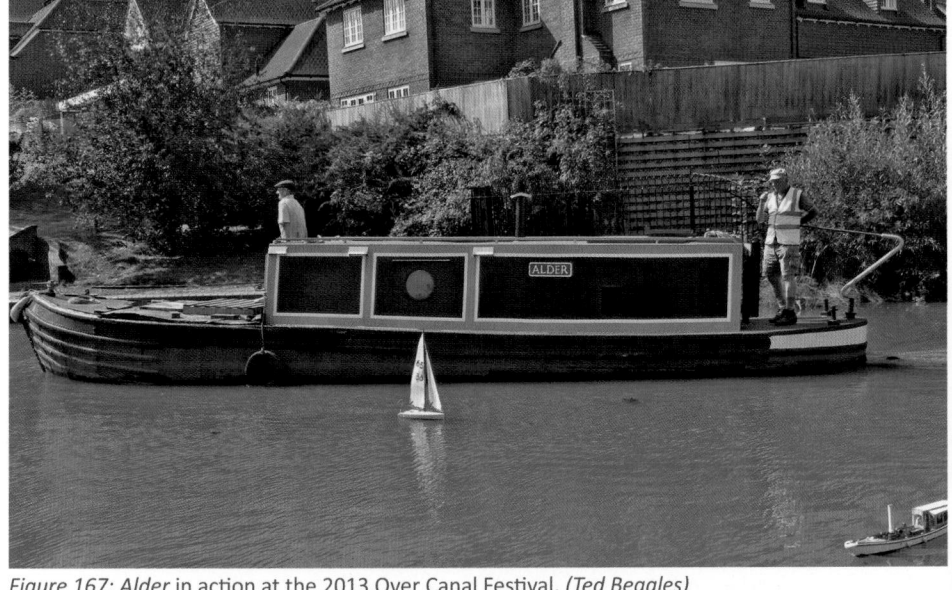

Figure 166: Alder moored by the Feature Wall at Over. (Ted Beagles)

Figure 167: Alder in action at the 2013 Over Canal Festival. (Ted Beagles)

The second member of the BW Heritage Fleet to be acquired is the tug *Renton*. Also built by Yarwoods, *Renton* began life in 1936 as a full length motor in the Grand Union Canal Carriers fleet, a Large Northwich Town Class. After work on the Grand Union between London and Birmingham she was converted by the War Department in 1943 into a 48' ice-breaker, subsequently acquiring a more conventional bow. In 2009 the Trust secured the lease and was able to bring the boat by water under her own power from Marsworth, on the Grand Union to Gloucester. This was a trip of 147 miles and 165 locks, undertaken by a Trust director and her family, complete with dog, in eight days, even though the tug was not fitted out with living accommodation.

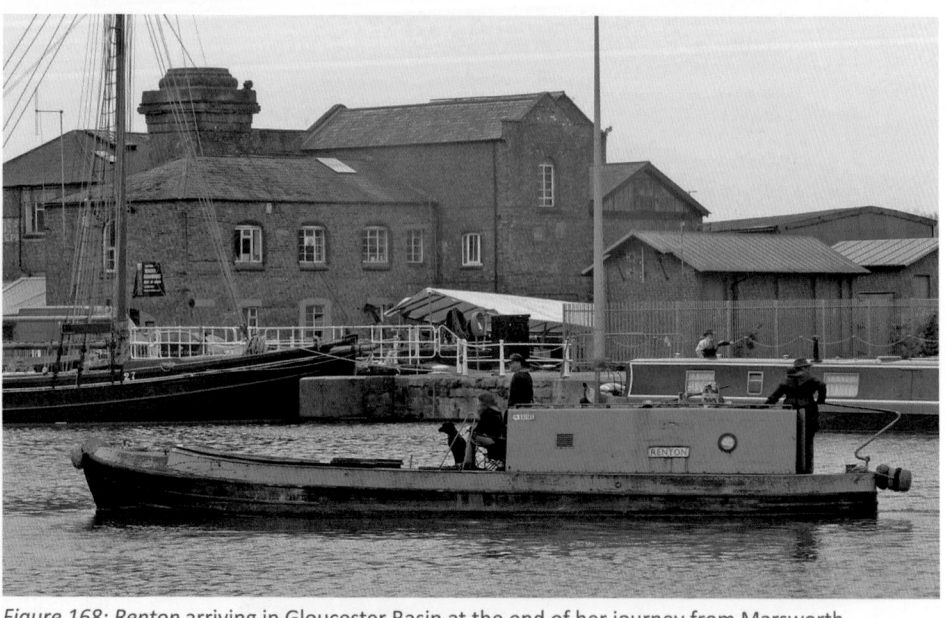

Figure 168: Renton arriving in Gloucester Basin at the end of her journey from Marsworth. (Maggie Jones)

While in Gloucester Docks undergoing restoration *Renton* was called upon to assist with several tasks on the Gloucester and Sharpness Canal including the rescue of the National Waterways Museum's large trip boat *Boadicea* which was drifting around in the Docks having suffered an engine failure with a party of schoolchildren aboard.

In 2011 *Renton* arrived by low-loader at Over and was craned into the basin, where she now acts as a trip boat on open days and cruises up and down the canal, her 23" propeller helping to control the weed which summer weather inevitably encourages.

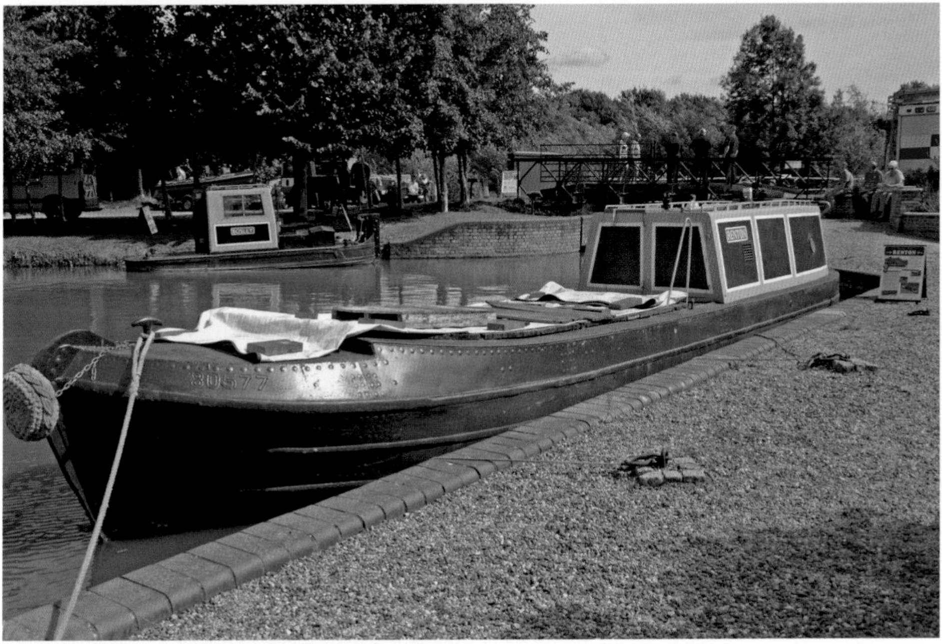

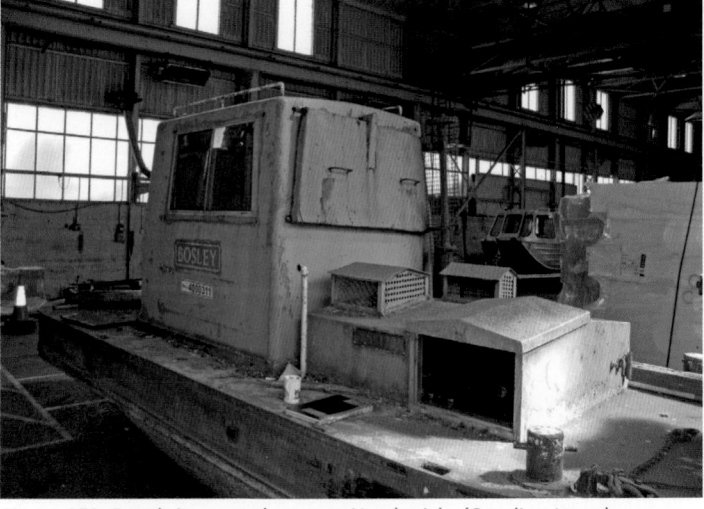

Figure 169: Renton at Over Basin. (Ted Beagles)

The third of the Heritage Boats is the smallest, and newest. *Bosley*, a push tug was built in 1986 and used by British Waterways on the Trent and Mersey Canal and the River Weaver. She has a large winch at the bows and will be a useful small vessel as restoration of the canal continues. She was acquired by the Trust in 2011.

British Waterways was clearly content that the Trust was caring for and using the boats to its satisfaction. All three leases were terminated early and the boats sold to the Trust for one pound each.

Figure 170: Bosely in a warehouse at Northwich. (Caroline Jones)

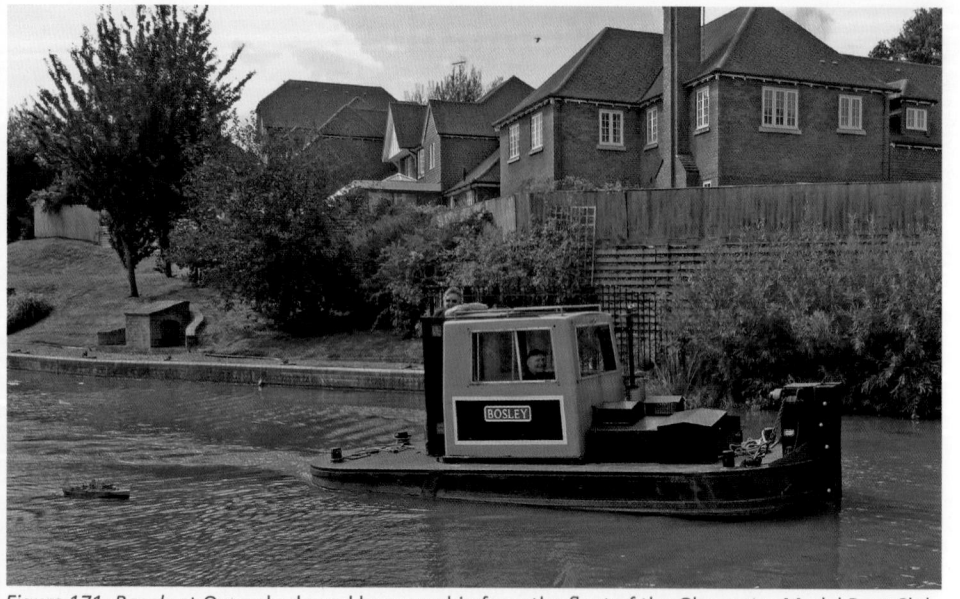

Figure 171: Bosely at Over, shadowed by a warship from the fleet of the Gloucester Model Boat Club. *(Ted Beagles)*

Other Reminders

While the Trust has been working to restore navigation along the canal, others have quietly been preserving some of the remaining buildings and other features which were to be seen along the towpath in years gone by. These are not museum pieces – they are privately owned homes and part of the vernacular architecture of the two counties. Most are now quite isolated, being built where they were needed to perform a particular function.

The only cluster of buildings is to be found close to the site of the wharf at Withington Marsh. The house of William Bird, the Wharfinger, has been sensitively restored in recent years and within a few yards of this is a terrace of houses which may well have been lengthsman's cottages. Another house which stood at the end of an arm at the wharf bore the word SALT on its end wall, almost invisible today. This would have indicated that there was a salt warehouse at the wharf.

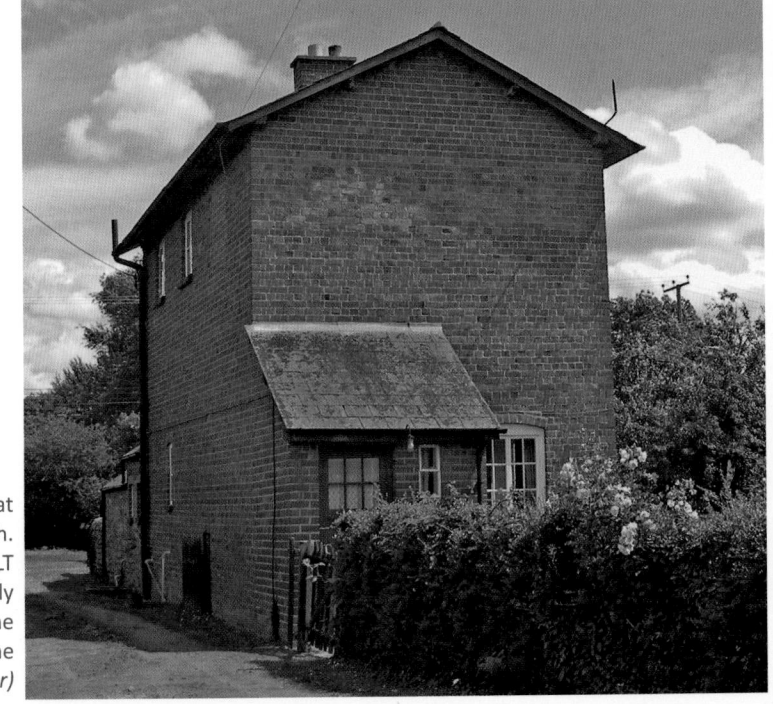

Figure 172: House at Withington Marsh. The word SALT is now barely discernible on the end wall above the porch. *(Author)*

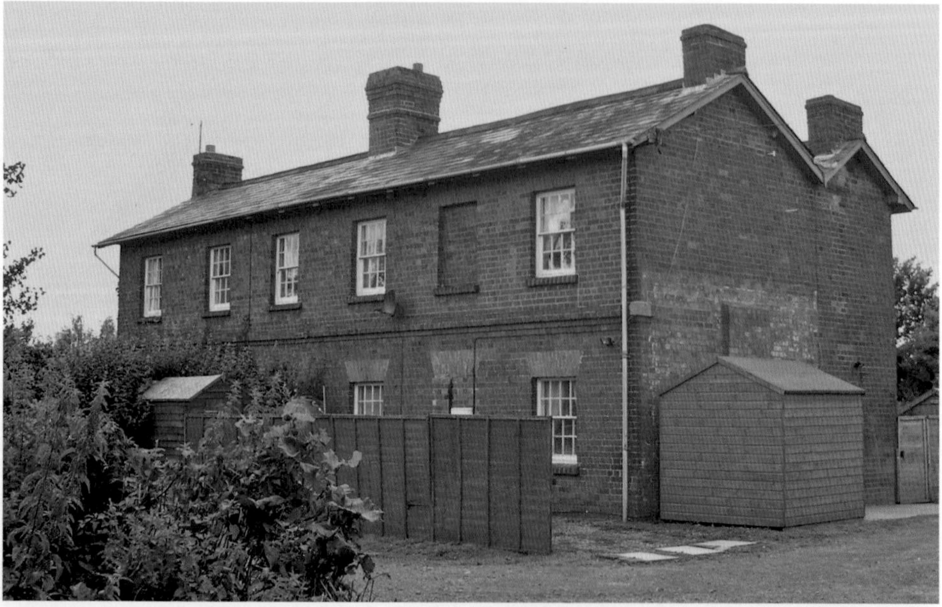

Figure 173: Wharf buildings at Withington Marsh – possibly lengthsmen's cottages. *(Author)*

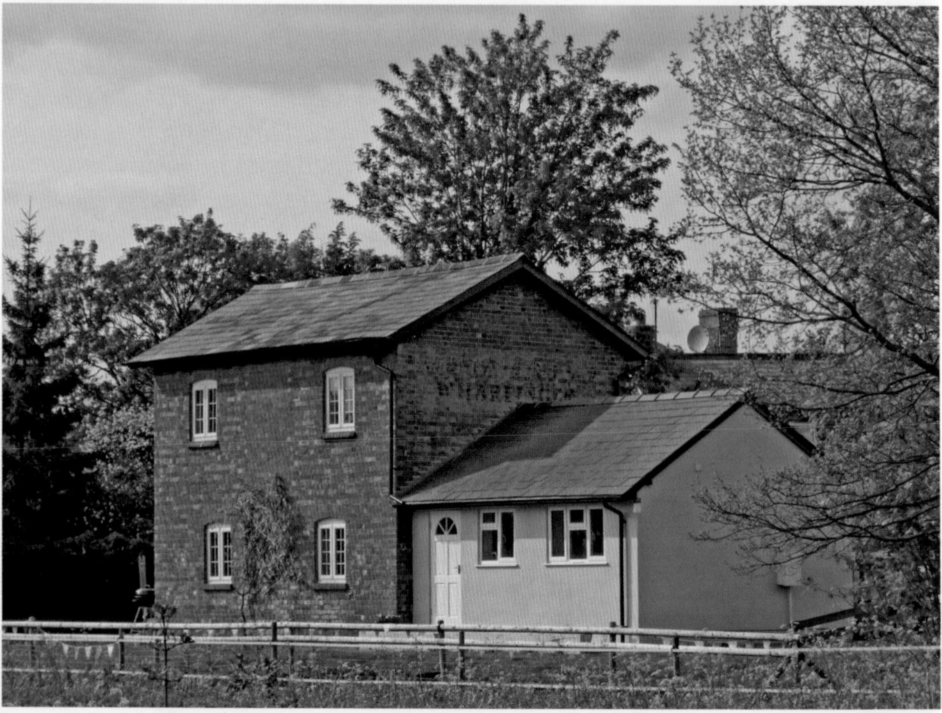

Figure 174: The Wharfinger's House, Withington Marsh in 2014. *(Author)*

Two miles away at Kymin is "Canal House" almost certainly another wharfinger's house, now an attractive home.

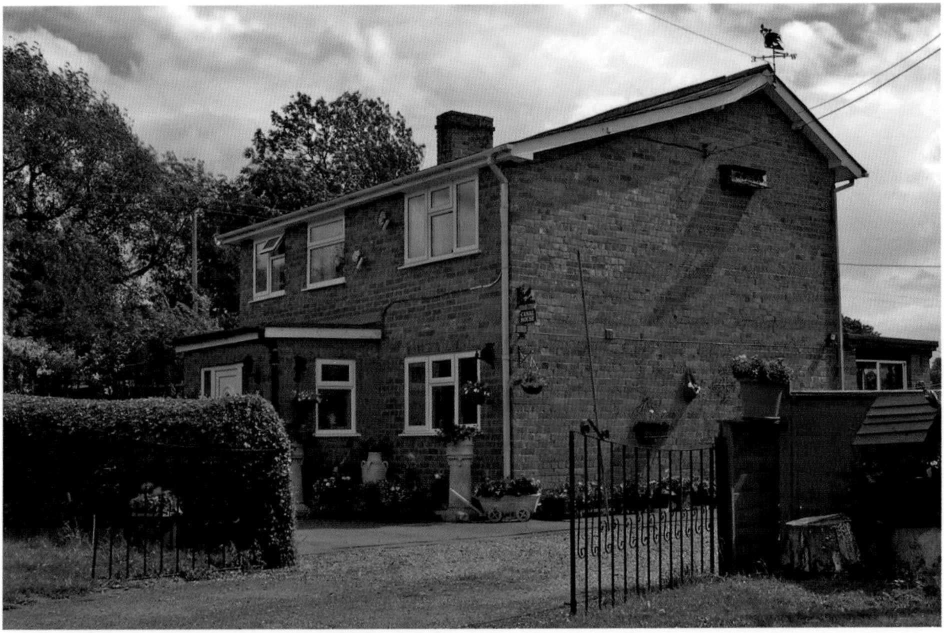

*Figure 175:*Canal House, Kymin. *(Author)*

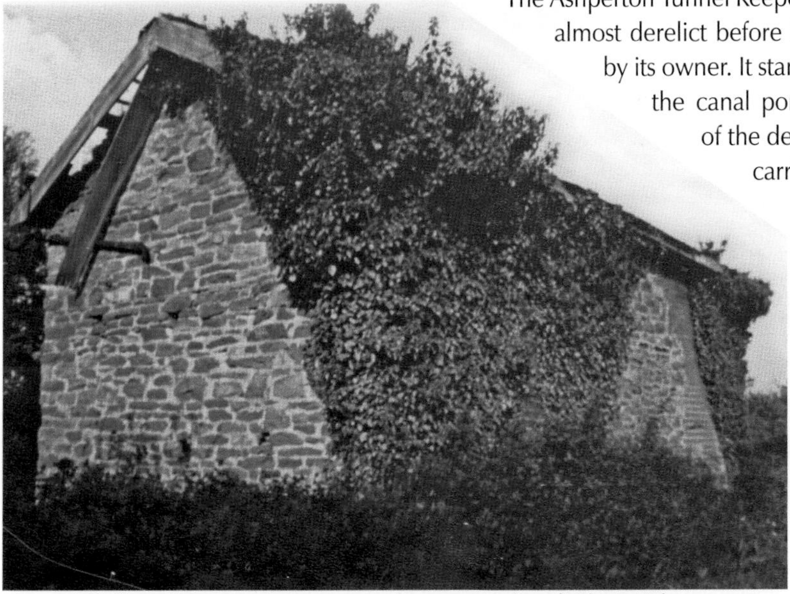

The Ashperton Tunnel Keeper's House was almost derelict before being restored by its owner. It stands high above the canal portal at the top of the deep cutting and carries a plaque reminding passers-by of its function, the tunnel being out of sight from the road.

Figure 176: Tunnel Cottage, Ashperton before restoration. *(Mike Potts)*

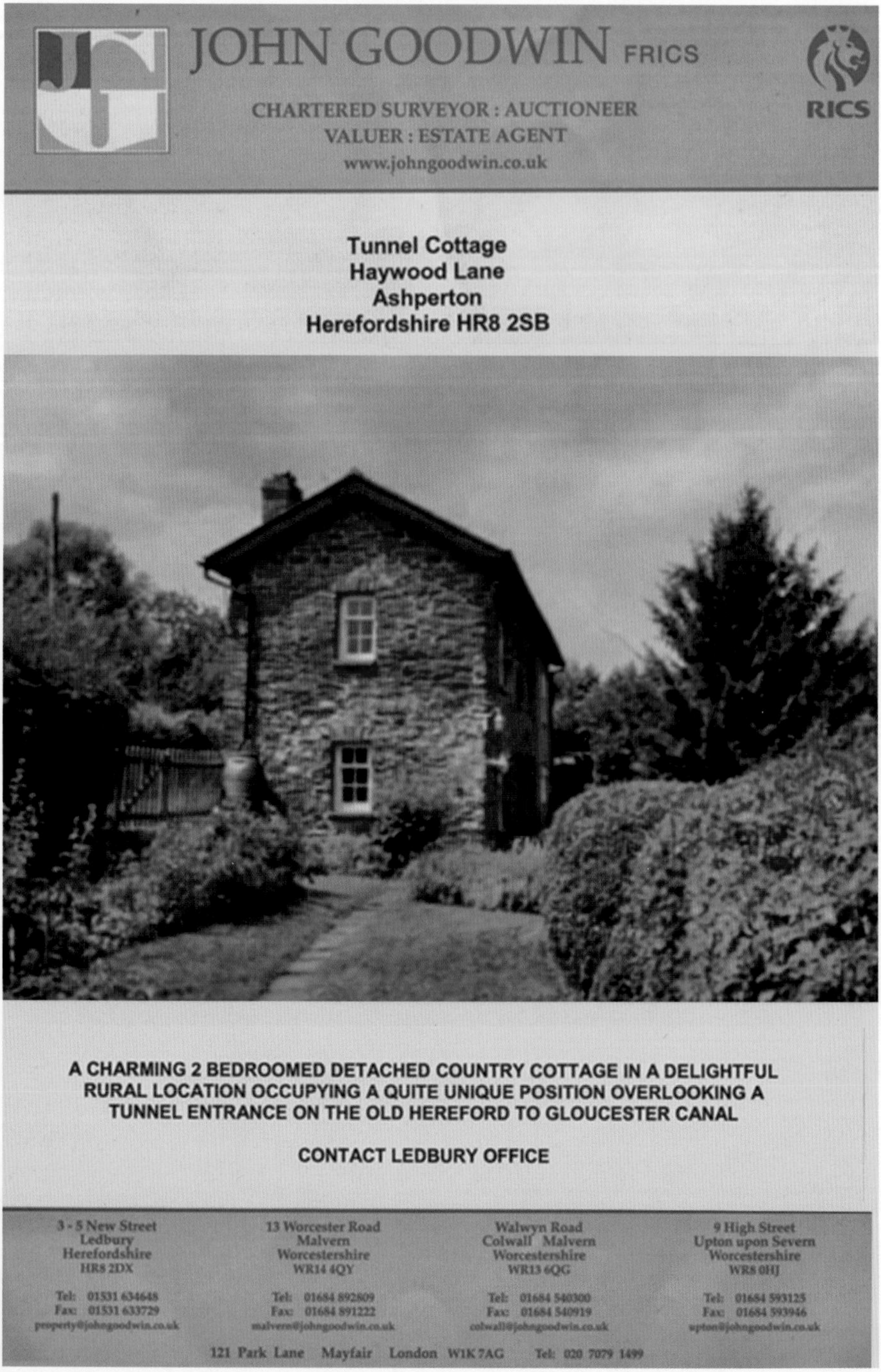

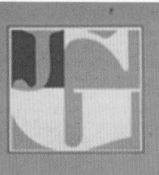

JOHN GOODWIN FRICS

CHARTERED SURVEYOR : AUCTIONEER
VALUER : ESTATE AGENT
www.johngoodwin.co.uk

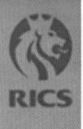

RICS

Tunnel Cottage
Haywood Lane
Ashperton
Herefordshire HR8 2SB

**A CHARMING 2 BEDROOMED DETACHED COUNTRY COTTAGE IN A DELIGHTFUL
RURAL LOCATION OCCUPYING A QUITE UNIQUE POSITION OVERLOOKING A
TUNNEL ENTRANCE ON THE OLD HEREFORD TO GLOUCESTER CANAL**

CONTACT LEDBURY OFFICE

3 - 5 New Street	13 Worcester Road	Walwyn Road	9 High Street
Ledbury	Malvern	Colwall Malvern	Upton upon Severn
Herefordshire	Worcestershire	Worcestershire	Worcestershire
HR8 2DX	WR14 4QY	WR13 6QG	WR8 0HJ
Tel: 01531 634648	Tel: 01684 892809	Tel: 01684 540300	Tel: 01684 593125
Fax: 01531 633729	Fax: 01684 991222	Fax: 01684 540919	Fax: 01684 593946
property@johngoodwin.co.uk	malvern@johngoodwin.co.uk	colwall@johngoodwin.co.uk	upton@johngoodwin.co.uk

121 Park Lane Mayfair London W1K 7AG   Tel: 020 7079 1499

Figure 177: John Goodwin's Sale Brochure for Tunnel Cottage. *(John Goodwin)*

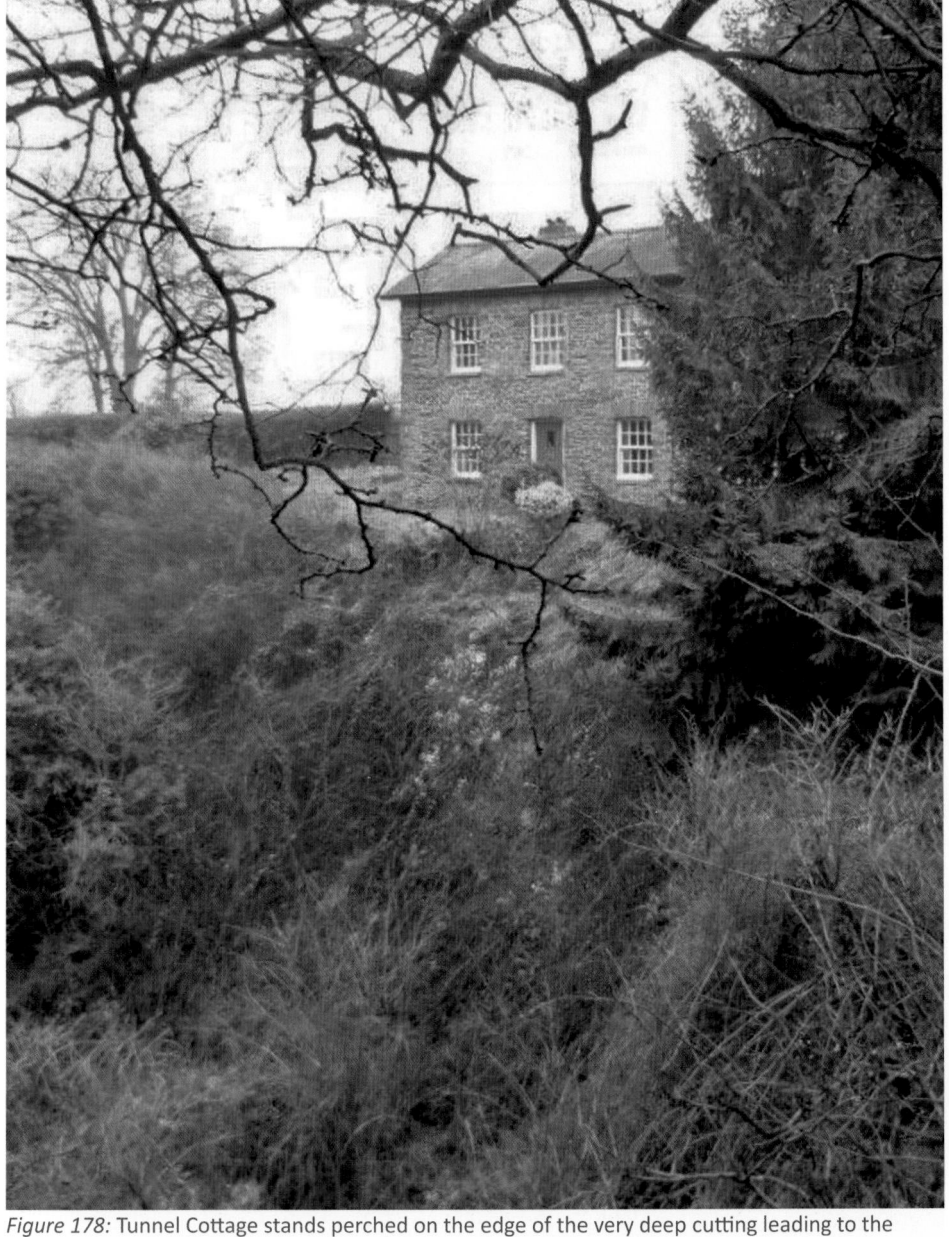

Figure 178: Tunnel Cottage stands perched on the edge of the very deep cutting leading to the tunnel itself. *(John Goodwin)*

Further along the canal towards Ledbury there stands a pair of canal cottages on Swinmore Common, with no road access. These were almost certainly lengthsman's cottages as there was no wharf or lock nearby.

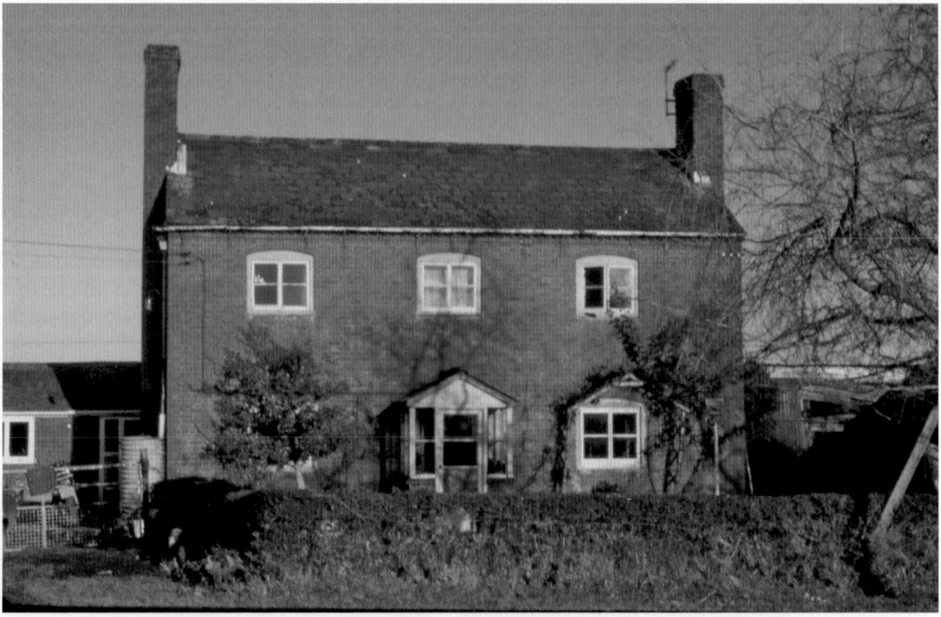

Figure 179: Lengthsman's Cottage, Swinmoor. *(Nigel Jefferies)*

A much finer building saved from dereliction is the wharf house at Staplow, one of Stephen Ballard's most elegant houses.

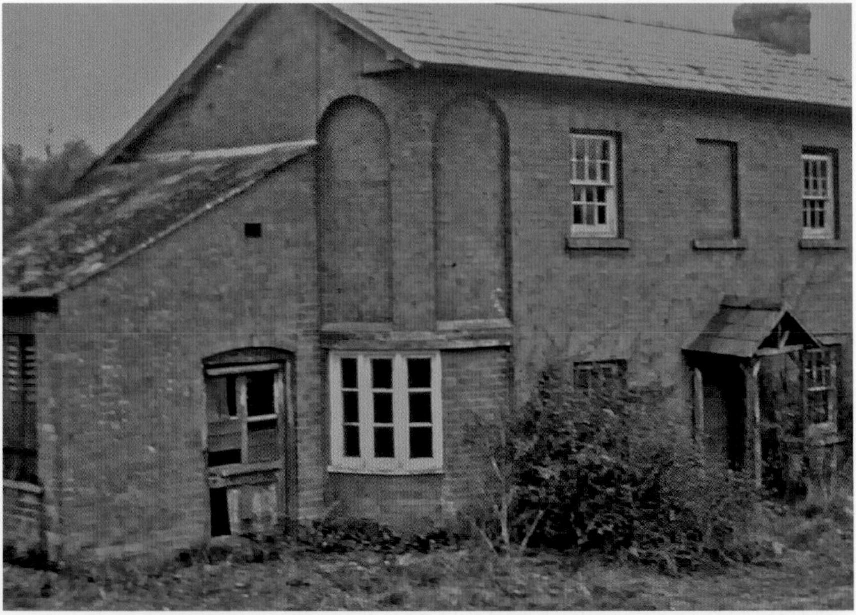

Figure 180: Staplow wharf house, almost derelict. *(David Bick – Peter Moore)*

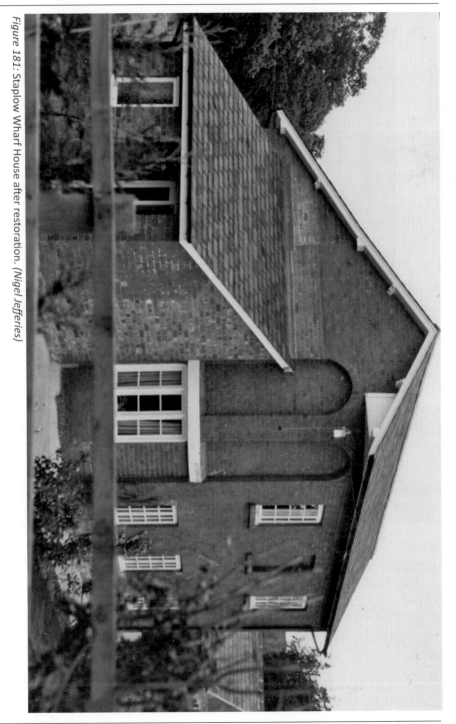

Figure 181: Staplow Wharf House after restoration. (Nigel Jefferies)

Some of the property associated with the canal passed to British Railways which then sold it off during the 1960s. An example was the Lock Cottage at Oxenhall, the building having survived a lightning strike in 1956. It was built by Stephen Ballard in 1838 and for a lock cottage, it is extremely elegant in its design with a number of interesting architectural features. It is, however, essentially a "two up and two down", and at the time of the 1851 census apparently housed the lock keeper, Richard Goode, and his wife Eliza, their five children and two lodgers who were colliers!

Newent District Council had issued a Demolition Order on the semi-derelict property, probably because the tenant's wife had recently had a baby and this was the surest way of getting the family to the top of the waiting list for Council housing. There was no electricity to the property and the only water supply was a polluted well and the sanitation an outside privy.

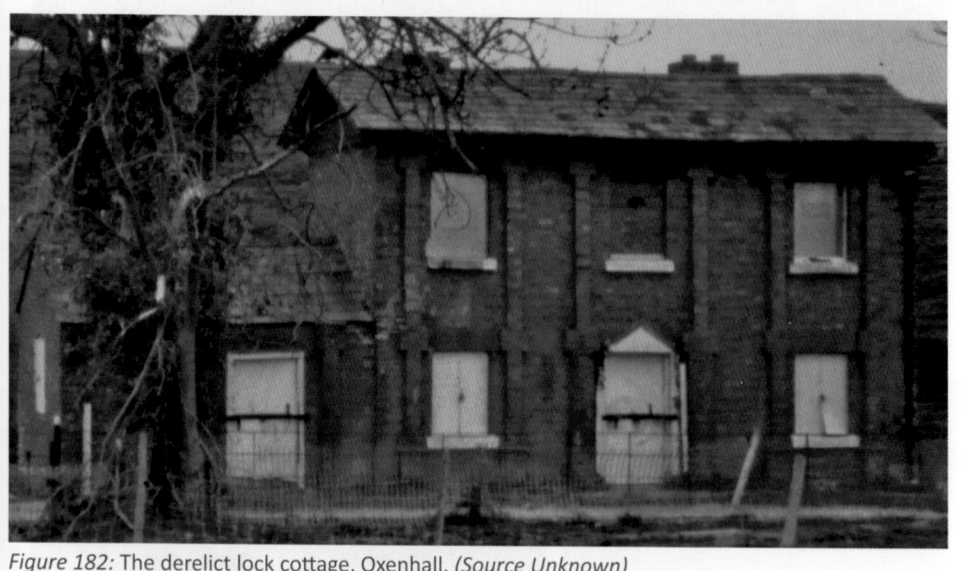

Figure 182: The derelict lock cottage, Oxenhall. *(Source Unknown)*

Unaware that they were selling the property to one of their employees, which, had they known, would have complicated matters greatly, British Railways finally completed the sale to Robin Stiles in 1967. The new owner carried out an agreed Schedule of Works including repairs to the roof and installation of water and septic tank drainage. The Demolition Order was revoked in 1969. The building was listed Grade II on 18th October 1985. It was later fully restored and became a family home once again – but less crowded than in 1851!

Stiles, Robin: Unpublished autobiography

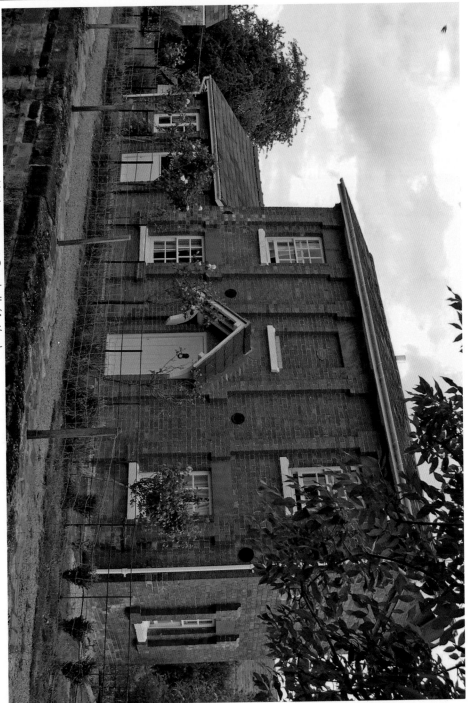

Figure 183: The beautifully restored lock cottage at Oxenhall. (Author)

The Road Ahead

It would be a brave and perhaps foolish person who would commit any view of the future of any canal restoration to print. Hopes are raised and dashed in equal measure and success in one area is often accompanied by delays in another. About the only forecast one can make with any confidence is that it will always take much longer than we would ever imagine. If we are like Mrs. Dashwood and Marianne, for whom "to wish was to hope, and to hope was to expect" we will almost certainly be disappointed.

Austen, Jane: Sense and Sensibility, Chapter 4

But, because many readers will be as much interested in the future as the past, something must be said about the road ahead. Experience elsewhere has shown us that, while canal restoration is almost always a long process, nothing should be written off as "impossible" – a lesson learned from the restoration of the Huddersfield Narrow Canal, which "impossibly" re-opened in 2001.

While, in strictly engineering terms, the Hereford and Gloucester Canal is not an easy restoration, there is nothing needing to be done that has not been achieved elsewhere. Between Hereford and Ledbury parts of the canal remain in water, albeit at variable levels, most of the bridges still stand, the two tunnels are believed to be in relatively good condition and only three locks need to be built. One new main road bridge, on the Roman Road, has already been provided, as well as those at Farriers Way. The greatest engineering challenge will be to design a new aqueduct over the Lugg which will pass over the river without impedance of its flood flows. Although some of the masonry of the original culvert under the railway embankment at Shelwick still exists, the best solution will be take the canal off-line and thrust-bore a new culvert. The embankment is high and thrust-boring beneath it does not constitute a particularly major feat of engineering.

New main road bridges under the A4103 at Monkhide, the A465 at Withington, the A438 at Ledbury and the A417 at Canon Frome will be required. However, these main roads are not like main roads in other parts of the Midlands where Herefordshire main roads would generally considered to be country lanes. All of these bridges can be built without a significant change in road level.

The canal line through Ledbury, with its five deep locks, is too obstructed to afford a practical route for restoration, but the River Leadon corridor, which bypasses the town to the west through the Riverside Park offers a pleasant alternative route which is protected in the County Development Plan. The canal will fall through twice the number of the original locks to better fit in with the landscape and assist in water management.

Between Ledbury and Gloucester restoration will be far more difficult. Much less of the canal is in water, most of the line having been infilled for the railway. Of the 22 original locks, 14 are on this section including the very deep river lock at Over. The canal crosses the B4215 no less than four times. Here the repositioning of some locks and the restoration of the canal at a higher level offer possible solutions.

This section also includes the mile and a quarter long Oxenhall Tunnel which caused so much grief to the original builders of the canal. A major threat to restoration was the planned route of a high pressure gas pipeline of four feet diameter. The construction of this, crossing just above the tunnel and with the subsequent restricted zone around it, would have prevented work on the tunnel and even its use for navigation. Negotiations with Transco's project manager at The Wharf House, with views of Over Basin and maps of the canal on the wall, led eventually to an agreement in 2008 that the pipeline specification would be modified, at a cost of some £300,000, to allow the Trust unrestricted access to the tunnel for both restoration and navigation. The masonry at the southern end is thought to be in remarkably good condition and this gives way to a long section which is unlined and formed by the natural rock. The northern portal has almost completely disappeared. The restoration of Oxenhall Tunnel is likely to be eye-wateringly expensive but every large successful canal restoration has had a similar project to contend with and has found ways to achieve success.

By far the greatest challenge is not one of engineering at all, it is of land ownership. Following the closure of the canal, the land in Herefordshire was sold, or even given away. On the nationalisation of the railways in 1948 the Ledbury-Gloucester line passed into the ownership of British Railways and this land was sold off piecemeal after the railway closed in 1964. Possession of the line of the canal is now shared by over 100 landowners, some sympathetic towards restoration, some indifferent and a few who oppose it. The Trust has acquired and now has access to some short lengths, but one of the major priorities over the coming years must be to build up its land holding wherever it can.

This may be achieved by outright purchase, if the necessary capital is available, and the Trust has a Land Fund for this purpose. A recent anonymous donation of £100,000 was a most helpful contribution, as were several donations of £10,000. But land may also be obtained under agreements with developers or other individuals where a mutual benefit will be secured. The Trust's canal and basin at Over was acquired by this means.

Adjacent to the partly restored canal in Aylestone Park is a length of canal beside to the Holmer Trading Estate which in 2009 was the subject of a planning application proposing a mixed development for residential, employment and retail purposes. The application was rejected on the grounds that it conflicted with the Council's planning policy to retain existing employment land unless there were benefits to outweigh it.

On appeal this decision was overturned, the Inspector arguing as follows:

> 66 I do not consider that the benefits arising from land remediation, affordable housing provision and local highway improvements would be sufficient to outweigh the harm I have identified. However, the likely benefits associated with the re-opening of the Canal would be substantial. It seems to me that this is an important section of the Canal in terms of achieving the UDP's long-term restoration aims. The Canal to the east of the site is being restored and passes through a substantial park, and there is an important tunnel portal to the west of the site. Restoration of the length of Canal indicated in the obligation would add substantially to the significance of the Canal as a feature within the City. In my judgement, the benefit of the scheme to the restoration of the Canal is sufficient to tip the balance in favour of allowing the appeal, notwithstanding the conflict with the provisions of UDP Policy E5 99
>
> *Herefordshire Council: Appeal Decision APP/W1850/A/09/2098857*

Clearly the appeal would have not been allowed if the proposal had not included the restoration of the canal. Under the Section 106 Agreement, ownership of both the restored canal and the adjacent Aylestone Tunnel will be transferred to the Trust. Construction work on this proposal has not yet begun but the planning application was successfully renewed in 2012.

Another development greatly influenced by the Trust is that of a residential development at Dymock. Here the Trust led a partnership of Dymock Parish Council, Two Rivers Housing Association and the owner of land

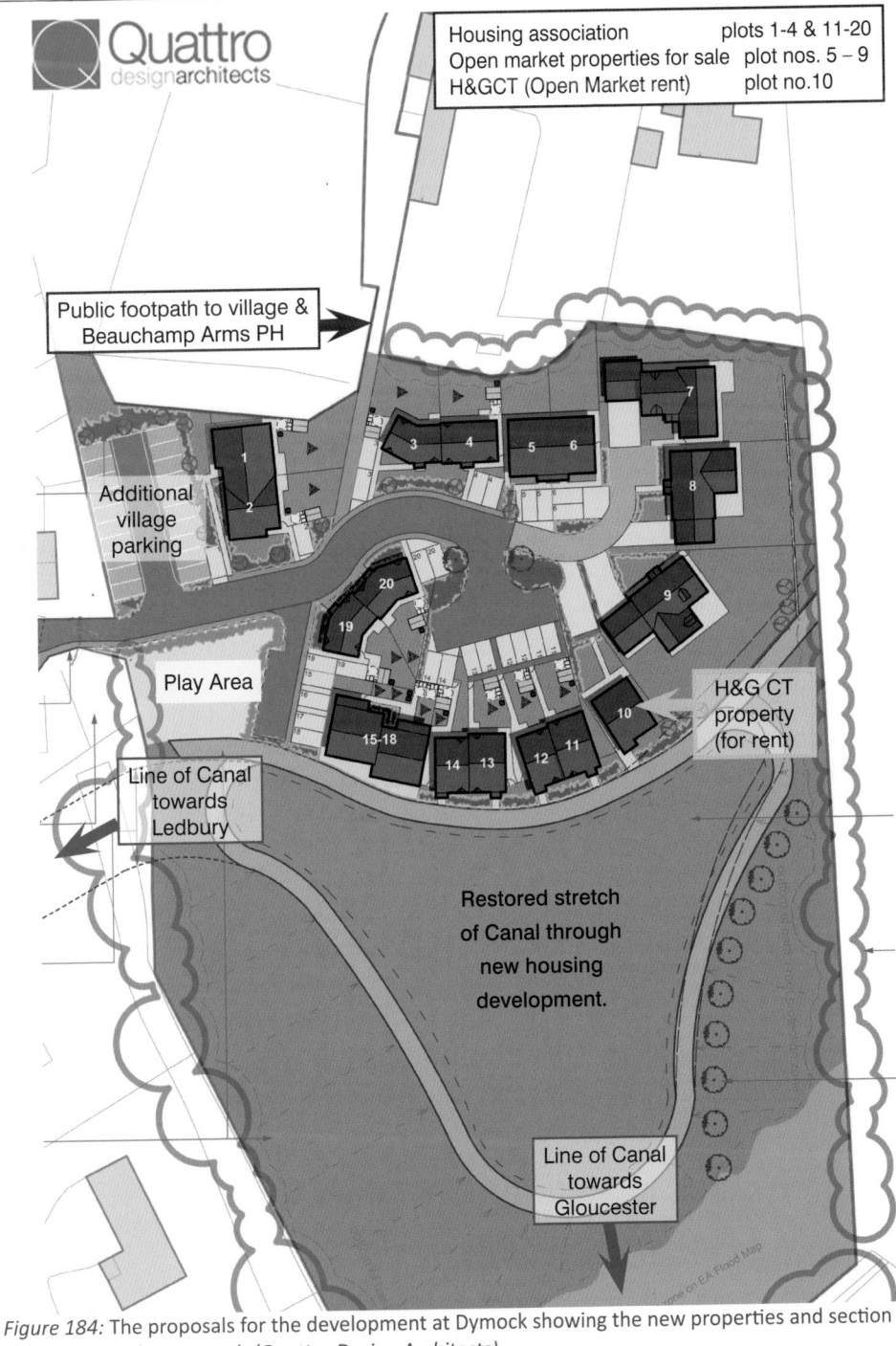

Figure 184: The proposals for the development at Dymock showing the new properties and section of canal to be restored. *(Quattro Design Architects)*

in the centre of the village. The development includes much needed affordable housing properties, a new children's play area and a short restored stretch of the canal. Against the recommendations of Planning Officers, the Forest of Dean Councillors approved the application by 12 votes to 2.

An opportunistic approach, however, will to lead to a number of short stretches of unconnected canal across the two counties which have little practical use in the short term but will require constant maintenance. While the Trust will still have to seize such opportunities as they arise, it will focus on acquiring and gaining access to land adjacent to its present holdings, thus enabling restoration of continuous sections of canal.

The demands of sustainability and the establishment of continuing income streams, will be a high priority. The Wharf House and plans for the Llanthony Hydro are examples of this and no doubt many more will emerge over the coming years.

As part of the agreement for all developments taking place where the canal forms a significant feature, all properties are required to make an annual, index-linked contribution in perpetuity towards the maintenance of the waterway. While this is not a large amount for an individual householder, as the number of developments grows the income stream from these arrangements will become increasingly important. When the projected redevelopment of the city takes place, new commercial properties in Hereford which will benefit from the restored canal basin will make a more significant contribution.

As part of the restoration process it is necessary to develop the infrastructure necessary to support the management of the canal in the future. A case in point is the reconstruction of the Mill Barn at Over. Long before the Hospital was built, indeed since the 13th century, there had a mill at Over, powered by water from the Leadon. The mill itself was worked until 1885 and was finally demolished in 1903. It had two barns, one of which survived until the hospital was demolished and restoration of the canal basin was begun in 1998. This stone barn was about to be destroyed, but the developer allowed the Trust to dismantle it carefully for rebuilding at a later date. Proposals have been developed and discussed with the residents of Staunton's Hill with a view to using the salvaged materials to provide a new building to house maintenance equipment and provide proper facilities for those working on the site or using it for recreational purposes. The upper floor will provide for a meeting and training room and much-needed office space for the Trust's Legal and Project Development Team.

Bailey, Nigel: Over and Over Again Red Osier Publishing, 2000 pp.14-15

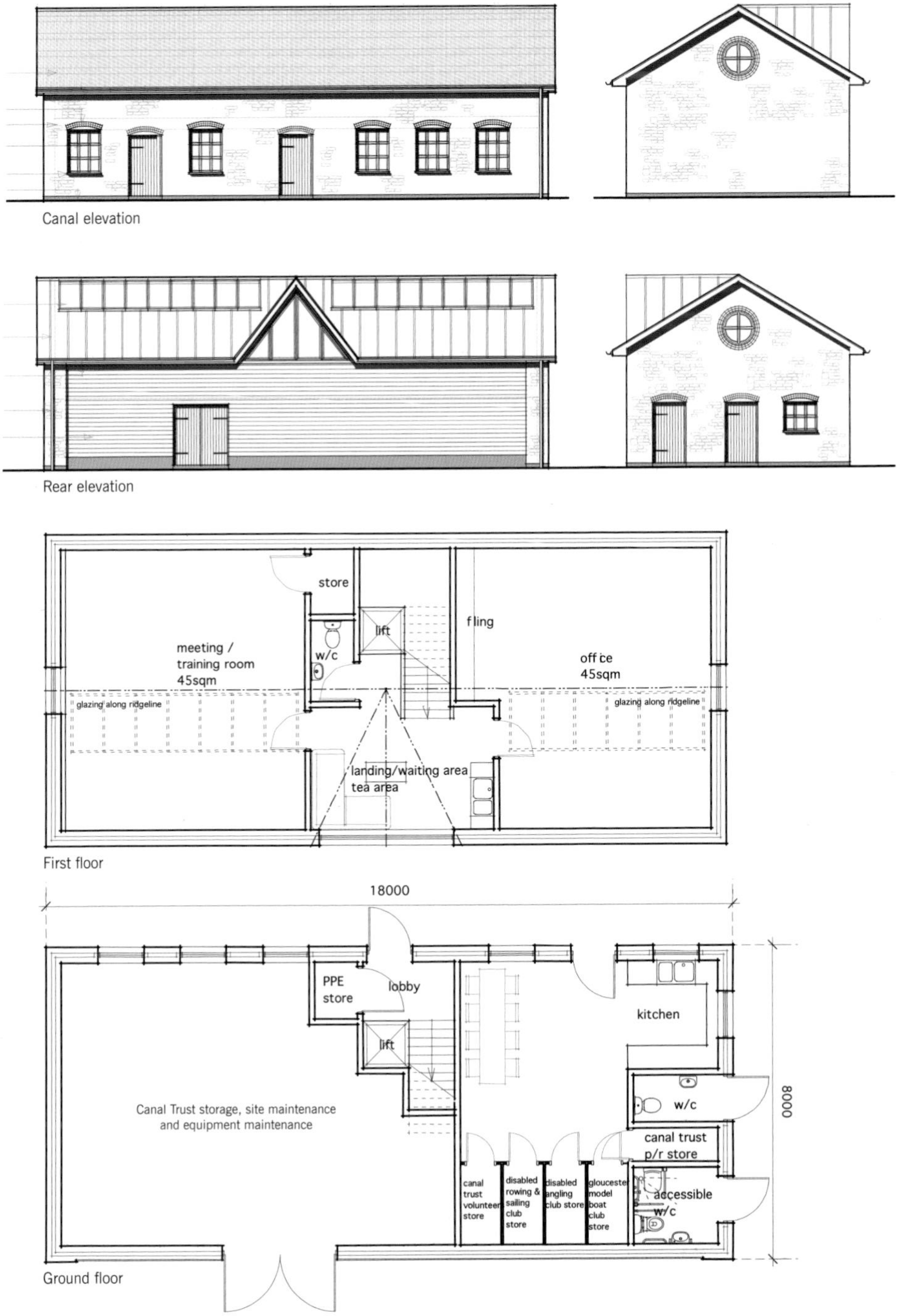

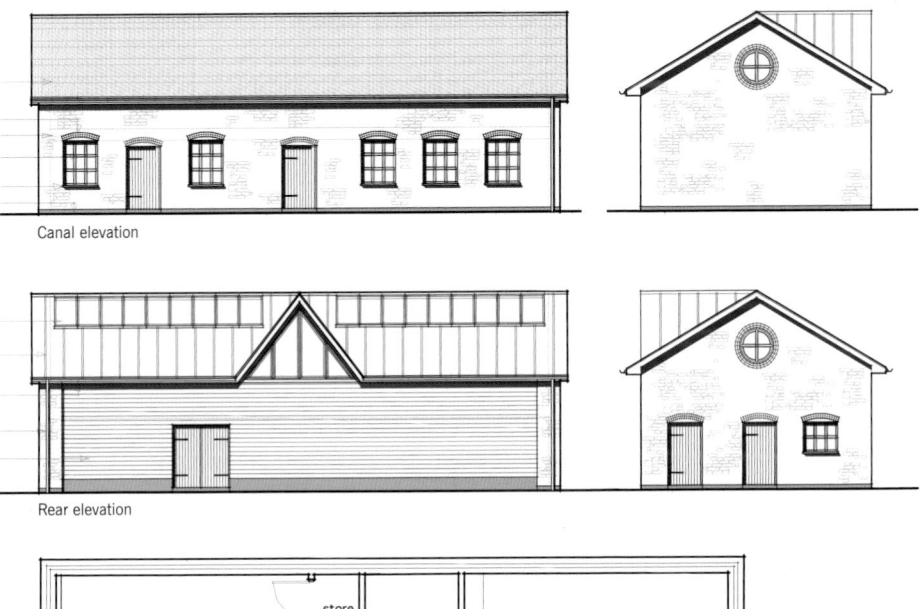

Canal elevation

Rear elevation

First floor

store

meeting /
training room
45sqm

glazing along ridgeline

w/c

lift

f ling

off ce
45sqm

glazing along ridgeline

landing/waiting area
tea area

18000

PPE
store

lobby

lift

kitchen

Canal Trust storage, site maintenance
and equipment maintenance

w/c

canal trust
p/r store

canal
trust
volunteer
store

disabled
rowing &
sailing
club
store

disabled
angling
club store

gloucester
model
boat
club
store

accessible
w/c

8000

Ground floor

Figure 185: The plans for the restoration the Mill Barn. *(H&GCT)*

Another project which is currently under active development is the canal crossing of the B4215 near the site of Newent Station. The canal originally passed under Bridge Street but the road level has been lowered considerably and restoration on the original level is considered impractical. The alternative is to use the existing railway bridge abutments to support an aqueduct carrying the canal over the road and thence over a long embankment on the site of the former Willows Nursery, over the restored Ell Brook aqueduct to the pound below House Lock omitting Devin's Lock and the first lock of the Oxenhall flight. The Trust owns much of the land in question.

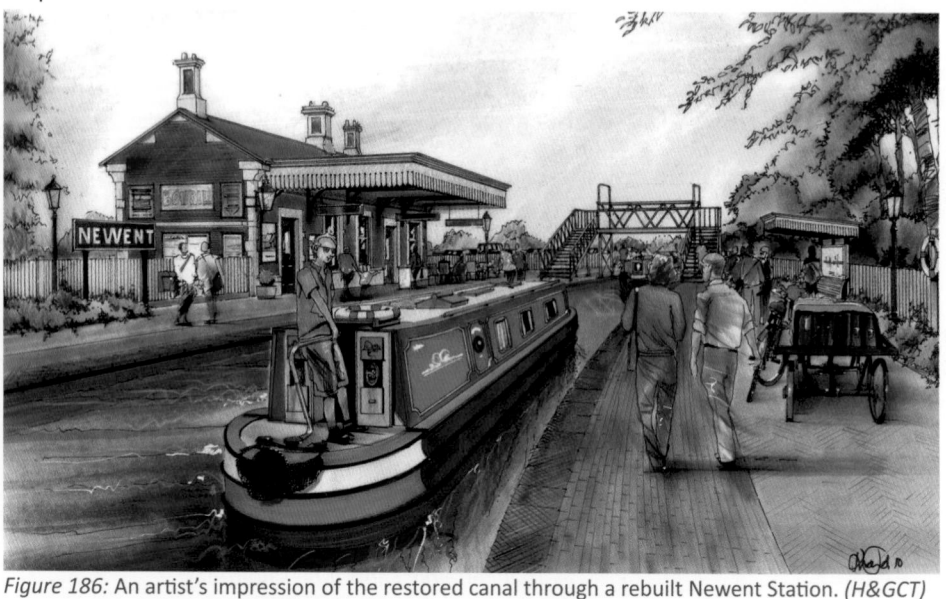

Figure 186: An artist's impression of the restored canal through a rebuilt Newent Station. *(H&GCT)*

Given that the canal would now run along the former railway line through the station, the platforms of which are still in existence, consideration is being given to the rebuilding of the station itself with the canal passing through the platforms.

The aim, of course, is to provide a visitor attraction only a few hundred yards from the centre of Newent with the rebuilt station providing facilities in a unique situation. The project, with its embankment, may well prove controversial but it shows the Trust's ability to "think outside the box" which already marks it apart from many other restoration groups.

It is a strategy which undoubtedly carries considerable risks, but it may also reap great rewards. With an ever-growing number of restoration schemes being considered, competition for funding will increase and it is

the projects which stand out from the rest which will benefit the most.

The Trust's efforts, achievements and strategy have been noticed. The Nicholson's Waterways Guide, familiar to all boaters, notes that the canal "is now firmly fixed in the sights of a very professional and dedicated canal trust, committed to its complete restoration" and asserts "the sheer dogged determination and tenacity shown in the face of not inconsiderable adversity, whilst meeting a demanding schedule, will surely stand as an inspiration to all those engaged in future waterway restoration." The latter quote appears also in Times Waterways of Britain (2010), which selects the Hereford & Gloucester Canal as the only example in the section "The Future". Waterways World, in its annual review of the 60 national waterway restoration projects, placed the Trust in the top five in 2014 and in the equivalent top group in 2013 and 2012, noting "the impressive achievements to date bode well for success in the future."

It will, no doubt, be a long time before boats from Gloucester arrive in Hereford Basin again, but when they do, it will be because of the hundreds of people who worked tirelessly over those many years to make it happen.

As I wrote in my introduction, it does not matter whether they have been out getting muddy, at a desk preparing paperwork, representing the Trust in negotiations or promoting the Trust at a show – all will have played a vital role in bringing this beautiful canal back to life.

Writing in 1979, David Bick was right in observing that:

> 66 Throughout the length and breadth of England, no major navigation is so lost in obscurity as the Hereford and Gloucester Canal. 99

That certainly cannot be said today!

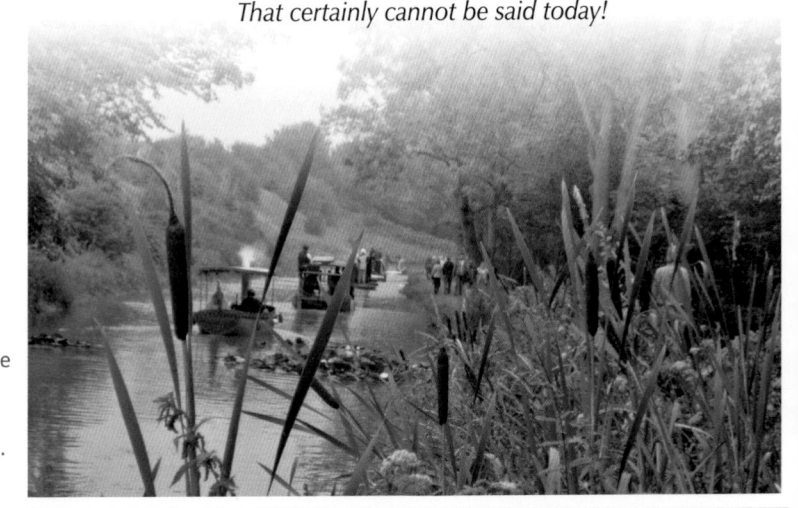

Figure 187:
A flotilla of boats marks the opening of the Vineyard Hill stretch in 2012.
(Ted Beagles)

The Hereford & Gloucester Canal

Appendix

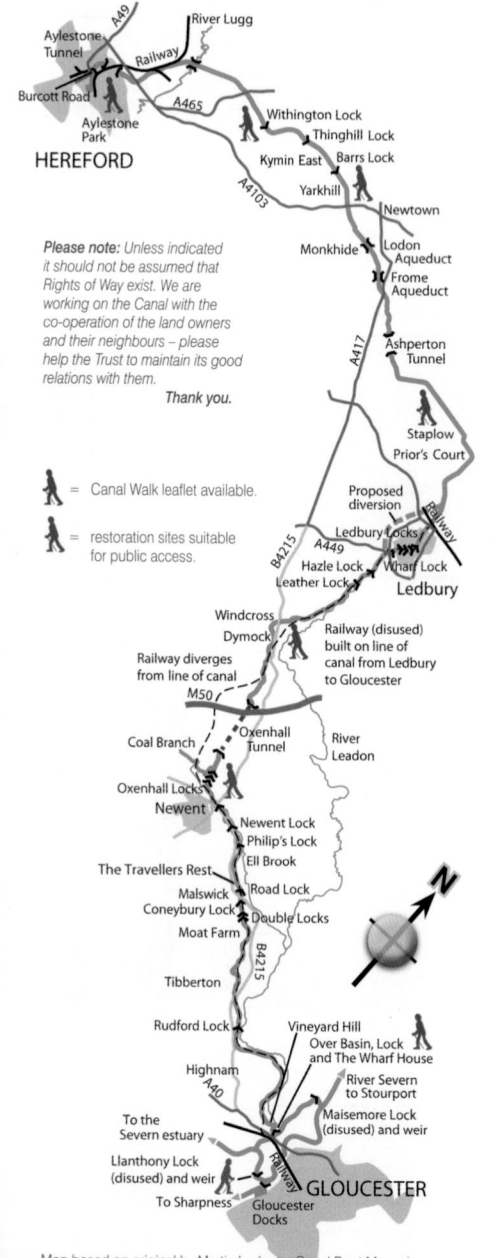

Please note: Unless indicated it should not be assumed that Rights of Way exist. We are working on the Canal with the co-operation of the land owners and their neighbours – please help the Trust to maintain its good relations with them.

Thank you.

🚶 = Canal Walk leaflet available.

🚶 = restoration sites suitable for public access.

Map based on original by Martin Ludgate, Canal Boat Magazine.

Mileage Table: Miles from Over

HEREFORD 34

Miles	Location
3½	Rudford Lock
3¾	Rudford Bridge
6	Double Locks
6¼	Coneybury Lock
6½	Road Lock
7½	Philip's Lock
8	Newent Lock
8¾	Newent Wharf
9	Devin's Lock (Oxenhall Bottom Lock)
9¼	Oxenhall Top Lock
9¾	Oxenhall Tunnel South Portal
11	Oxenhall Tunnel North Portal
11½	Boyce Court
12	Dymock
15	Leather Lock
15¾	Hazle Lock
16¼	Old Wharf, Ledbury
17	New Wharf, Ledbury
19½	Prior's Court
20	Staplow Wharf
22½	Ashperton Tunnel East Portal
22¾	Ashperton Tunnel West Portal
24	Canon Frome Wharf
26	Crews Pitch, Monkhide
26¾	Barr's Lock
27¾	Kymin Lock
28¾	Withington Lock
29½	Withington Marsh Wharf
31	Lugg Aqueduct
31¾	Shelwick Green
32¾	Aylestone Tunnel South Portal
33	Aylestone Tunnel North Portal
34	Hereford, Barr's Court Basin

Boats moored on the Canal on April 7th 1861

Compiled by John Chappell from 1861 Census data

Boat Name	Tonnage	Home Wharf	Location on April 7th
Colina	30	Gloucester	Canal Wharf Hereford
Lion	30	Newent	Canal Wharf Hereford
Mary	30	Gloucester	Canal Wharf Hereford
Mary Ann	28	Hereford	
Perseverance	28	Hereford	Canal Wharf Hereford
Perseverance	30	Hereford	Canal Wharf Hereford
Ralph	30	Gloucester	Canal Wharf Hereford
The Hereford	30	Gloucester	Canon Frome Wharf
Lady of the Lake*	27	Staplow	Dymock
Unknown			Staplow Wharf
Thomas			Newent
Useful			Newent
Betsy			Newent
Sand Bank			Newent
Ellen	20	Hereford	Gloucester Docks
William	22	Gloucester	Gloucester Docks
Perseverance			Over
Perseverance No. 3			Over

*Details of Lady of the Lake are as of 1871

The four boats named Perseverance were owned by members of the Whitehouse family who seem to have used this as a fleet name. Presumably they were numbered, but this were not always recorded by the enumerator. They were associated with the canal for the whole of its operational life.

In the census of 1871 the distribution of boats was as follows:

Hereford	0
Gloucester	1
Newent	4
Oxenhall	1

People from Newent recorded as involved with boats in 1861

Compiled by John Chappell from 1861 Census data

Address	Name	Age	Dependants	Job	Notes
New Street	Charles Jones	35	4	Boatman	
Gloucester Street	Pamphrey	23	2	Boatman	
Gloucester Street	Charles Mayo	14	0	Boatman	
Gloucester Street	John Mayo	21	0	Boatman	
Gloucester Street	Charles Wood	19		Boatman	
Rocks Ally	Whitehouse	23	0	Boatman	
Rocks Ally	Charles Pitt	16		Boatman	
Church Street	William Chandler	26	3	Boatman	
Church Street	George Williams	21	0	Boatman	
Broad Street Police Station	Francis Cousier	24	0	Boatman	In custody
Lower New Street	Charles Thomas	49	0	Boatman	
Lower New Street	James Jones	71	1	Boatman	
Lower New Street	Edward Thomas	21	0	Boatman	Edward and Henry are brothers
Lower New Street	Henry Thomas	19	0	Boatman	
Lower New Street	Henry Jones	29	4	Boatman	
New Street	William Hatch	45	2	Grocer and Boat Owner	
New Street	Fredrick Hatch	20	0	Boatman	William's Nephew
Hill Top (Near Stardens)	William Jones	26	0	Boatman	

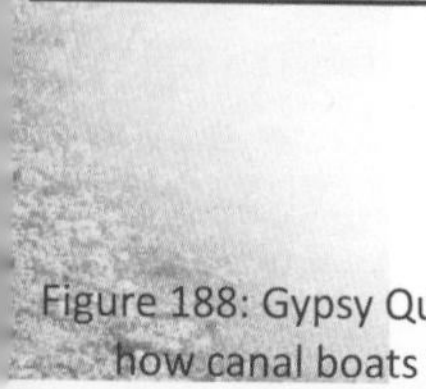

Figure 188: Gypsy Queen demonstrates at Over Festival how canal boats were towed years ago. *(Ted Beagles)*

Index

Alder   122,156,171

Alney Island   28–30,33,80,165

Ashperton   8,20,30,46,47,60,83,87,178, 179,193,

Aylestone   87,130–134,187,193

Ballard, Phillip   62,67,69,76–79

Ballard, Stephen   9,38–48,50–52,55–64, 70, 71,91,97,100,105,108,124,126,160, 181,183

Barbers Bridge   26

Barr's Lock   127–129,134,193

Bick, David   3,6,8–10,106,110,111,181,192

Biddulph, John   38,98

Bill, Ernest   75–76

Bosely   174,175

Boyce Court   91,95,193

Brassey, Thomas   58

Brindley, James   13,17,20,24

British Waterways   102,117,118,120,156, 165,168,170,171,174

Bunning and Gibson   48,50

Canon Frome   39,47,48,61,94,96, 97,102,104,185,193,194

Carne, John   28–30

Clowes, Josiah   19–21,24–6,28,30,47

Cross-Rudkin, Peter   29

Danks, Venn and Sanders   66,76,79

Double Locks   69,81,193

Drownings   66,67

Dymock   26,29,30,36,66,69,73,81,83,91,94, 95,122,146,159,187–188,194

Eastnor Castle   8,35,67

Ell Brook   144–146

Ell Brook Aqueduct   141,144–146,191

Environment Agency   120,136,168

Foley, Lady Emily   63

Frome, River   19,20,35,41,42,87,89

Gloucester   8,10,13,15,17,18,20,24,26,27, 33,34,43,55,58,66,69,70,72,73,75,77,79, 80,83–85,87,112,118,121,148,156,158, 165,173,192,194

Gloucester Model Boat Club   121,175

Hadfield, Charles   33,42,110,111

Hall, Richard   19,20

Henshull, Hugh   13,24,25,26

Hereford   10,13,14,15,17–20,22–24,26,27, 32,35,39,41-3,46,50-5,58,60,62,64–68, 71,76,79,83,84,90,106,110,112,113,124, 126,130,132,134–136,189,192–194

Hereford and Gloucester Canal Society   9,105-107,111–112,114,119,132,137

Hereford and Gloucester Canal Trust   6,8,9,10,96,114–122,148,164,165,174, 183,190

Heritage Fleet   121,170–175

Holmer Trading Estate   52,189

Inland Waterways Association   111,112,120,132,148,170

Jefferies, Nigel   31, 107,183

Kymin   10,110,134,178,193

Leadon, River   20,150,153,156,186,189

Ledbury   8,19,20,22,23,25,33–35,38–40, 45,47,50,53,57,58,60,66,75,76,79, 82–84,98,99,185,186,193

Leominster Canal   18,19,41–43

Llanthony Hydro 168–169
Llanthony Lock 103,122,165–169
Lock Cottages 98,100,102,104,140–142, 144,148,160,165,183
Lock Keepers 36,70,71,80,160,167,183
Locks, damage to 36,38,77,78
Lugg, River 14–16,19,20,41,42,52,87,88, 112,185,193
Maisemore 73,75,102,111,165,168
Malswick 37,81,158,163
Malvern Hills 58,62,63
Masefield, John 84,85
Maysey, William 30,36–38,153
Mileposts 87
Mill Barn, Over 189,190
Mister Maysey 121,153,154,170
Moat Farm, Malswick 158
Monkhide 37,108,123,125,127,185,193
Newent 10,17,19,20,22-6,30,33,36,37, 58,66,67,68,70,81,91,95,106,113,191, 193–195
Newent Station 191
Over Basin 20,149,150,152,153,155,157, 162,164,170,171,174
Over Mill 27
Oxenhall 24,31,33,35,47,67,68,69,70,79, 83,98,100,101,104,113,122,125,137, 140,141,143,144,145,170,183,186,191, 193,194
Oxenhall Tunnel 8,30,66–70,82,91,92,125, 137,139,186,193
Price, William 27,71,72,85
Prior's Court 41,105,193

Railways 42,46,51,52,57–60,64,65,70–73, 83,91,141,185,186,191
Renton 173,174
Rudford 27,28,101,193
Salt 50,75,96,97,176
Scales, Prunella 153,154,156
Severn, River 13,18,19-22,23,25,28,32–34, 43,51,73,79,84,102,111,113,115,128, 148,157,162,165,167,168
Skew Bridge 108–110,163
Staplow 79,105,122,181,182,184,193,194
Stiles, Robin 98,99,113,140,183
Swan Hill Homes 161
Swinmore Common 180
The Travellers Rest, Malswick 163–164
The Wharf House, Over 157,160–164,186, 189,200
Walker, James 41,42
Walker, Ralph 37
Walsopthorne Tunnel 47
Waterway Recovery Group 120,128,130, 131,134,135,150,153,154,156,167
Watkins, Alfred 83,84,101
West, Timothy 153,154,156
Wharfinger, The 10,114,119,120,183
Whitworth, Robert 18,19,24,25,30,33
Williams, Howard 79,80,158
Willows Nursery, The 146,148,191
Withington 50,51,55,65,66,76,77,96,97, 100,106,176,177,193
Wye, River 13–15,17,18,21–23,41,42, 48,66,79
Yarkhill 128,129,134

Canal Walks

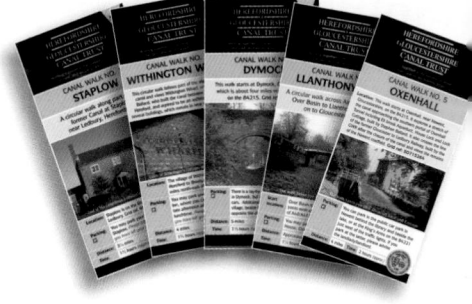

The Canal Trust has produced a series of walk leaflets which explore various parts of the **Hereford & Gloucester Canal.**

CANAL WALK NO. 1 **STAPLOW**

A circular walk along part of the former Canal at Staplow, near Ledbury, Herefordshire, which includes a number of former canal buildings. The walk is largely across grassland and field boundaries. You will have to cross some stiles and uneven ground.

CANAL WALK NO. 2 **WITHINGTON WHARF**

This circular walk follows part of the alignment of the canal and views Withington Wharf, where Stephen Ballard, who built the canal between Ledbury and Hereford and aspired to be an architect, constructed several buildings which remain in near original condition.

CANAL WALK NO. 3 **DYMOCK**

This walk starts at the village of Dymock, Gloucestershire, which is about four miles north of Newent, on the B4215. It takes in part of the doffodil way and the deep canal cutting at Boyce Court, and up to the former entrance to the north portal of Oxenhall Tunnel.

CANAL WALK NO. 4 **LLANTHONY LOCK**

A circular walk from Over Basin across Alney Island nature reserve to Llanthony Lock, showing the remains of a large river lock and the lock cottages. The walk continues on to Gloucester Docks before returning to The Wharf House at Over.

CANAL WALK NO. 5 **OXENHALL**

This walk starts at Oxenhall, near Newent, Gloucestershire, on the B4215. It explores a stretch of the canal approaching the southern portal of Oxenhall Tunnel including Ell Brook Aqueduct, House Lock and Lock Cottage, built by Stephen Ballard. It also crosses the line of the former Gloucester to Ledbury Railway, built by the GWR after the closure of the canal, and views the remains of the Newent coalfield.

Further walks in this series are planned for the future.

30p per walk leaflet, available from The Wharf House, sales stands or via our website. All proceeds towards the promotion and restoration of the **Hereford & Gloucester Canal.**

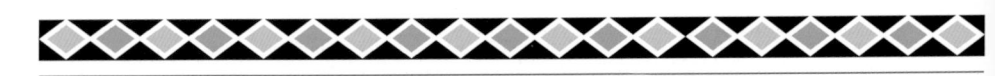

Helping to fund the restoration

You might like to consider making a gift to the H&G CT during your lifetime? Alternatively, remembering the H&G CT in your Will would be a lasting legacy helping towards the restoration of the H&G Canal into a 34 mile working waterway? This will be enjoyed for leisure activities by current and future generations of visitors and in the local communities through which it passes, bringing economic and employment benefits to these areas and to the two counties.

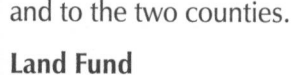

HEREFORDSHIRE
&
GLOUCESTERSHIRE
CANAL TRUST

Working together in the present, to revive the past, and secure a better future.

Land Fund

The Land Fund will provide the means to negotiate the crucial new sites along the line of the **Hereford & Gloucester Canal** where there is no new development present or where we cannot acquire the line of the Canal by other opportunities. It is a vital fund to help us eventually restore the full length from Gloucester to Hereford.

H&G CT
LAND FUND

What it is and how you
can help us restore the
Hereford & Gloucester Canal
by contributing to it.

Gift Aid

This can benefit the charity further through an income tax rebate, providing you are a relevant tax payer and meet the simple rules of Gift Aid. Additionally, if you are a higher rate tax payer, you will be eligible to reclaim tax at the higher rate. Such lifetime gifts to a charity do not count as part of your estate should you be unfortunate enough to die within seven years of making the gift, unlike gifts to individuals or non-charitable bodies. Alternatively, you might like to consider donating to the H&G CT a monthly sum paid by standing order.

Bequests

Remembering the H&G CT in your Will would be a lasting legacy helping towards the restoration of the H&G Canal. As the H&G CT is a registered charity, your legacy is subtracted from the value of your estate for tax purposes. This reduces the amount of your estate that is chargeable to inheritance tax as well as benefiting the work of the H&G CT.

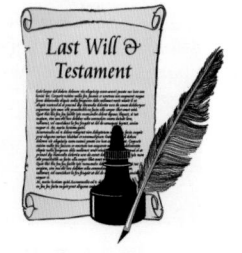

Last Will &
Testament

The H&G CT is most grateful to everyone who has made and is considering a donation, large or small, towards the restoration of the H&G Canal.

For more details please pick up a leaflet at one of our stands or contact us via our website: **www.h-g-canal.org.uk**

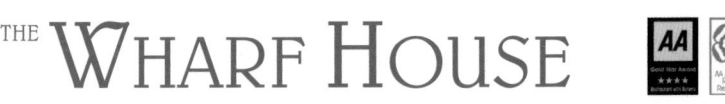
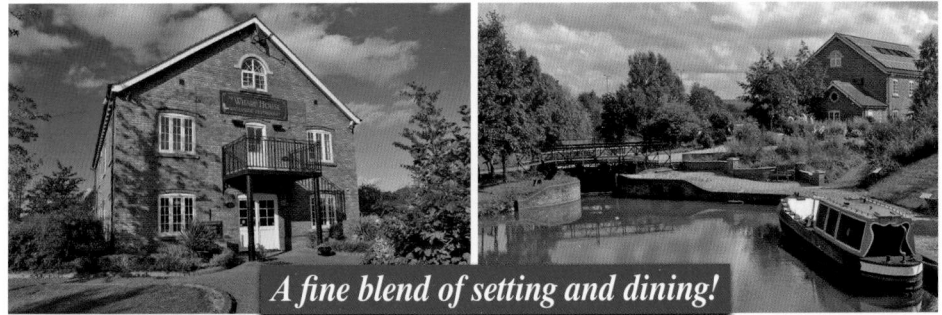